CW01671589

Daily Telegraph

ATLAS OF THE UNITED STATES OF AMERICA

Contributors:
Compiled: M W Dempsey B A
Additional research: N S Barrett M A

Published by The Daily Telegraph
135 Fleet Street, London EC4P 4BL

First published 1986

Hardback ISBN 0-86367-058-X

Paperback ISBN 0-86367-057-I

Colour separations by Paramount Litho Ltd., England
and Trilogy, Italy

Printed in Italy

The Atlas of the United States of America

Created and produced by Nomad Publishers Ltd.,
The Grange, Grange Yard, London SE1 3AG.

Daily Telegraph
ATLAS OF THE UNITED STATES OF AMERICA

Compiled by M W Dempsey B A

with an Introduction by

David Adamson

Diplomatic Correspondent of The Daily Telegraph
specialist in The United States of America

A Nomad Book

Daily Telegraph

CONTENTS

INTRODUCTION

In outline, on a conventional two-dimensional map, the United States would easily win a contest for the world's most boring country. It has a northern border with Canada that runs straight along a parallel for most of the way (even Alaska's frontier with Canada is mostly straight), huge box-like states in the middle and west, and an eastern shore that boasts hardly a cliff, being mainly long beaches broken here and there by great, sluggish rivers. There are few of the quirks, the seismic wanderings from the median, that history has imposed on European boundaries. But this atlas is something rather different. It is a statistical holograph, a three-dimensional picture whose purpose is to show as many significant aspects of the country as possible: the geology and the minerals, the vegetation, the weather which with indifferent ferocity bakes and freezes, and the human diversity which persists, and even grows, in a nation whose founding fathers pledged it to homogeneity and equality.

All these aspects are related. Look at the map showing the natural watersheds, for instance, and you will see in the east the natural boundary of the 13 states which declared independence from Britain. The rivers, which were often the main means of communication, concentrated a still eastward-looking population between the mountains and the sea until expansionist policies and the urge for new, cheaper lands to farm and exploit pushed and tugged people west.

The world has become so conditioned by the saga of the American West, the restless pursuit of manifest destiny that eventually took America beyond its boundaries and out of isolationism, that it tends to see it as a country for ever in the process of rapid change. That may be true in many ways, but in one very major way it is quite untrue. Politically, the United States has changed less than any other Western country in the past 200 years, and that includes conservative, unrevolutionary Britain. America's democracy is older than that of anyone else. Since the revolutionary war, when the rebellious colonists succeeded in giving King George III the boot, the constitution and the underlying ideals have remained virtually intact. It may have taken blacks nearly 200 years to win their full rights as citizens, but there is no deep cynicism about either the constitution or the ideals. They maintain their hold on the imagination and loyalty of people in a way that often surprises European newcomers, unused to displays of emotion about such matters. Those endless roads leading into American cities lined with the illuminated totems of fast-food establishments, carpet and furniture discount stores, banks built like mausoleums and supermarkets whose entrances are graced by classical porticos, may seem like the natural shrines of the popular ethic, where the priesthood really resides, but in fact America is a lawyer's country, a place which in the end, whatever the detours on the way, obeys the legal imperatives.

That to a very great extent accounts for its stability, a condition which has allowed great wealth to flourish and encouraged investment ($32.5 billion from Britain, top of the foreigners' league) on an appropriately massive scale. If you examine the section on personal wealth you will see that in 1983 the median family income was $24,580. However, you may also note that below the poverty threshold, fixed at a fairly generous $10,178 for a family of four, were 12 per cent of whites, 36 per cent of blacks and 28 per cent of Hispanics. The gap between the wealthiest and the poorest in the United States is very, very wide indeed, and a disproportionate number of the poor are black or of Spanish-speaking origin. Remember, though, that opportunity and betterment are words which shine bright in the American lexicon and that many of the poor, notably the Hispanics, have come from poorer places to improve their lot. The pressures generated by inequalities of wealth have not led to the creation of left-wing class parties of the sort prevalent in Europe and the two-party system has remained intact and without major challenge. The success of the American education system plays a considerable part in this, indoctrinating and bringing together children from all classes. The reasonably clever are virtually certain to go on to higher education (16 per cent completed four-year courses in 1980). Crime has told a different story in the past few decades, with violence a commonplace, particularly in the major cities. But here there has been a marked improvement in the past few years, leaving New Mexico in the unhappy position of being the only state which has experienced an increase. The decreases elsewhere have often been sharp, indicating that America has crested this particular epidemic.

America's political structure may be relatively unchanging, but this is true of little else. People pull up their roots and move in the United States with a readiness and frequency that is found in few other places. On the whole, the trend is away from the regions of long cold winters towards places where the sun shines all the year round (with the exception of Alaska, where the oil boom will continue to draw in people until the end of the century, if the projections are correct). New York's population has shrunk while that of California has boomed, so that it is now the largest state in the Union. In Florida it was the elderly in search of sea and year-round warmth who started its move into the top brackets of population increases, a process which new industries are topping up. Even in the chilly north-east, though, the picture is not uniform. New Hampshire and Vermont look for increases between 1980 and 2000 which will rival California's in percentage terms, while New England as a whole may just be beginning to see a return to population growth. But that does not change the significance of the figures which show that New York State which was first in value of manufacturing output in 1967 fell to fifth in 1981. California and Texas took the first two places.

American remains a dynamic country where there are fewer inhibitions to expansion and enterprise than there are in Western Europe, but it is nevertheless in decline as an exporter. Its percentage of world trade has fallen since the end of the war as dramatically as those of Japan and Western Europe have risen. Trade deficits combined with huge budget deficits are a new American experience and their impact will no doubt show up when the statistical cartographers tackle the next edition of this atlas.

DAVID ADAMSON

THE UNITED STATES

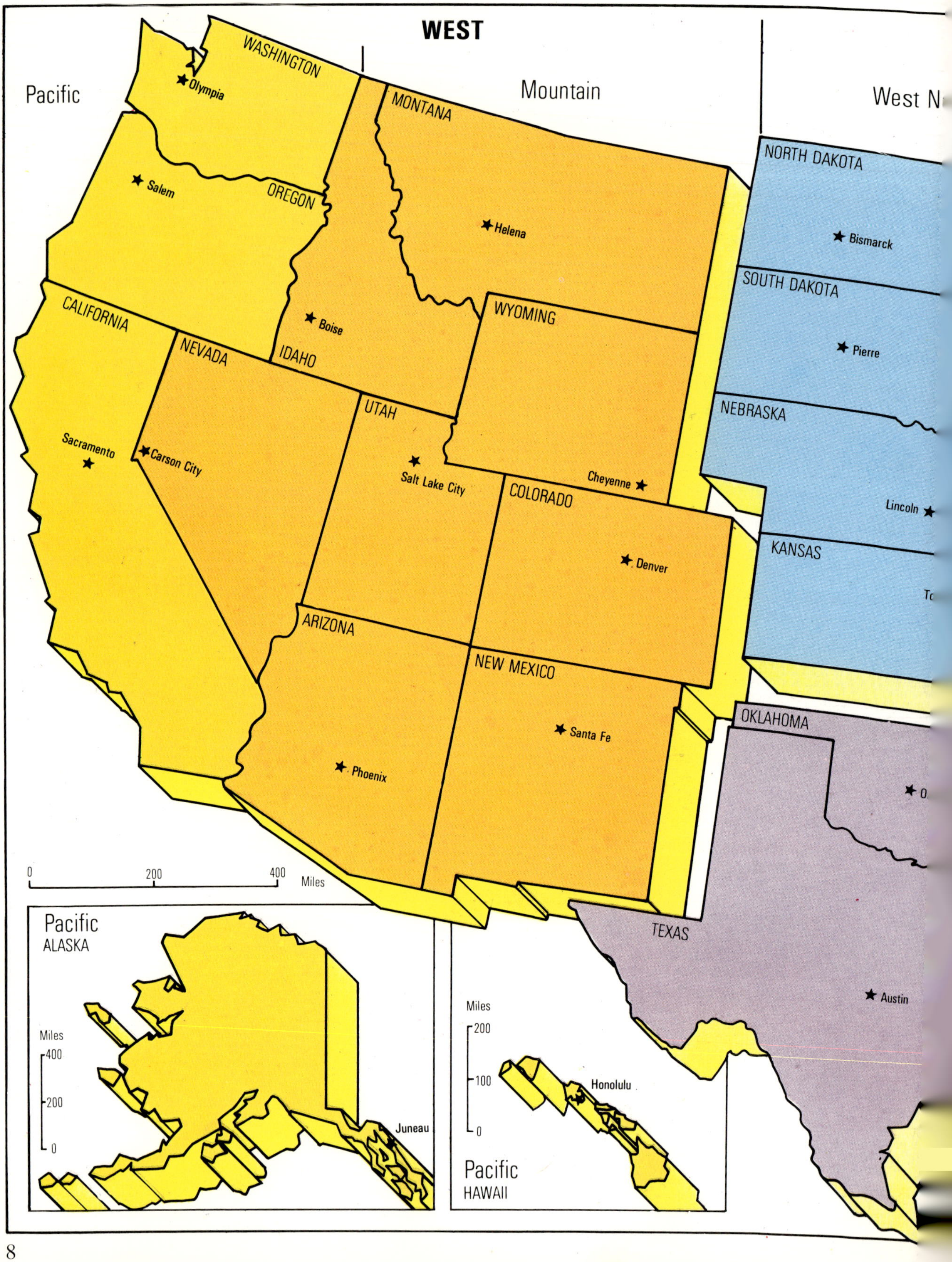

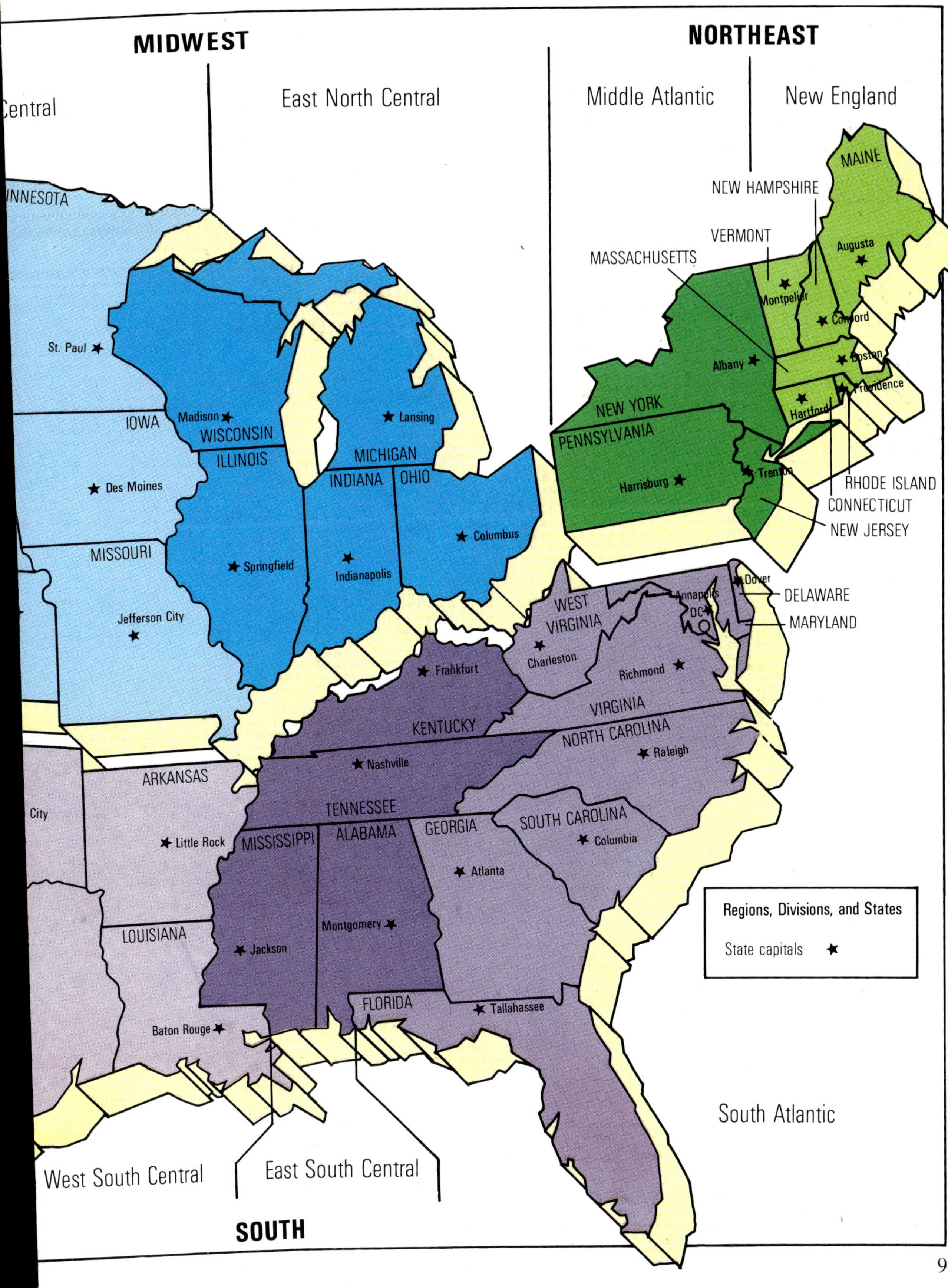
MIDWEST
NORTHEAST
Central
East North Central
Middle Atlantic
New England
MINNESOTA
St. Paul
IOWA
Des Moines
MISSOURI
Jefferson City
WISCONSIN
Madison
ILLINOIS
Springfield
MICHIGAN
Lansing
INDIANA
Indianapolis
OHIO
Columbus
NEW YORK
Albany
PENNSYLVANIA
Harrisburg
Trenton
NEW JERSEY
MAINE
Augusta
NEW HAMPSHIRE
Concord
VERMONT
Montpelier
MASSACHUSETTS
Boston
CONNECTICUT
Hartford
RHODE ISLAND
Providence
DELAWARE
Dover
MARYLAND
Annapolis
DC
WEST VIRGINIA
Charleston
VIRGINIA
Richmond
KENTUCKY
Frankfort
TENNESSEE
Nashville
NORTH CAROLINA
Raleigh
SOUTH CAROLINA
Columbia
GEORGIA
Atlanta
ALABAMA
Montgomery
MISSISSIPPI
Jackson
FLORIDA
Tallahassee
ARKANSAS
Little Rock
LOUISIANA
Baton Rouge
City
Regions, Divisions, and States
State capitals
South Atlantic
West South Central
East South Central
SOUTH

THE UNITED STATES

The United States is made up of fifty states and the District of Columbia, which contains the federal capital of Washington. These political units are not always convenient for economic, social, or other analyses, and the map shows larger units ("regions" and "divisions"), which are adopted on occasion in this atlas. (These larger units are also used by the Bureau of the Census and by other federal agencies concerned with national statistics.)

TOP TEN: LARGEST STATES BY POPULATION

1 California
2 New York
3 Texas
4 Pennsylvania
5 Illinois
6 Ohio
7 Florida
8 Michigan
9 New Jersey
10 North Carolina

POPULATION AND AREA OF THE UNITED STATES BY REGION, DIVISION, AND STATE

Region, Division, and State	Population (1983) (thousands)*	Area (square miles)*
NORTHEAST	**49,519**	**168,875**
New England	**12,489**	**66,672**
Maine	1,146	33,265
New Hampshire	959	9,279
Vermont	525	9,614
Massachusetts	5,767	8,284
Rhode Island	955	1,212
Connecticut	3,138	5,018
Middle Atlantic	**37,029**	**102,203**
New York	17,667	49,108
New Jersey	7,468	7,787
Pennsylvania	11,895	45,308
SOUTH	**79,539**	**898,575**
South Atlantic	**38,805**	**278,927**
Delaware	606	2,044
Maryland	4,304	10,460
District of Columbia	623	69
Virginia	5,550	40,767
West Virginia	1,965	24,231
North Carolina	6,082	52,669
South Carolina	3,264	31,113
Georgia	5,732	58,910
Florida	10,680	58,664
East South Central	**14,946**	**181,947**
Kentucky	3,714	40,409
Tennessee	4,685	42,144
Alabama	3,959	51,705
Mississippi	2,587	47,689
West South Central	**25,788**	**437,701**
Arkansas	2,328	53,187
Louisiana	4,438	47,751
Oklahoma	3,298	69,956
Texas	15,724	266,807

The four regions are the traditional ones of Northeast, South, Midwest, and West, which appear on the map as separate blocs. Each is further divided into two or three divisions, which are indicated on the map by colour.

The capital city is shown for each state.

Alaska and Hawaii, geographically separated from the rest of the states, are included in the Pacific section of the Western bloc.

Source: U.S. Bureau of the Census

Region, Division, and State	Population (1983) (thousands)*	Area (square miles)*
MIDWEST	**58,953**	**766,365**
East North Central	**41,531**	**248,540**
Ohio	10,746	41,330
Indiana	5,479	36,185
Illinois	11,486	56,345
Michigan	9,069	58,527
Wisconsin	4,751	56,153
West North Central	**17,422**	**517,825**
Minnesota	4,144	84,402
Iowa	2,905	56,275
Missouri	4,970	69,697
North Dakota	680	70,703
South Dakota	700	77,116
Nebraska	1,597	77,355
Kansas	2,425	82,277
WEST	**45,970**	**1,784,955**
Mountain	**12,331**	**863,563**
Montana	817	147,046
Idaho	989	83,564
Wyoming	514	97,809
Colorado	3,139	104,091
New Mexico	1,399	121,593
Arizona	2,963	114,000
Utah	1,619	84,899
Nevada	891	110,561
Pacific	**33,639**	**921,392**
Washington	4,300	68,138
Oregon	2,662	97,073
California	25,174	158,706
Alaska	479	591,004
Hawaii	1,023	6,471
United States	**233,981**	**3,618,770**

* Rounding population figures to the nearest thousand and area figures to the nearest square mile means that state, division and region totals do not always agree exactly.

TOP TEN: LARGEST STATES BY AREA

1 Alaska
2 Texas
3 California
4 Montana
5 New Mexico
6 Arizona
7 Nevada
8 Colorado
9 Wyoming
10 Oregon

THE SHAPE OF THE LAND

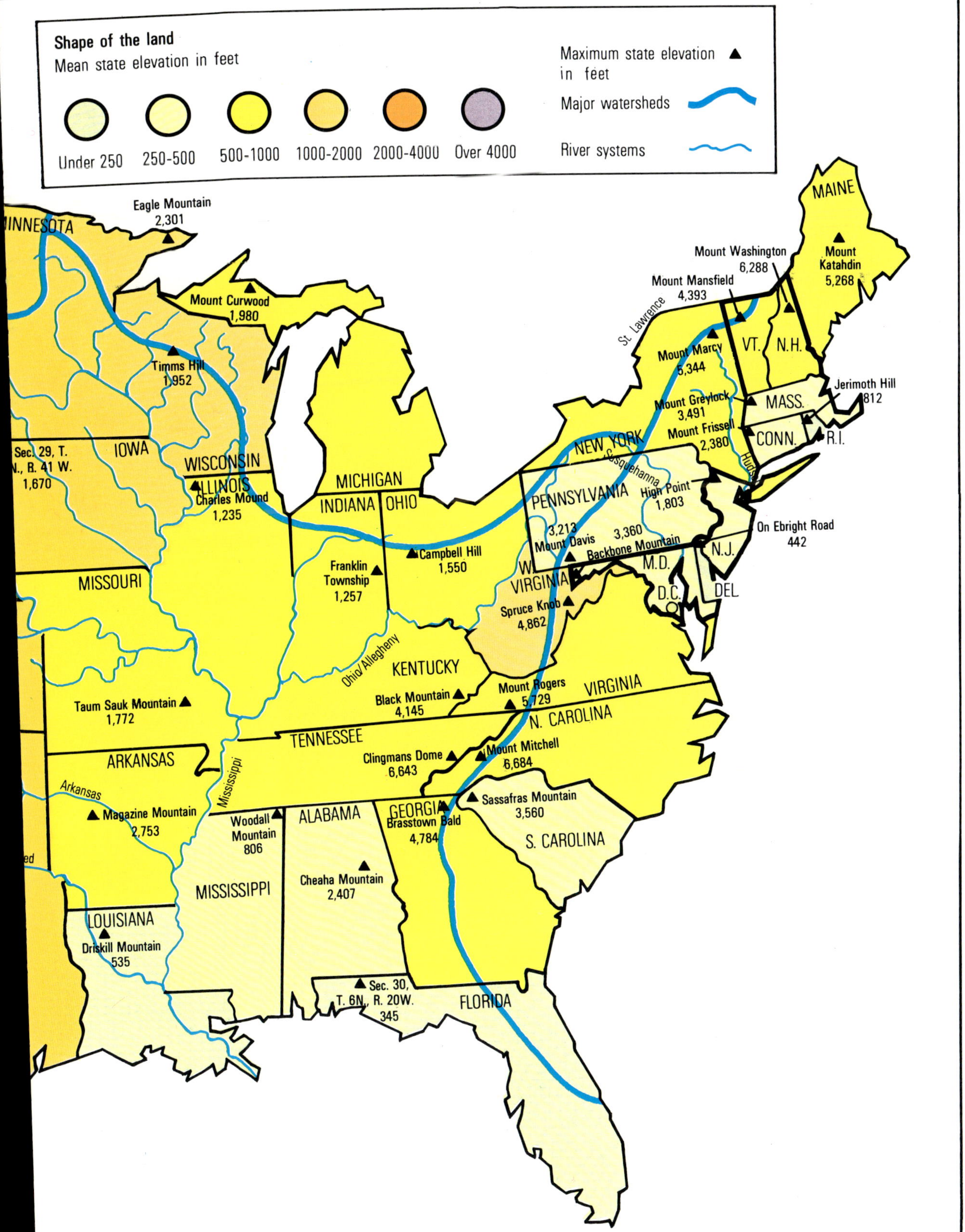
Shape of the land
Mean state elevation in feet
Under 250
250-500
500-1000
1000-2000
2000-4000
Over 4000
Maximum state elevation in feet
Major watersheds
River systems
MINNESOTA
Eagle Mountain 2,301
Mount Curwood 1,980
Timms Hill 1,952
IOWA
Sec. 29, T. N., R. 41 W. 1,670
WISCONSIN
ILLINOIS
Charles Mound 1,235
MICHIGAN
INDIANA
OHIO
Franklin Township 1,257
Campbell Hill 1,550
MISSOURI
Taum Sauk Mountain 1,772
KENTUCKY
Black Mountain 4,145
Ohio/Allegheny
TENNESSEE
Clingmans Dome 6,643
ARKANSAS
Arkansas
Magazine Mountain 2,753
Mississippi
Woodall Mountain 806
MISSISSIPPI
ALABAMA
Cheaha Mountain 2,407
LOUISIANA
Driskill Mountain 535
Sec. 30, T. 6N., R. 20W. 345
FLORIDA
GEORGIA
Brasstown Bald 4,784
Sassafras Mountain 3,560
S. CAROLINA
Mount Mitchell 6,684
N. CAROLINA
Mount Rogers 5,729
VIRGINIA
W. VIRGINIA
Spruce Knob 4,862
PENNSYLVANIA
Mount Davis 3,213
Backbone Mountain 3,360
M.D.
D.C.
DEL
N.J.
On Ebright Road 442
High Point 1,803
Susquehanna
NEW YORK
Mount Marcy 5,344
St. Lawrence
Mount Mansfield 4,393
Mount Washington 6,288
MAINE
Mount Katahdin 5,268
VT.
N.H.
MASS.
Mount Greylock 3,491
Jerimoth Hill 812
CONN.
R.I.
Mount Frissell 2,380
Huds

THE SHAPE OF THE LAND

Diagram A: Natural regions of the United States

- Pacific mountain system
- Intermontane plateaus
- Rocky mountain system
- Interior plains
- Interior highlands
- Coastal plain
- Appalachian region
- Canadian shield
- Volcanic region

The terrain of the contiguous United States can be simply divided into three: two mountain chains running parallel with the coasts, with a large lowland plain between them. This is reflected in the map opposite which shows the mean elevation of the states.

The map below reveals that the layout of the land is more complicated. The mountains in the West are not a single range but a wide mountainous system consisting of three distinct, major regions: the Pacific mountain system, the intermontane plateaus, and the Rocky Mountains. These mountain systems in turn consist of series of associated ranges, such as the Sierra Nevada or the Cascades in the Pacific system. The whole region makes up about one-third of the area of the United States.

The Rocky Mountains, running through Canada, extend into Alaska and form the Aleutian island chain. There are two main mountain ranges in the north: the Alaskan and Brooks ranges. Between them lies the Yukon plateau, with the smaller Arctic plateau north of the Brooks range.

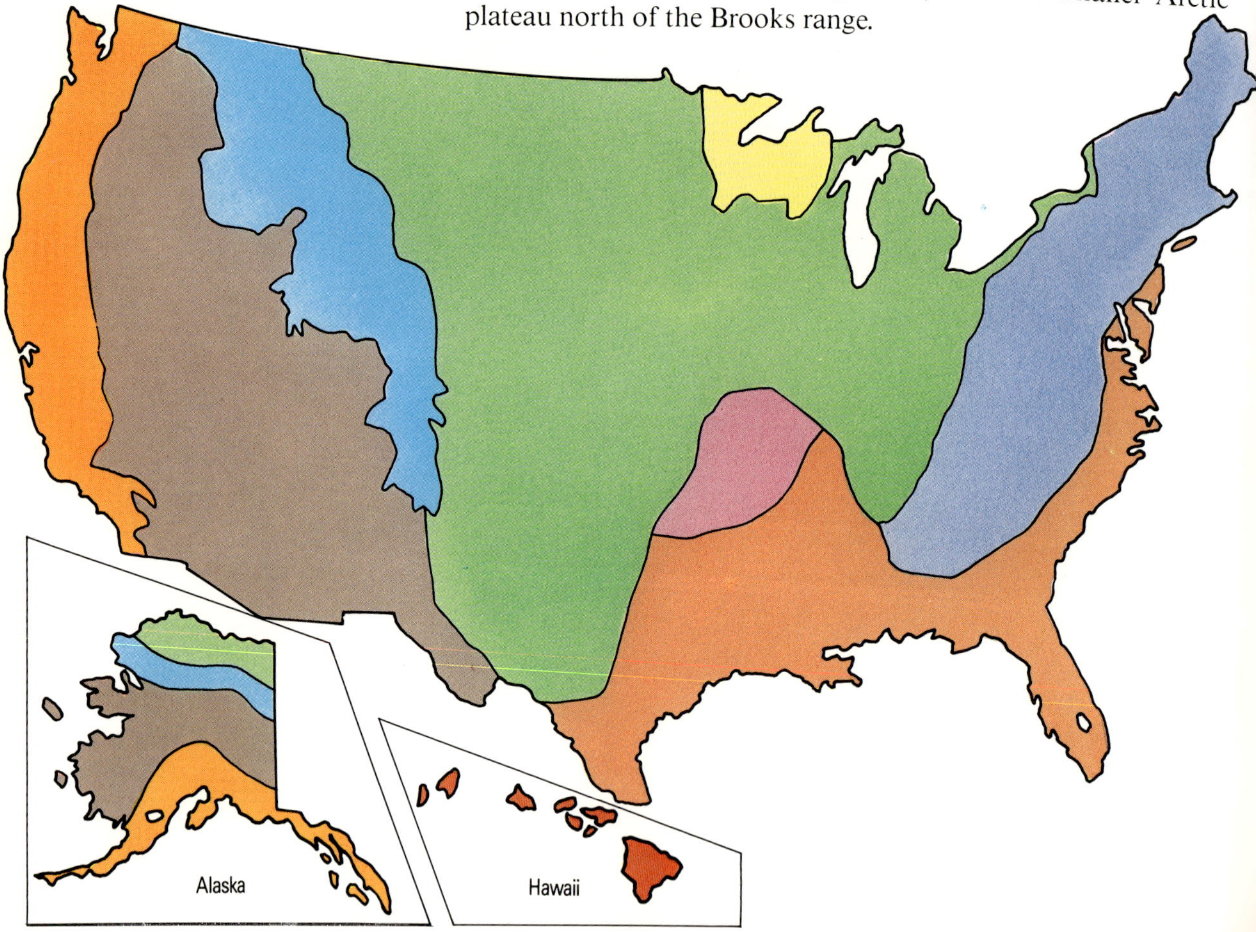

The central lowland and plains region, east of the Rockies, contains the Great Plains and associated regions, including part of the Canadian Shield (an area of ancient rocks) and a number of upland areas. Though generally level, the Great Plains have an overall downward slope from west to east.

The Ozark plateau of southern Missouri and northwestern Arkansas forms an interior highland region separating the interior plains from the wide Atlantic plain of the South and East. Farther north, the Atlantic coastal plain is narrow or nonexistent.

Appalachia is the second major highland system, and, like the Rocky Mountains, it is made up of a series of ranges, including the Blue Ridge, Adirondack, Catskill, and Allegheny Mountains.

The islands of Hawaii are of volcanic origin, built up from the ocean floor by successive deposits of lava. On the larger islands, there are small plateaus between the volcanic peaks.

The map on the opposite page illustrates the main drainage basins. Much the largest is that of the Mississippi River and its tributaries. The Mississippi basin encompasses almost the entire region between the Rocky Mountains and the Appalachians, from the Canadian border down to the Gulf of Mexico. Areas that do not form part of the Mississippi system include a few small regions in the South, which are drained by rivers flowing directly into the Gulf, and the Great Lakes region in the Northeast, which belongs to the Canadian St. Lawrence River system.

East of the Appalachian region, the Hudson, Susquehanna, and many short streams cross the coastal plain to the Atlantic. In the West, the principal drainage basins are those of the Columbia system in the north, the Sacramento-San Joaquin system in the Central Valley of California, and the Colorado and the Rio Grande in the south.

The major part of the central plateau of Alaska is drained by the Yukon River.

The table gives the length of principal U.S. rivers. The St. Lawrence and other primarily Canadian rivers are not included. Measuring rivers is always controversial; rivers sometimes change course or have their courses altered, and the pinpointing of their source is often impossible. These figures, however, are the most reliable available.

The point of highest elevation above sea level in each state is also marked on the map. The highest point in the United States is Mount McKinley in Alaska, 20,320 feet. Highest in the contiguous United States is Mount Whitney in the Sierra Nevada, California, 14,494 feet. Less than 100 miles to the east is the lowest point in the United States, in Death Valley, 282 feet below sea level.

Source: U.S. Geological Survey

TOP TEN: LONGEST RIVERS
(in miles)

Mississippi/Missouri	3,710
Yukon	1,900
Rio Grande	1,885
Arkansas	1,459
Colorado	1,450
Ohio/Allegheny	1,306
Red (southern)	1,270
Columbia	1,243
Snake	1,038
Platte/North Platte	930

WEATHER

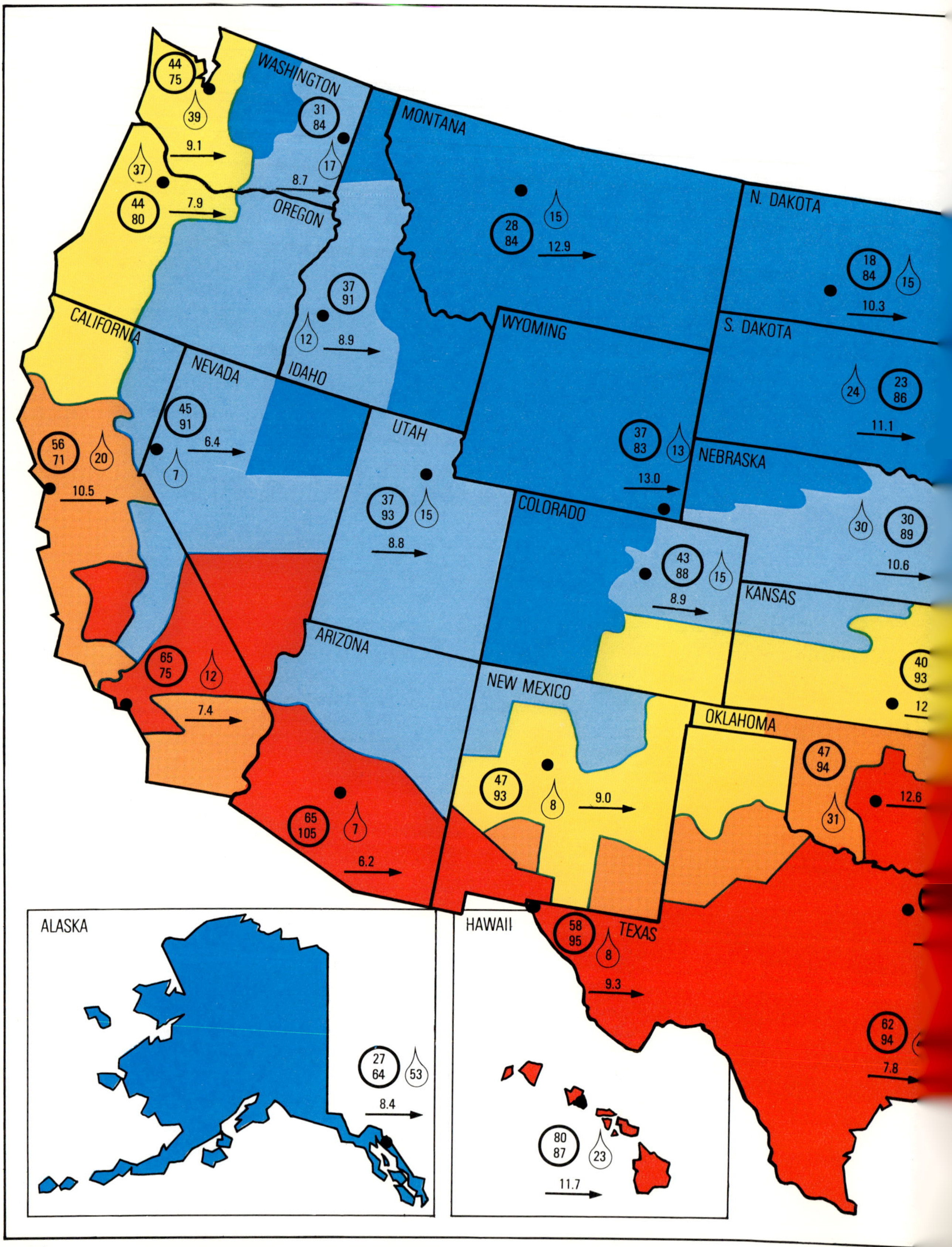
WASHINGTON
MONTANA
N. DAKOTA
OREGON
CALIFORNIA
NEVADA
IDAHO
WYOMING
S. DAKOTA
UTAH
NEBRASKA
COLORADO
KANSAS
ARIZONA
NEW MEXICO
OKLAHOMA
TEXAS
ALASKA
HAWAII
44 75 39
31 84 17
9.1
8.7
37
44 80
7.9
28 84 15
12.9
18 84 15
10.3
37 91
12
8.9
23 86 24
11.1
45 91
6.4
7
37 83 13
13.0
56 71 20
10.5
37 93 15
8.8
30 89 30
10.6
43 88 15
8.9
40 93
12
65 75 12
7.4
47 94 31
12.6
47 93 8
9.0
65 105 7
6.2
58 95 8
9.3
62 94
7.8
27 64 53
8.4
80 87 23
11.7

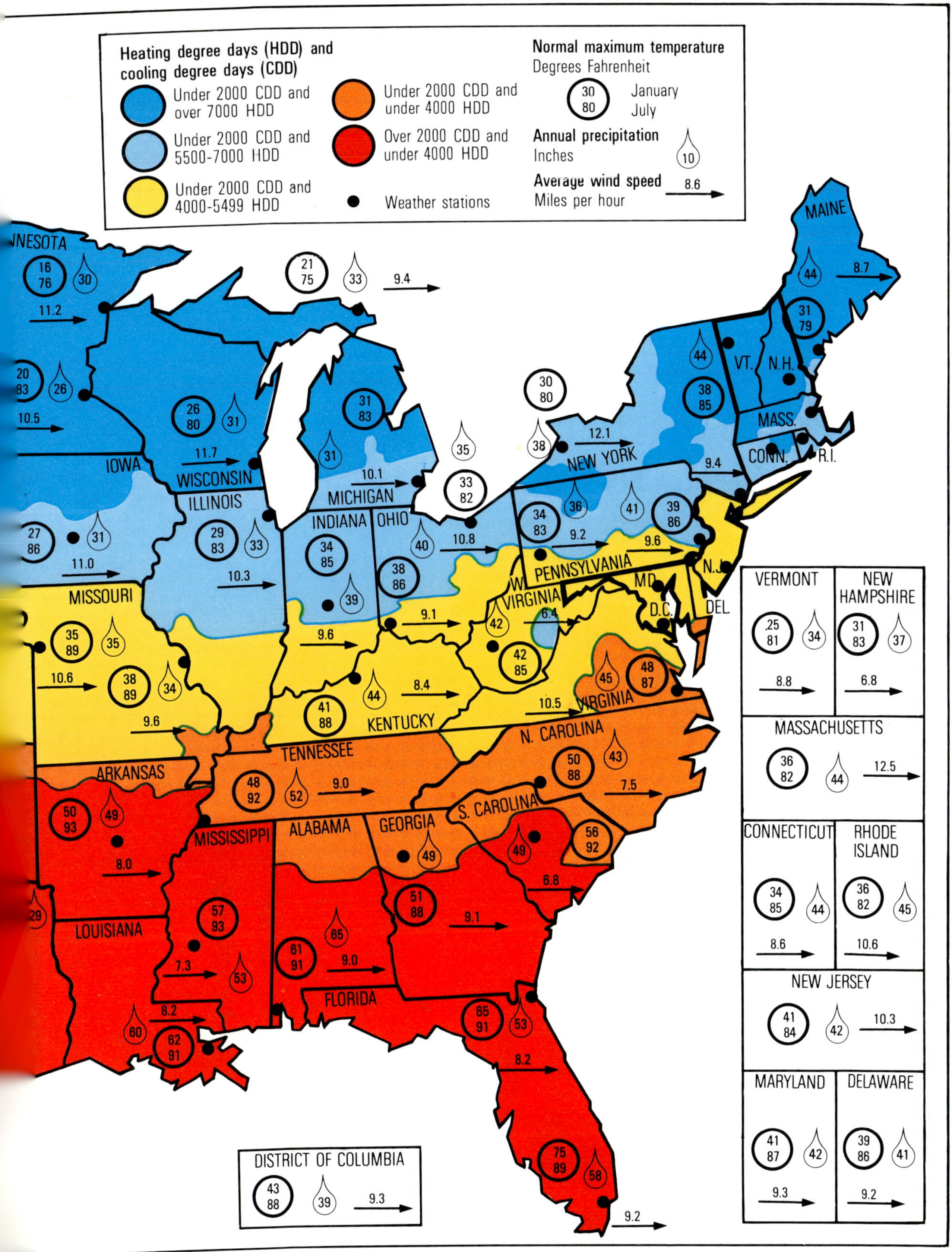
Heating degree days (HDD) and cooling degree days (CDD)
Under 2000 CDD and over 7000 HDD
Under 2000 CDD and 5500-7000 HDD
Under 2000 CDD and 4000-5499 HDD
Under 2000 CDD and under 4000 HDD
Over 2000 CDD and under 4000 HDD
Weather stations
Normal maximum temperature
Degrees Fahrenheit
30 80
January
July
Annual precipitation
Inches
10
Average wind speed
Miles per hour
8.6
MAINE
VT.
N.H.
MASS.
CONN.
R.I.
NEW YORK
PENNSYLVANIA
N.J.
MD.
D.C.
DEL
W. VIRGINIA
VIRGINIA
N. CAROLINA
S. CAROLINA
GEORGIA
FLORIDA
ALABAMA
MISSISSIPPI
LOUISIANA
ARKANSAS
TENNESSEE
KENTUCKY
OHIO
INDIANA
ILLINOIS
MICHIGAN
WISCONSIN
IOWA
MISSOURI
NESOTA
VERMONT
NEW HAMPSHIRE
MASSACHUSETTS
CONNECTICUT
RHODE ISLAND
NEW JERSEY
MARYLAND
DELAWARE
DISTRICT OF COLUMBIA

WEATHER

Temperature and precipitation are the chief elements of weather. The map measures temperature nationwide in terms of degree days. Heating degree days (HDD) refers to the number of degrees the daily average temperature is below 65° Fahrenheit. Cooling degree days (CDD) refers to the number of degrees the daily average temperature is above 65° Fahrenheit. For example, on a day when the highest temperature is 69°F and the lowest is 51°F, the average is 60°F, resulting in 5 HDD.

In addition, the normal maximum temperature in January and July is shown at one or more weather stations (mainly airports near large cities) in each state, together with the average wind speed in miles per hour. The figures represent an average over a recorded period of, in most cases, more than 30 years.

The map shows clearly that temperature is largely governed by latitude: it is warmer in the south and cooler in the north. The map also shows two other factors affecting temperature: proximity to the sea and elevation. Coastal regions, especially near the Pacific, have warmer winters and cooler summers than inland places at the same latitude, while temperatures in general decrease with altitude. The moderating effect of the sea on temperatures can be clearly seen in Diagram A.

The figures enclosed in raindrops on the map represent the normal annual precipitation at selected stations.

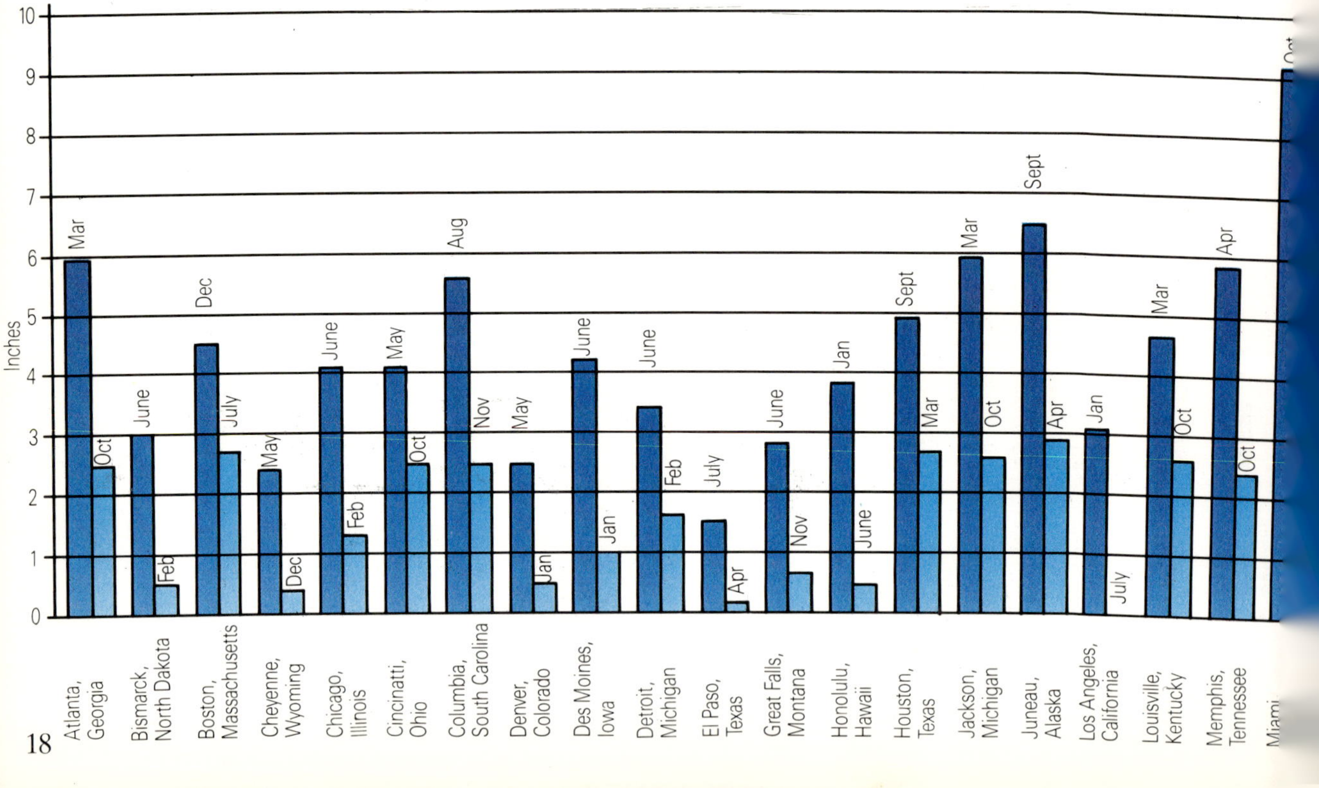

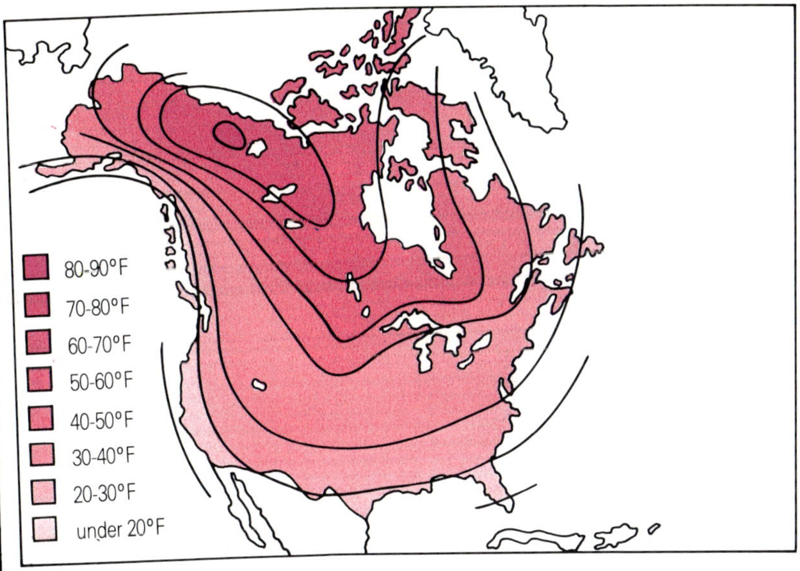

Diagram A: Mean annual range of temperature

The amount of precipitation is largely governed by two factors: the proximity of large bodies of water and the influence of mountain ranges. Areas near the sources of moisture and on windward slopes of mountains generally have the most precipitation.

The seasonal pattern of precipitation varies considerably. The diagram shows average precipitation in selected cities during the wettest and driest months of the year.

Sources: U.S. National Oceanic and Atmospheric Administration; U.S. Bureau of the Census

Diagram B: Seasonal precipitation of selected cities showing the wettest and driest months

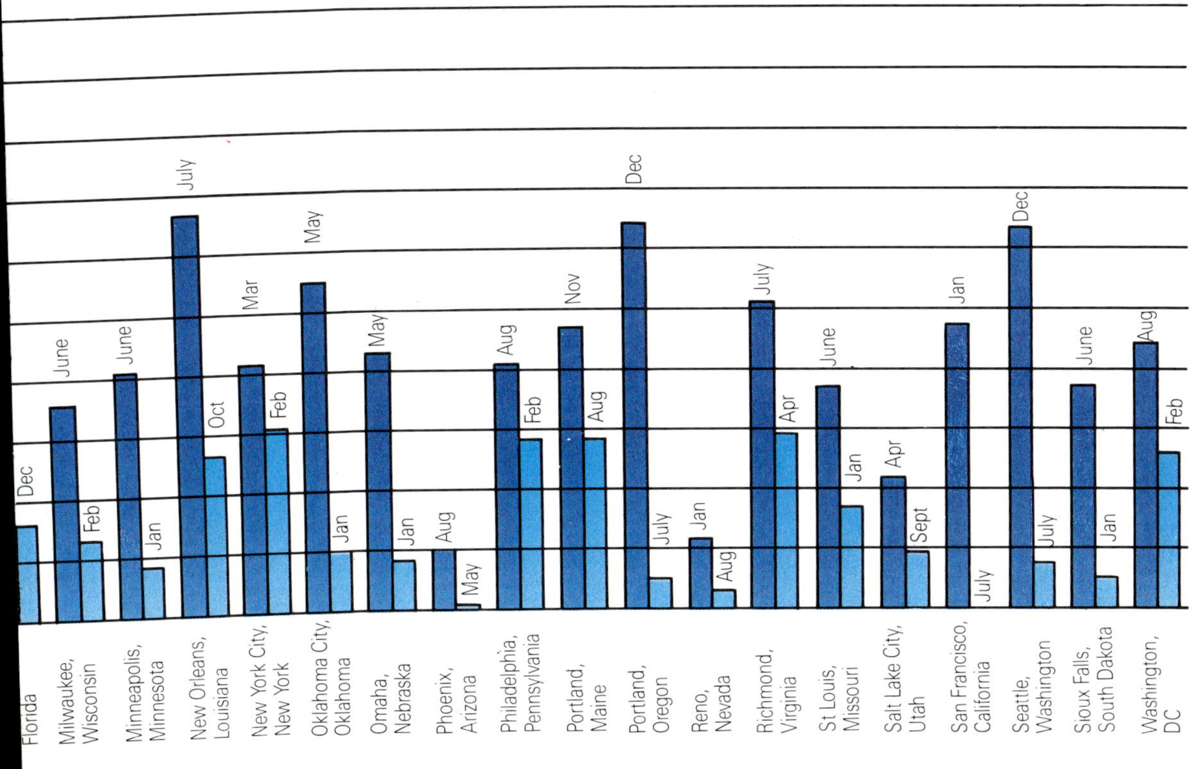

SOILS AND VEGETATION

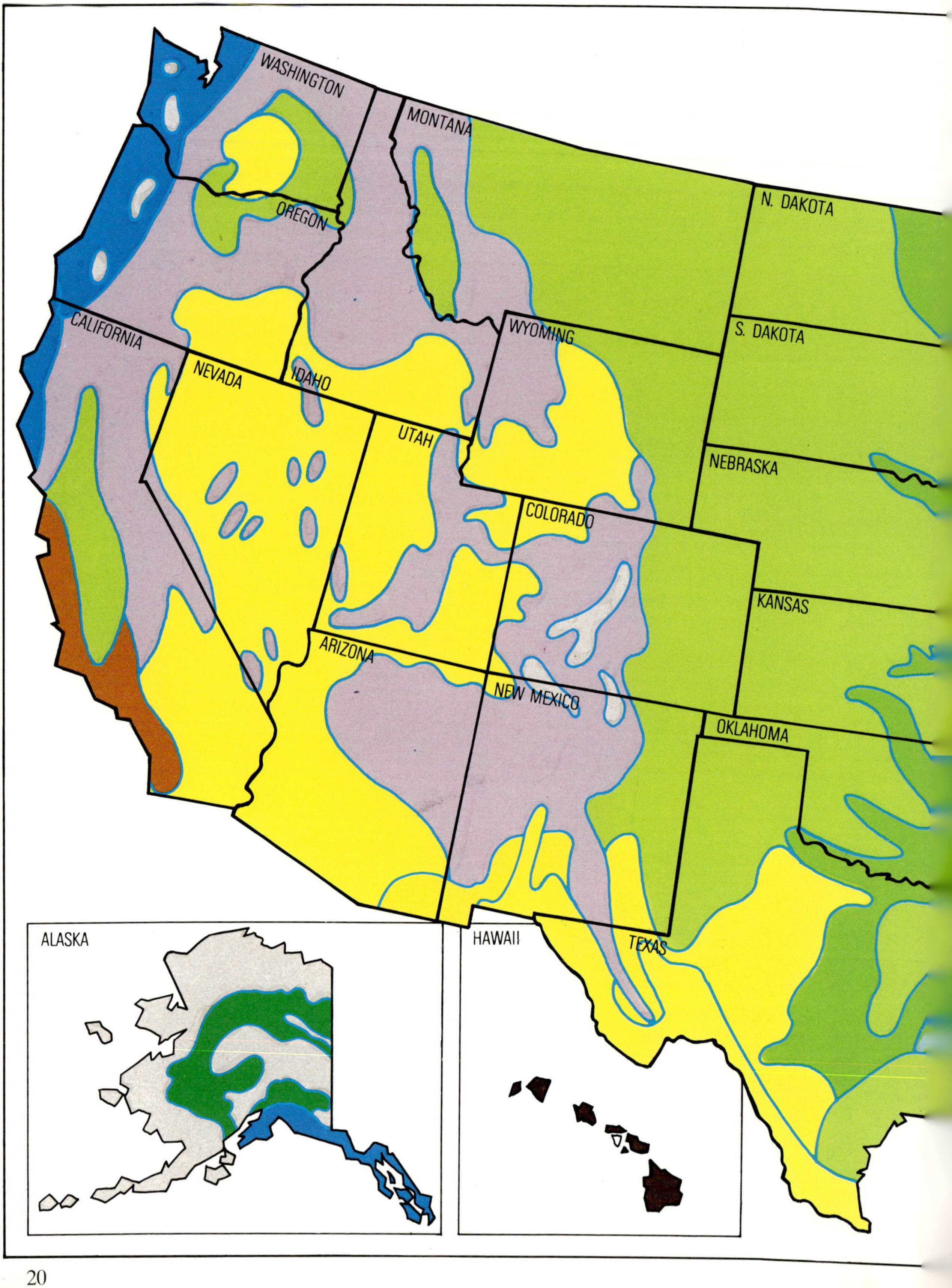

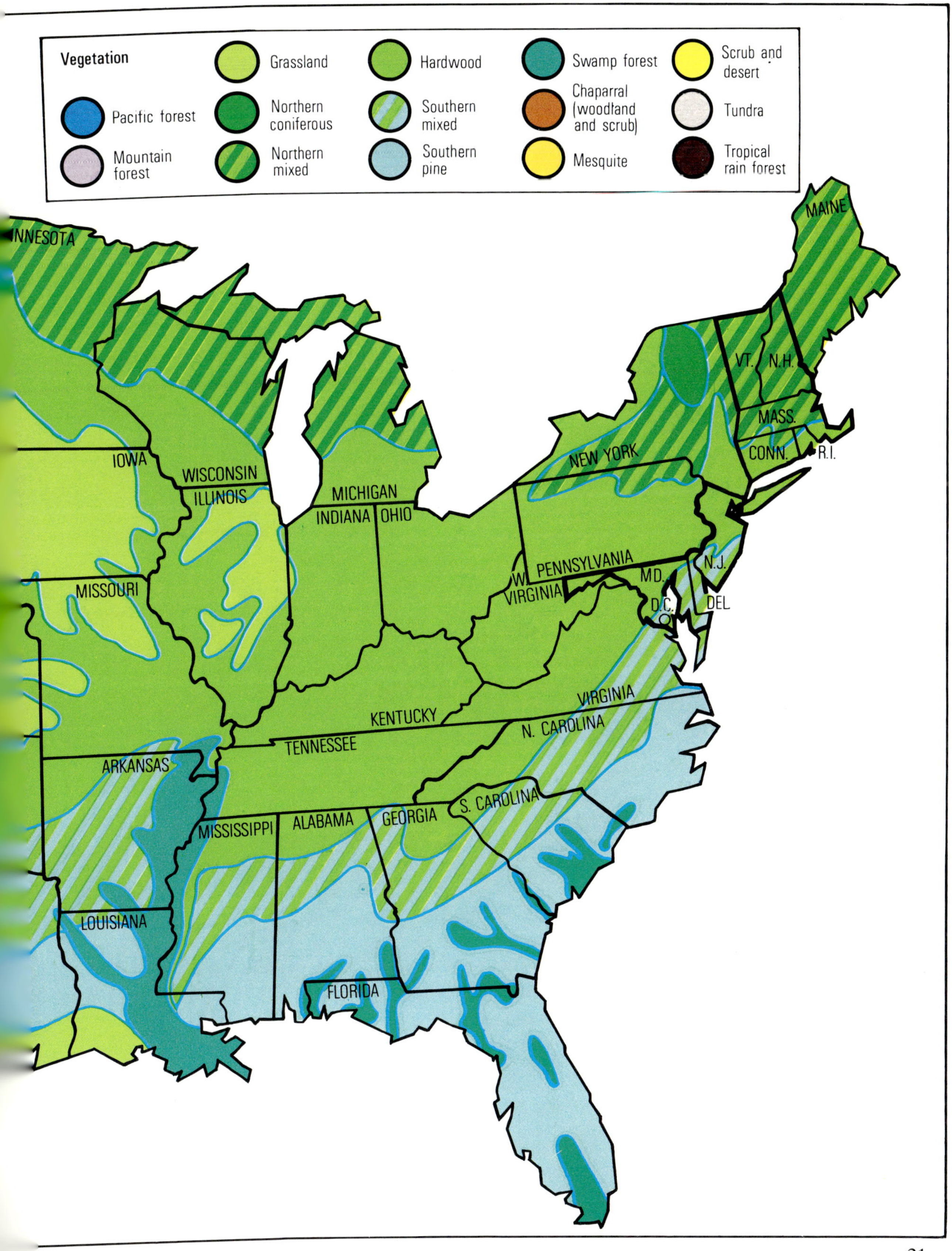

Vegetation
Grassland
Hardwood
Swamp forest
Scrub and desert
Pacific forest
Northern coniferous
Southern mixed
Chaparral (woodland and scrub)
Tundra
Mountain forest
Northern mixed
Southern pine
Mesquite
Tropical rain forest
MAINE
VT.
N.H.
MASS.
CONN.
R.I.
NEW YORK
PENNSYLVANIA
N.J.
MD.
DEL
D.C.
W. VIRGINIA
VIRGINIA
N. CAROLINA
S. CAROLINA
GEORGIA
FLORIDA
ALABAMA
MISSISSIPPI
LOUISIANA
ARKANSAS
TENNESSEE
KENTUCKY
OHIO
INDIANA
MICHIGAN
ILLINOIS
WISCONSIN
IOWA
MISSOURI
INNESOTA

SOILS AND VEGETATION

The United States is a land of great physical variety, and the variations of terrain and climate produce corresponding variations in soils and natural vegetation. There are more than 1,000 species or varieties of native forest trees and about 25,000 species of flowering plants (plus a great number introduced from other regions of the world).

In many regions, considerable differences in natural vegetation may occur within a small area; the map can show only the main divisions and approximate extents. Boundaries between zones are usually less sharp than they appear on the map, although abrupt changes do occur, particularly as a result of changes in altitude.

Natural vegetation consists generally of forest, grassland, or desert scrub. Alaska has a large area of Arctic tundra, which in the contiguous United States, is found only at high altitudes in the mountains.

Coniferous forests cover large parts of Alaska, occur in the Great Lakes region, the extreme Northeast, and the highest parts of Appalachia. Southwards the pines and spruces soon give way to a mixed forest and then to the true hardwood forest, which once extended uninterrupted from New England to Texas.

Southern pine forests grow in most of the coastal plain of the South and Southeast. In the southern mixed forest, the pines grow together with oaks, hickory, cedar, ash, and magnolia. The swamp forests contain the bald cypress as well as white cedar, tupelo gum, and brush vines.

Grassland is characteristic of the Great Plains, and it also occurs in large pockets among the Rocky Mountains. Mesquite grassland occurs in the dry Southwest.

The western forests contain a great variety of trees with different species dominating locally. The Pacific forest is limited to a narrow coastal belt where conditions are mild and humid. Chaparral is plentiful in California and scrub vegetation occurs in the arid basins and semidesert west of the Rocky Mountains. Sagebrush is the commonest plant in the northern areas and the thorny creosote bush in the southern areas. The desert, which stretches from southeastern California into Texas, is noted for the variety and abundance of cacti, notably the saguaro.

The United States has thousands of differently classified soils. The map on this page shows the main groups.

New England lost much topsoil to the glaciers which also deposited rocks so profusely. Patchy and often poor soils are characteristic of most of the Northeast.

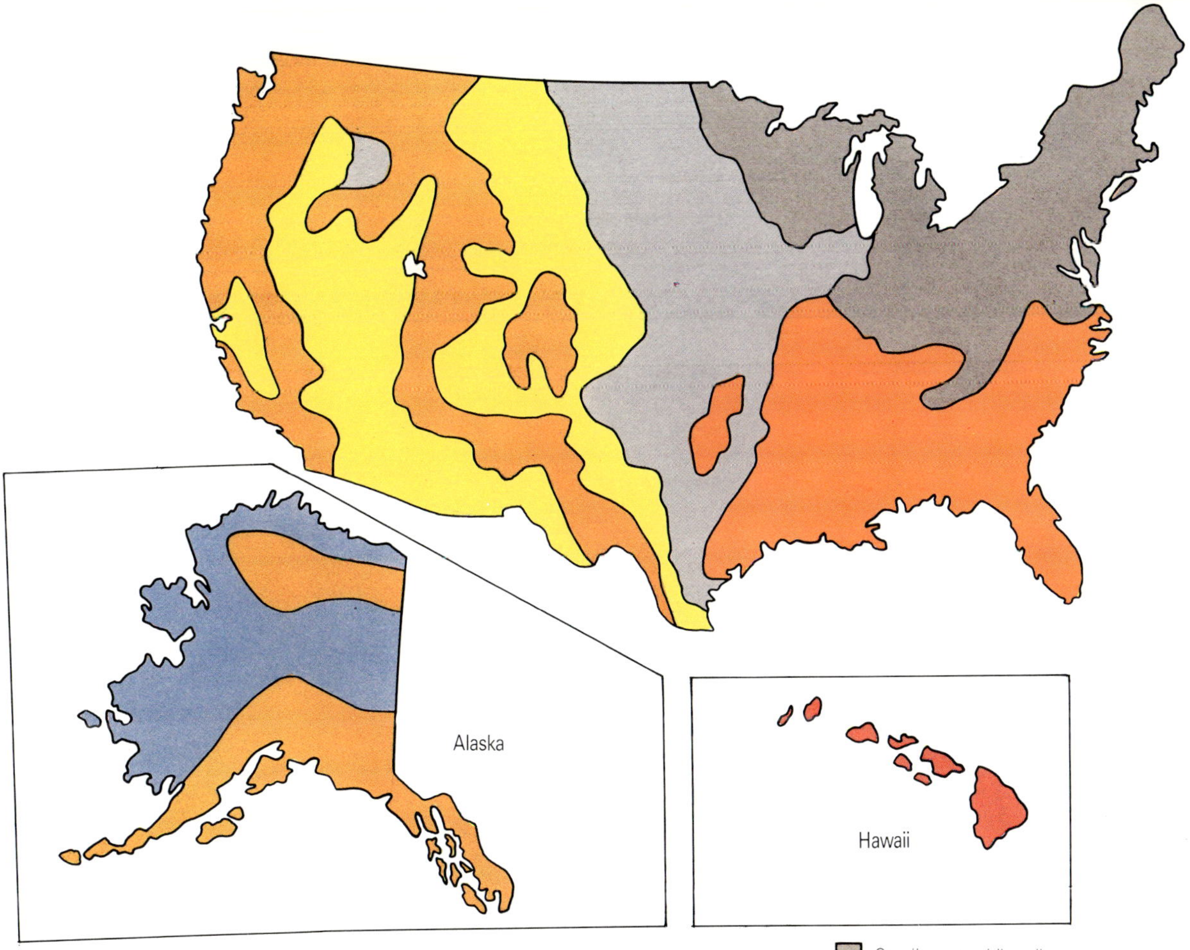

Diagram A: U.S. soils

The South is a patchwork of diverse soil belts, with generally low fertility. Along the coast and in much of Florida, the soil is sandy, with muddy flood plains and swamps. Alluvial soil makes an improvement in the Mississippi valley.

Farther west, in Texas and Oklahoma, many soils are too poor for anything but grazing, and drought is a constant problem. In the Ohio valley region, soils are much eroded, though there are better stretches in Kentucky and Tennessee. Extremely fertile, lime-rich soils are characteristic of the corn belt and the prairies but unreliability of water supply becomes a difficulty in the Great Plains.

The huge mountainous region of the West contains fertile soils in limited areas such as the Columbia plateau, but in general, soils are sparse, stony, or arid. The agricultural productivity of California, is largely dependent on irrigation.

Source: U.S. Dept. of Agriculture

NATIONAL PARKS

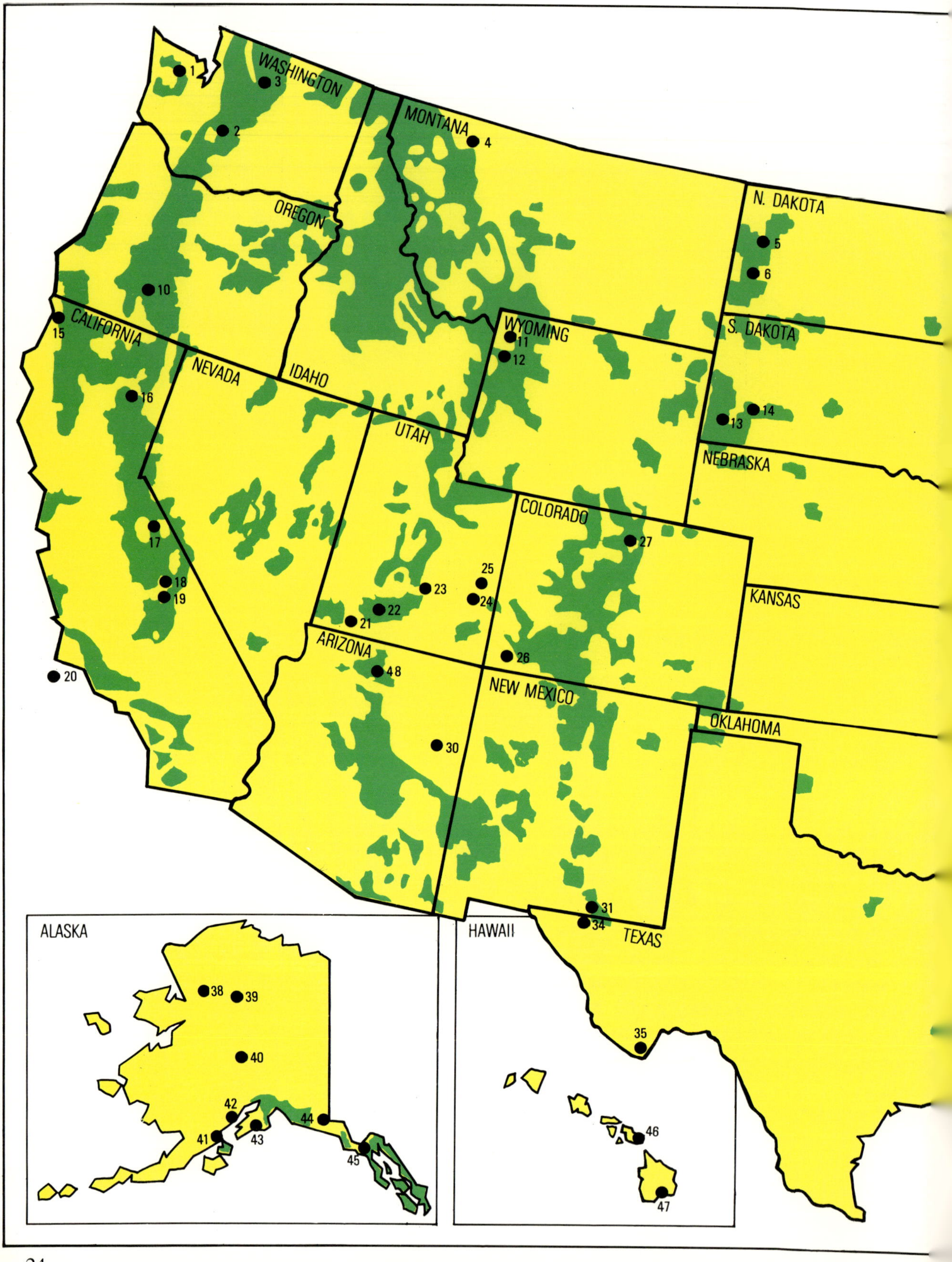

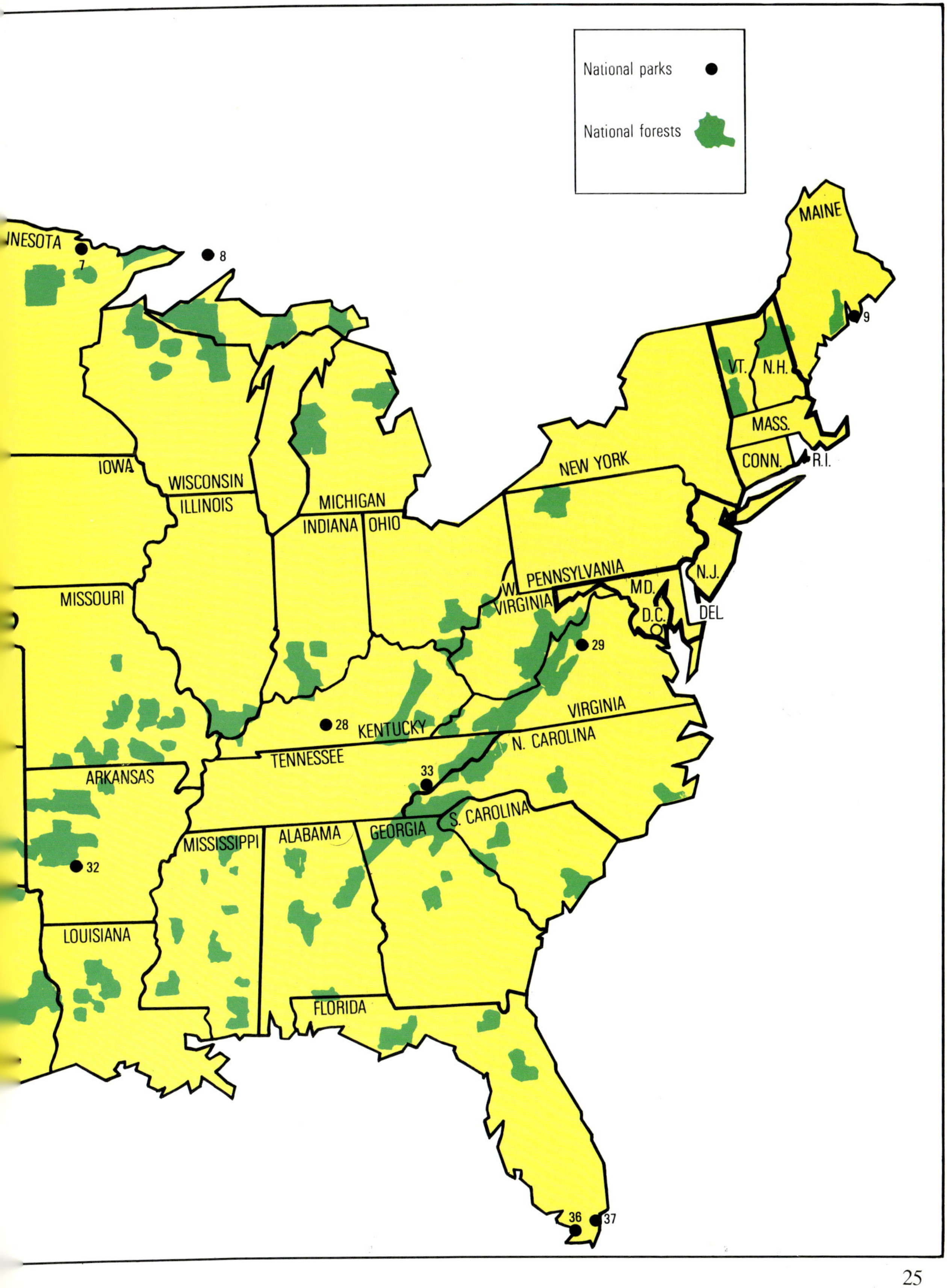
National parks
National forests
NESOTA
7
8
IOWA
WISCONSIN
ILLINOIS
MICHIGAN
INDIANA
OHIO
MISSOURI
KENTUCKY
28
TENNESSEE
33
ARKANSAS
32
MISSISSIPPI
ALABAMA
GEORGIA
S. CAROLINA
N. CAROLINA
VIRGINIA
W. VIRGINIA
29
PENNSYLVANIA
NEW YORK
MD.
D.C.
DEL
N.J.
CONN.
R.I.
MASS.
VT.
N.H.
MAINE
9
LOUISIANA
FLORIDA
36
37

NATIONAL PARKS

In 1872 President Ulysses S. Grant signed an act of Congress creating the Yellowstone National Park "as a pleasure ground for the benefit and enjoyment of the people". This marked the beginning of the concept of national parks under federal ownership. The protection of outstanding scenic areas, wildlife, and vegetation for posterity thus became part of national policy.

During the following decades the national park system grew, partly through the addition of huge natural areas, and partly through the acquisition of locations of historic interest. In 1916 an act of Congress established the National Park Service to administer the areas within the system. By 1983 the number of areas had grown to 335 and the total acreage to almost 75 million. The national parks are shown on the map.

Apart from the national parks themselves, there are many other protected areas within the national park system. National monuments include areas of scientific importance, such as the ecology of Death Valley and the rock arches of Utah. They also include remains of ancient Indian cultures and sites of importance in the development of the nation.

Other protected areas under the jurisdiction of the National Park Service include national parkways, trails, seashores and riverways, historical parks, and sites notable in the Revolutionary and Civil Wars.

The map also shows the extent of the national forest system in 1980. The dangers of forest clearance by settlers became obvious in the latter half of the nineteenth century and Congress passed legislation leading to the beginning of the national forest system in 1891. In 1983 this included a total of 230 million acres.

Source: U.S. National Park Service; National Association of State Park Directors; U.S. Forest Service

Diagram A: Distribution of visitors to national parks compared to distribution of total acreage by division, 1983. Figures for visitors and acreage are in thousands

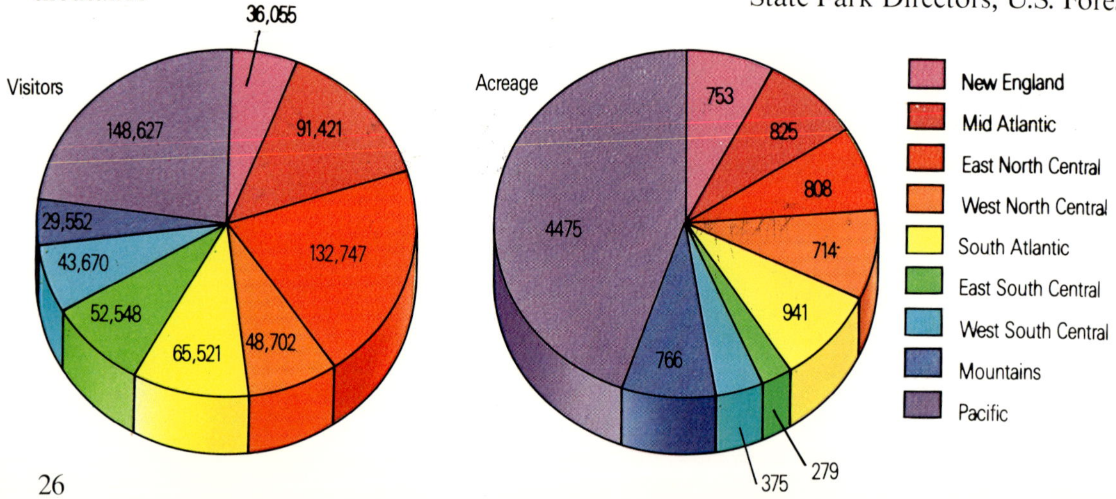

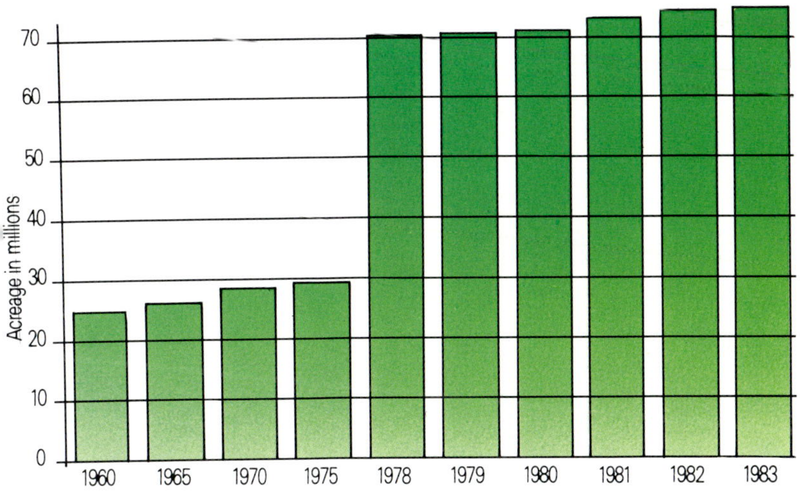

Diagram B: Acreage of National Park system (federal land only), 1960-1983. The leap in 1978 is accounted for by over 40 million acres of public domain land in Alaska being added to the system

NATIONAL PARKS (see map)

1 Olympic, Washington
2 Mount Rainier, Washington
3 North Cascades, Washington
4 Glacier, Montana
5 Theodore Roosevelt (North Unit), North Dakota
6 Theodore Roosevelt (South Unit), North Dakota
7 Voyageurs, Minnesota
8 Isle Royale, Michigan
9 Acadia, Maine
10 Crater Lake, Oregon
11 Yellowstone, Wyoming
12 Grand Teton, Wyoming
13 Wind Cave, South Dakota
14 Badlands, South Dakota
15 Redwood, California
16 Lassen Volcanic, California
17 Yosemite, California
18 Kings Canyon, California
19 Sequoia, California
20 Channel Islands, California
21 Zion, Utah
22 Bryce Canyon, Utah
23 Capitol Reef, Utah
24 Canyonlands, Utah
25 Arches, Utah
26 Mesa Verde, Colorado
27 Rocky Mountain, Colorado
28 Mammoth Cave, Kentucky
29 Shenandoah, Virginia
30 Petrified Forest, Arizona
31 Carlsbad Caverns, New Mexico
32 Hot Springs, Arkansas
33 Great Smoky Mountains, Tennessee
34 Guadalupe Mountains, Texas
35 Big Bend, Texas
36 Everglades, Florida
37 Biscayne, Florida
38 Kobuk Valley, Alaska
39 Gates of Arctic, Alaska
40 Denali, Alaska
41 Katmai, Alaska
42 Lake Clark, Alaska
43 Kenai Fjords, Alaska
44 Wrangell-St Elias, Alaska
45 Glacier Bay, Alaska
46 Haleakala, Hawaii
47 Hawaii Volcanoes, Hawaii
48 Grand Canyon, Arizona

RESIDENT POPULATION

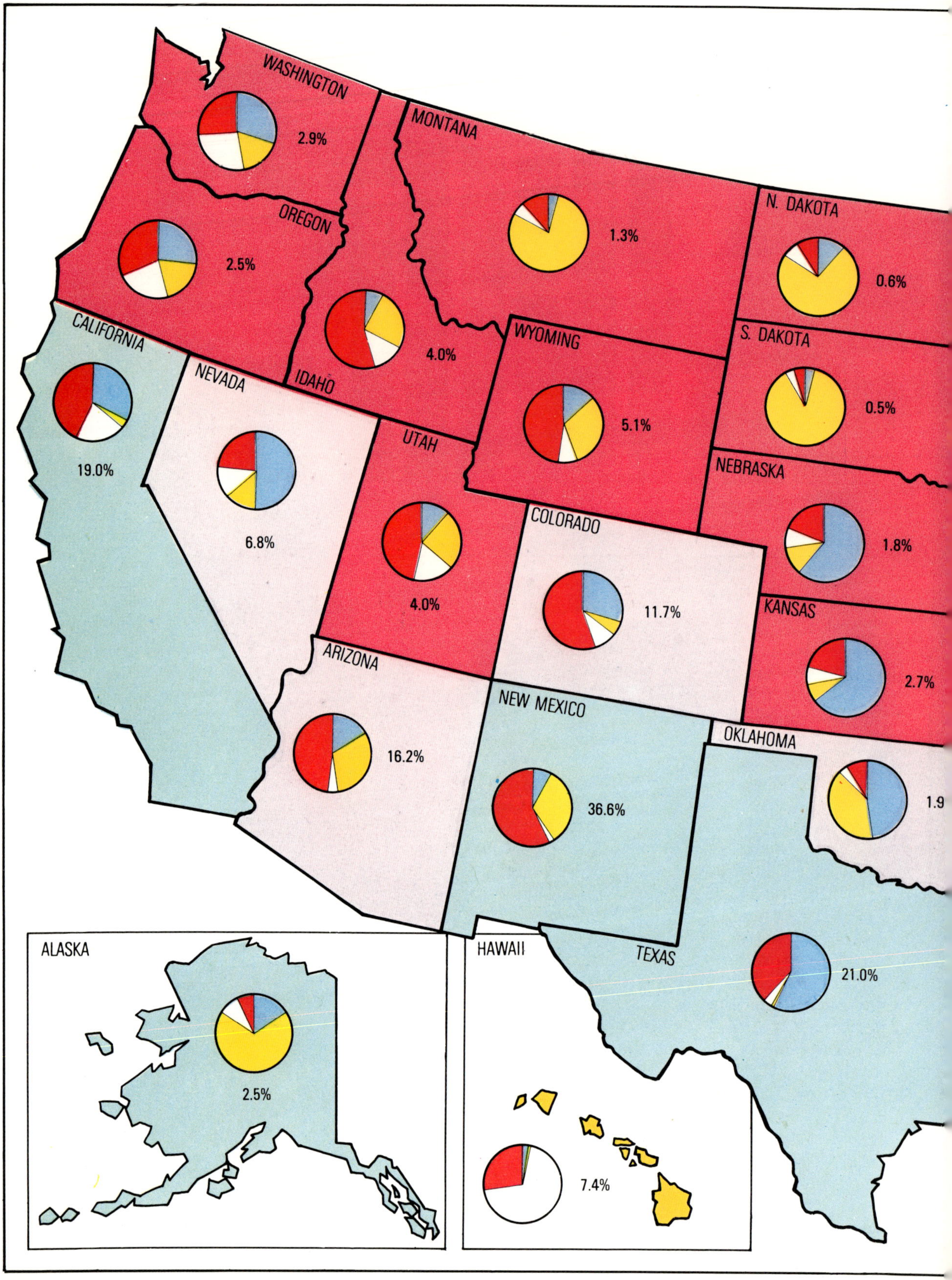

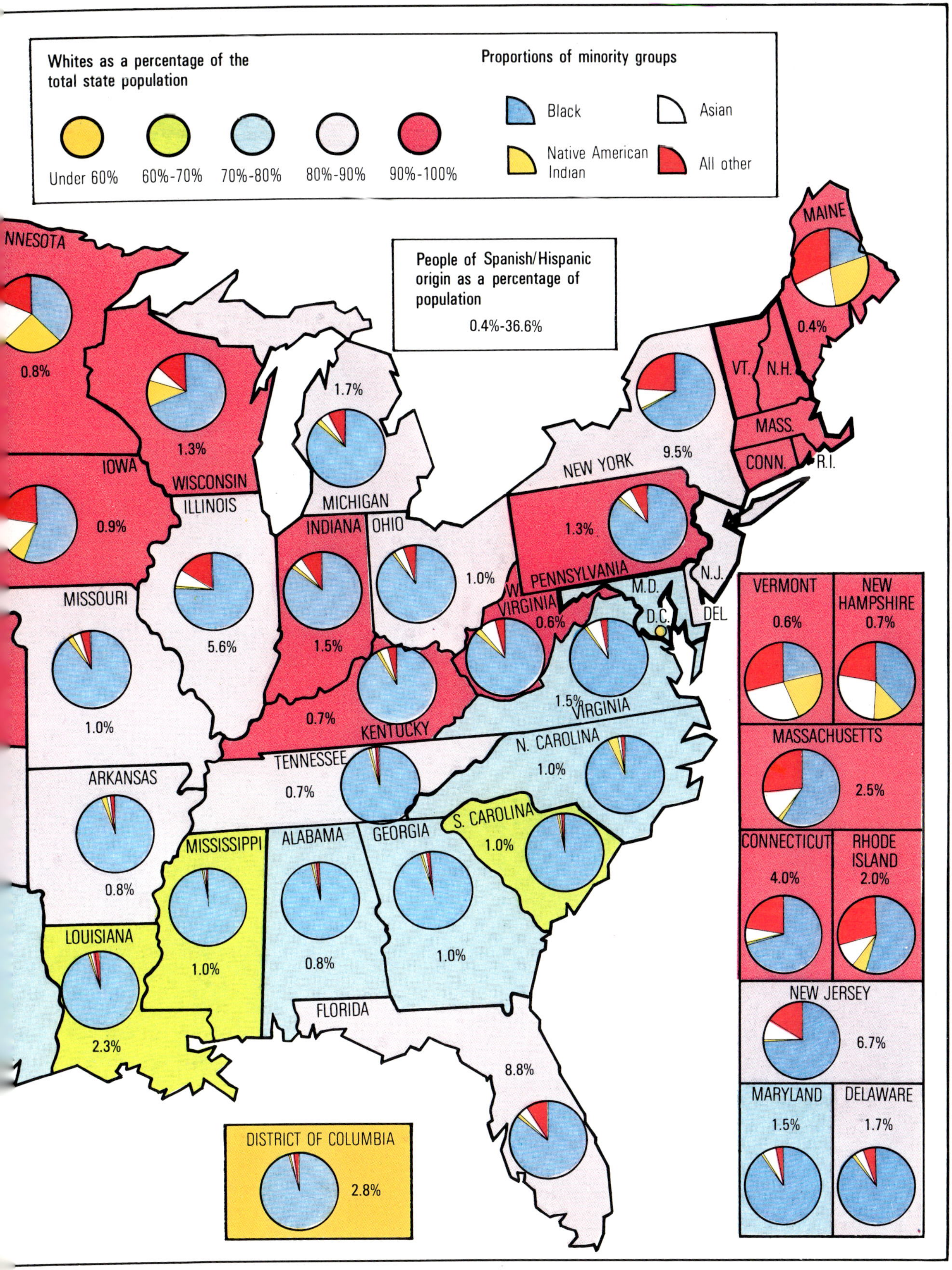

Whites as a percentage of the total state population
Under 60%
60%-70%
70%-80%
80%-90%
90%-100%
Proportions of minority groups
Black
Asian
Native American Indian
All other
People of Spanish/Hispanic origin as a percentage of population
0.4%-36.6%
NNESOTA
0.8%
WISCONSIN
1.3%
IOWA
0.9%
ILLINOIS
5.6%
MICHIGAN
1.7%
INDIANA
1.5%
OHIO
1.0%
MISSOURI
1.0%
KENTUCKY
0.7%
W VIRGINIA
0.6%
VIRGINIA
1.5%
PENNSYLVANIA
1.3%
NEW YORK
9.5%
MAINE
0.4%
VT.
N.H.
MASS.
CONN.
R.I.
N.J.
M.D.
D.C.
DEL
TENNESSEE
0.7%
N. CAROLINA
1.0%
ARKANSAS
0.8%
MISSISSIPPI
1.0%
ALABAMA
0.8%
GEORGIA
1.0%
S. CAROLINA
1.0%
LOUISIANA
2.3%
FLORIDA
8.8%
DISTRICT OF COLUMBIA
2.8%
VERMONT
0.6%
NEW HAMPSHIRE
0.7%
MASSACHUSETTS
2.5%
CONNECTICUT
4.0%
RHODE ISLAND
2.0%
NEW JERSEY
6.7%
MARYLAND
1.5%
DELAWARE
1.7%

RESIDENT POPULATION

A great mixture of ancestry groups makes up the resident population of the United States. The 1980 census classified people according to race, dividing them into "white," "black," "American Indian," several different Asian groups — Chinese, Filipino, Asian Indian, Korean, and Vietnamese — and "all other races." "American Indian" here includes Eskimo and Aleut people.

On the map, the states are coloured according to the percentage of the population classified as "white." The District of Columbia shows the lowest percentage, having only 27 percent in this category. Hawaii also has a low percentage, 33. South Carolina and Louisiana come next, with 69 percent each. At the other extreme, Maine, New Hampshire, and Vermont have over 99 percent.

Each state also shows the percentage classified by the census as "of Spanish origin." These people, the Bureau of the Census explains, may be of any race. Not surprisingly, New Mexico shows the highest percentage, 36.6, followed by 19 percent for California.

In addition, the map gives a pie chart for each state, dividing the non-"white" population between "black," "American Indian,"

Diagram A: Population by main ancestry groups, 1980

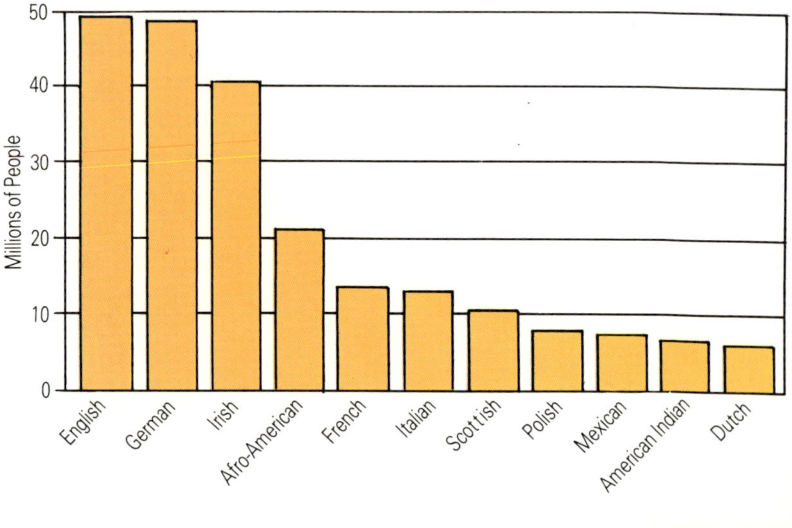

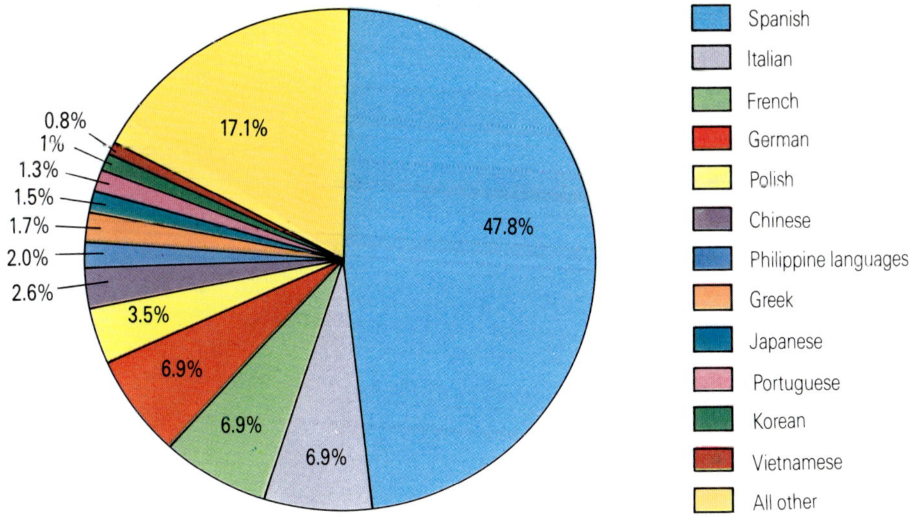

Diagram B: Percentage distribution of those aged 5 years and over, who currently speak a language at home other than English, by language

"Asian," and "all other." In most states "black" is by far the largest of these categories. The exceptions are North and South Dakota, Montana, and Alaska, where "American Indian" is the largest group, and New Mexico, where "all other" is the major group.

Because of the history of immigration into the United States from all over the world, people of similar ancestry groups have tended to settle in particular areas of the country. The 1980 census asked a sample of people about their ancestry. Those who answered either reported a single group, or gave multinational ancestry. Of those who gave "English" as their ancestry — either singly, or in combination with other nationalities — 40 percent live in the South; 41 percent of those who reported German ancestry live in the Midwest; 48 percent of those who said "Russian" are resident in the Northeast; and 53 percent of the group reporting Afro-American ancestry are in the South.

Remembering that multinational ancestry is common, we can use the same sample as a whole to estimate the numbers of people in the United States having foreign ancestry. See Diagram A.

The census also asked a sample of people whether they spoke a language other than English at home. It was estimated that, in 1980, there were 23 million such people. Diagram B gives the distribution of "foreign-speakers" omitting children aged less than 5 years. Spanish-speakers make up about 48 percent of the total, followed by Italian, French, and German, with about 7 percent each.

Source: U.S. Bureau of the Census

Note: Spanish origin — in the 1980 census, the Bureau of the Census collected data on the Spanish origin population in the United States by using a self-identification question. Persons of Spanish/Hispanic origin or descent are those who classified themselves in one of the specific Spanish origin categories listed on the questionnaire — Mexican, Puerto Rican, Cuban, or Other Spanish/Hispanic origin.

AMERICAN INDIANS

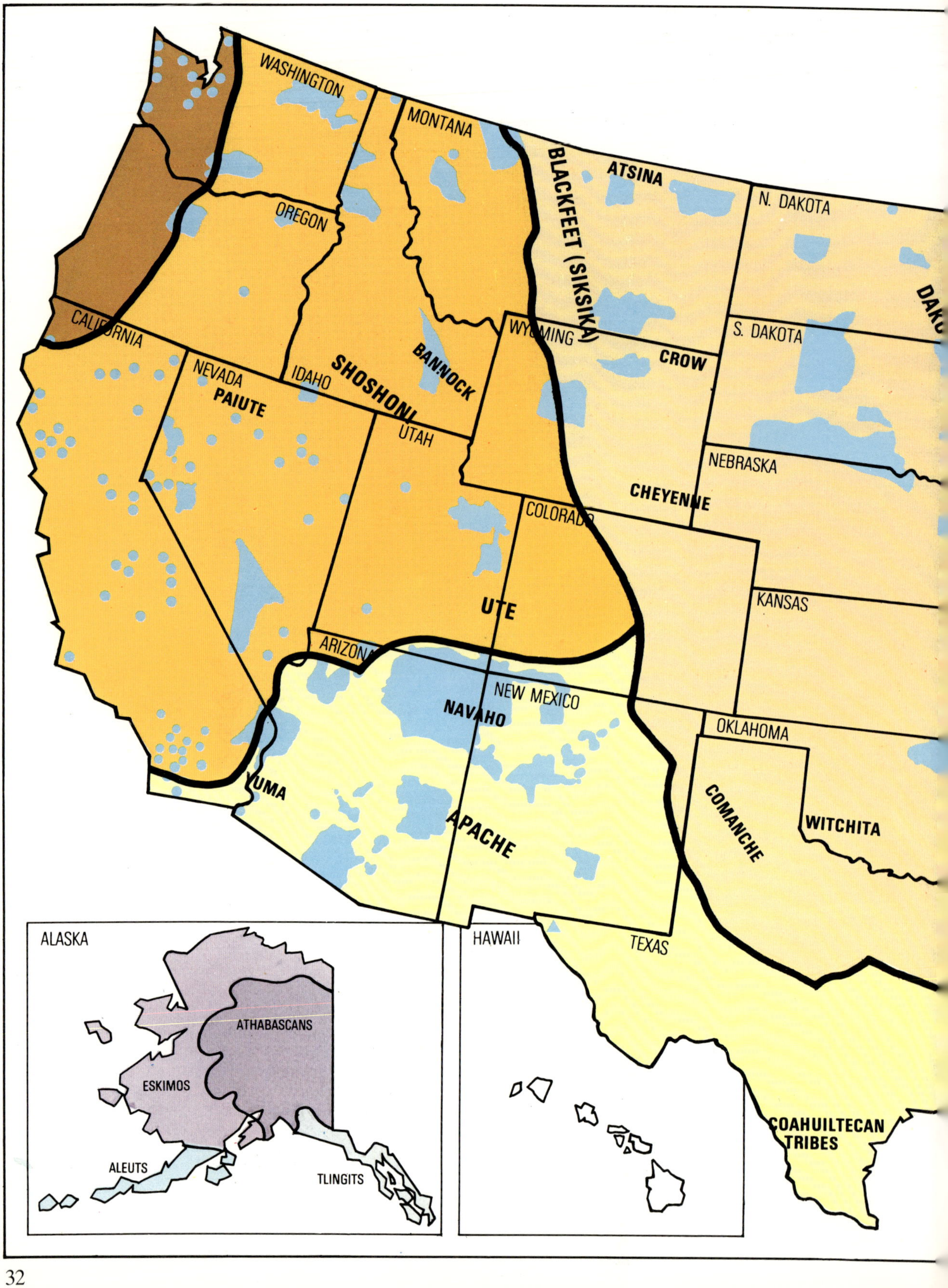

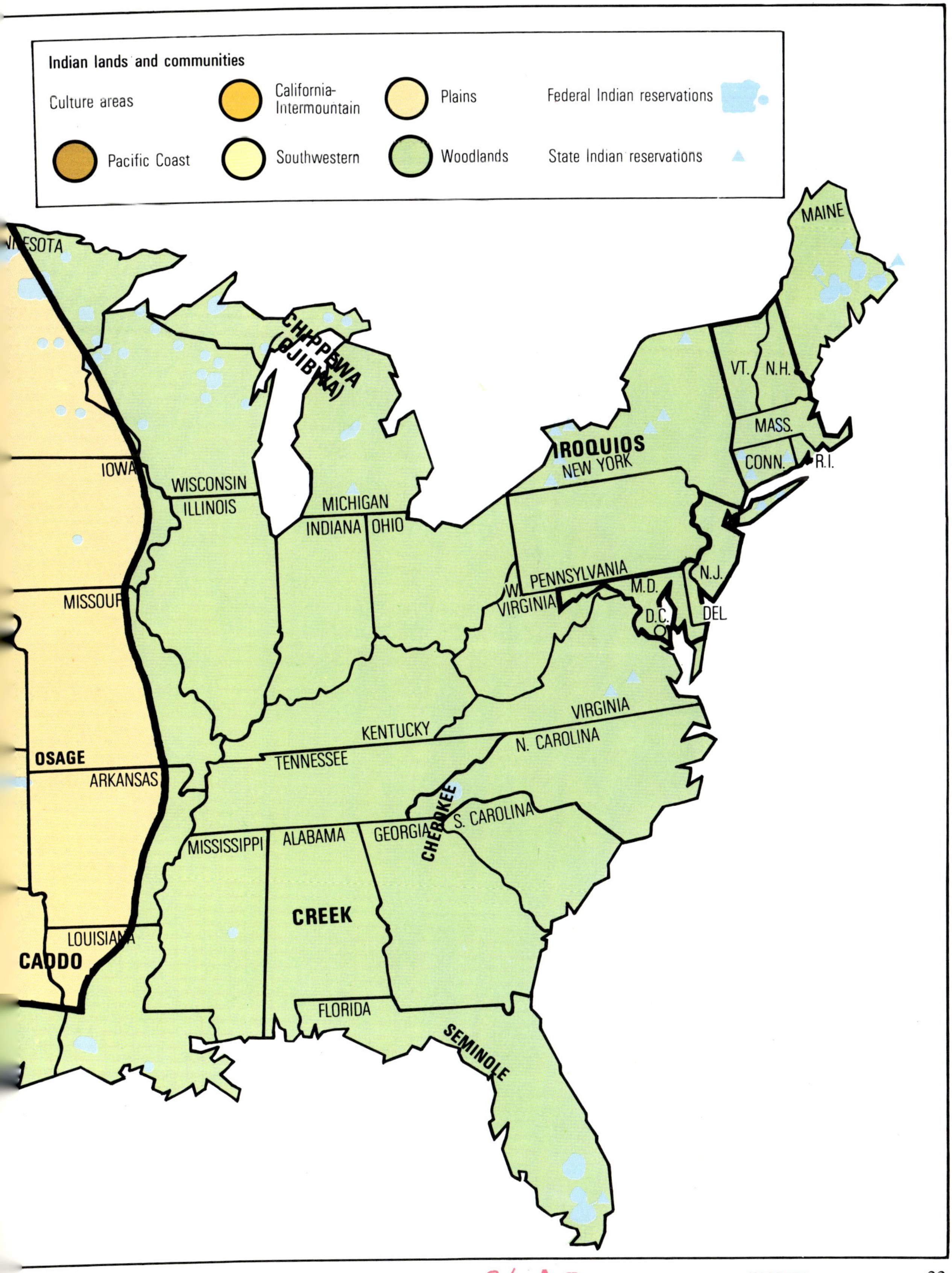

Indian lands and communities
Culture areas
Pacific Coast
California-Intermountain
Southwestern
Plains
Woodlands
Federal Indian reservations
State Indian reservations
CHIPPEWA (OJIBWA)
IROQUOIS
MAINE
VT.
N.H.
MASS.
CONN.
R.I.
NEW YORK
WISCONSIN
ILLINOIS
MICHIGAN
INDIANA
OHIO
PENNSYLVANIA
N.J.
M.D.
DEL
D.C.
VIRGINIA
KENTUCKY
N. CAROLINA
TENNESSEE
OSAGE
ARKANSAS
S. CAROLINA
CHEROKEE
MISSISSIPPI
ALABAMA
GEORGIA
CREEK
CADDO
FLORIDA
SEMINOLE

AMERICAN INDIANS

The map shows the main culture areas, and major tribes of the American Indians in early colonial times, together with Indian reservations in 1982. (Many descendants of the original inhabitants of North America object to the name "Indian," which is based on a 500-year-old error, but, as for the Eskimo peoples, no fully satisfactory alternative has yet been devised; the term "Native Americans" is sometimes used but is open to misinterpretation.)

The federal government currently recognizes a special obligation to, and trust responsibility for, approximately 500 "Indian entities" in the contiguous United States and Alaska. These Indian entities include tribes, other groups, pueblos, and other villages, which are organizations approved and recognized by federal statutes, plus other Indian organizations of traditional structure, which may or may not have formal federal approval.

The term "tribe" can also be misleading. Originally, it was an approximate equivalent of the term "nation," and it is chiefly in this sense that the names of major tribes appear on the map. Nevertheless, "Seminole," for example, is a Creek word meaning "separatist," which came into use after 1775 to describe a group united primarily by hostility to the United States. Since the relegation of Indians to reservations, the word "tribe" has developed a variety of meanings. It may imply a group within an Indian community, the community itself, or a group of — sometimes separated — communities.

Diagram A: Distribution of lands under the jurisdiction of the Bureau of Indian Affairs by region, 1982

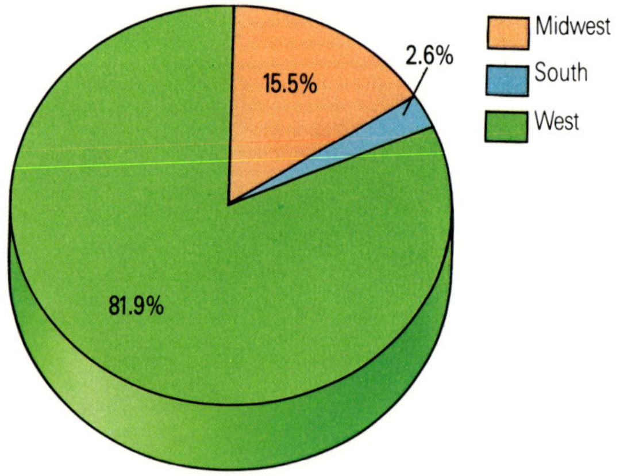

Indian-owned lands are known variously as reservations, communities, colonies, rancherias, pueblos, and so on, so that an exact accounting is difficult. In Oklahoma, where there is a high degree of assimilation with white culture, there are no reservations in the sense that the term is used in other parts of the United States. The map shows large reservations, such as the Navaho reservations in Arizona, New Mexico, and Utah, many of which have been enlarged by purchase to accommodate a growing population since the Indian Reorganization act of 1934.

The distribution of lands under the jurisdiction of the Bureau of Indian Affairs is shown in Diagram A. States containing less than 500,000 acres of land in this category have been excluded from the totals. The total for each region includes Trust allotted land (that is, landholdings of individuals), lands held by Indian tribes, and government-owned land. The amount of government-owned land is statistically insignificant except in the states of New Mexico (4.1 percent of the total), Indiana (3.9 percent), and Arizona (0.5 percent).

The proportion of lands held by tribes is 78.3 percent of all Indian lands in the United States as a whole. However, there are considerable variations from state to state. For example, in Alaska, the major part is held by individuals, and tribal lands account for only 18 percent of the state total. In South Dakota, tribal lands account for 52 percent of the total, in Montana, 56 percent. In Utah, on the other hand, the proportion of tribal land is 98 percent, and in New Mexico 91 percent (these figures exclude government-owned land).

The population of American Indians numbered 1,420,000 in 1980. The proportion of the total population in each region, is given in Diagram B.

Source: U.S. Bureau of Indian Affairs;
U.S. Bureau of the Census

Diagram B: Distribution of American Indians by division, 1980

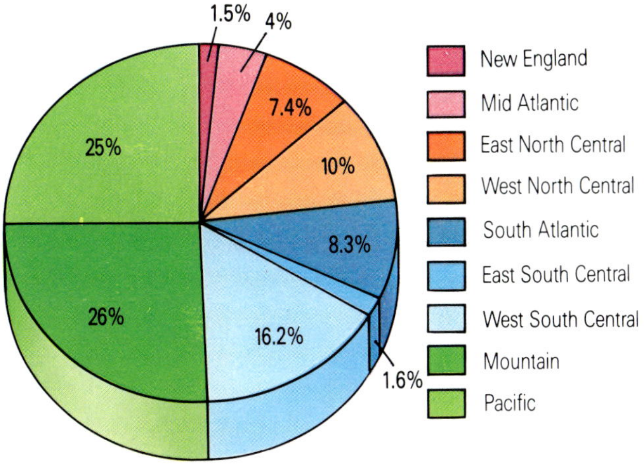

YOUNG AND OLD

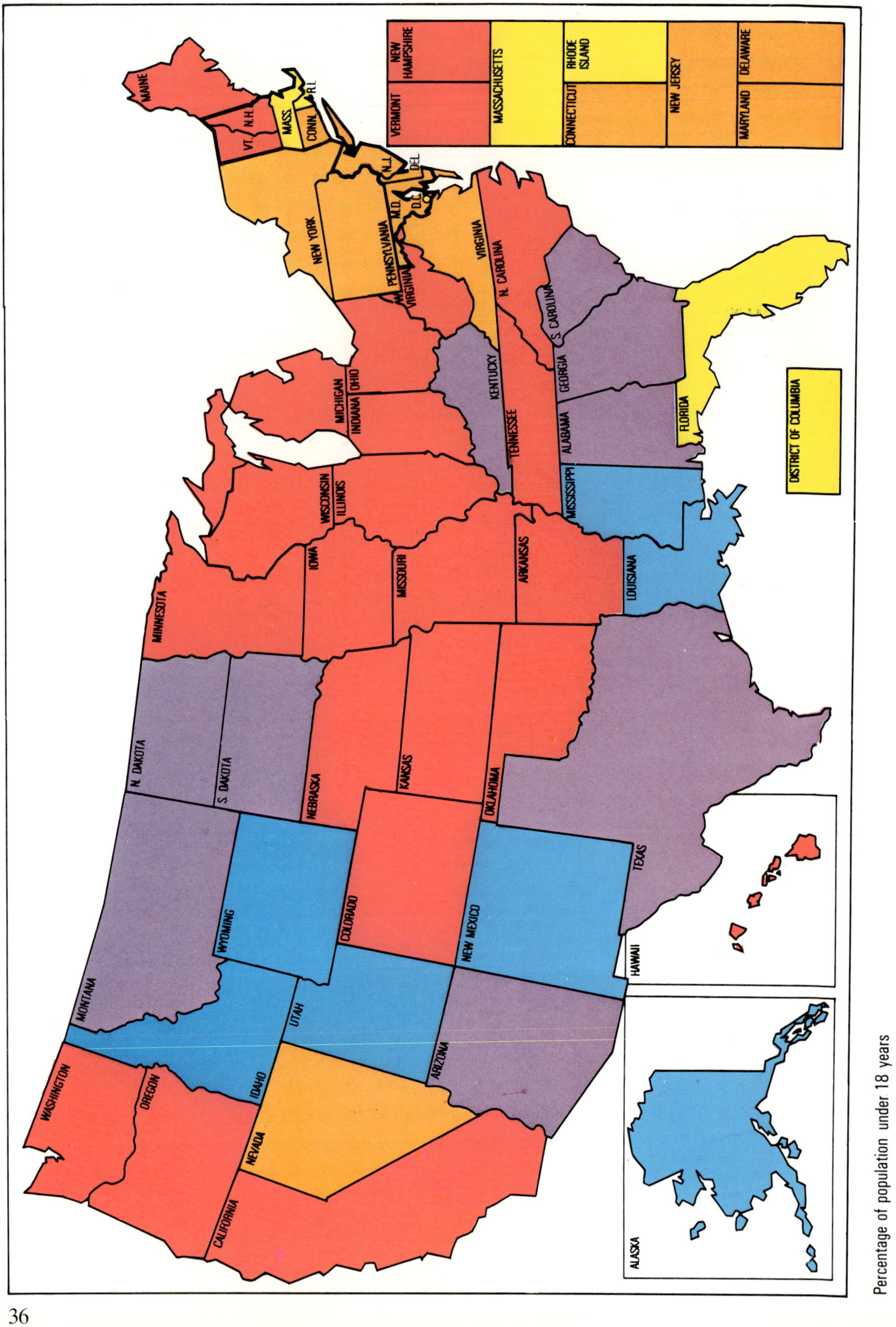

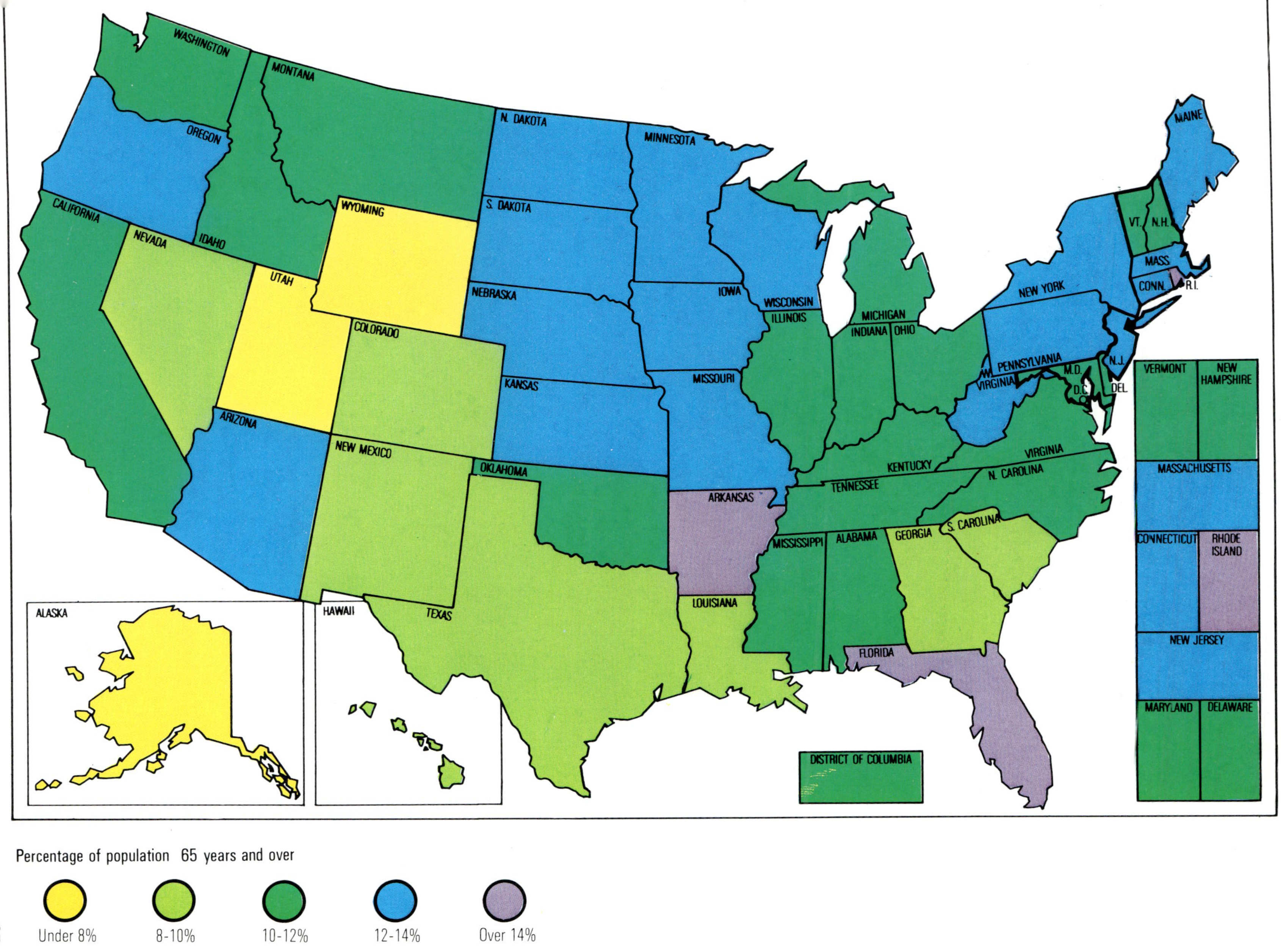
WASHINGTON
OREGON
CALIFORNIA
NEVADA
IDAHO
MONTANA
WYOMING
UTAH
ARIZONA
COLORADO
NEW MEXICO
N. DAKOTA
S. DAKOTA
NEBRASKA
KANSAS
OKLAHOMA
TEXAS
MINNESOTA
IOWA
MISSOURI
ARKANSAS
LOUISIANA
WISCONSIN
ILLINOIS
MICHIGAN
INDIANA
OHIO
KENTUCKY
TENNESSEE
MISSISSIPPI
ALABAMA
GEORGIA
FLORIDA
S. CAROLINA
N. CAROLINA
VIRGINIA
W. VIRGINIA
PENNSYLVANIA
NEW YORK
M.D.
D.C.
DEL
N.J.
CONN.
R.I.
MASS
VT.
N.H.
MAINE
ALASKA
HAWAII
DISTRICT OF COLUMBIA
VERMONT
NEW HAMPSHIRE
MASSACHUSETTS
CONNECTICUT
RHODE ISLAND
NEW JERSEY
MARYLAND
DELAWARE
Percentage of population 65 years and over
Under 8%
8-10%
10-12%
12-14%
Over 14%

YOUNG AND OLD

STATES WITH HIGHEST PERCENTAGE OF YOUNG PEOPLE
(under 18 years)

Utah	37.6
Idaho	32.2
Alaska	32.1
Wyoming	31.1
Mississippi	31.0

STATES WITH LOWEST PERCENTAGE OF YOUNG PEOPLE
(under 18 years)

Florida	23.0
Rhode Island	23.8
Massachusetts	23.9
Connecticut	24.2
Pennsylvania	24.7

STATES WITH HIGHEST PERCENTAGE OF OLD PEOPLE
(aged 65 and over)

Florida	17.5
Arkansas	14.1
Rhode Island	14.1
Iowa	13.9
Pennsylvania	13.8

STATES WITH LOWEST PERCENTAGE OF OLD PEOPLE
(aged 65 and over)

Alaska	3.0
Utah	7.6
Wyoming	7.9
Colorado	8.6
Hawaii	8.7

In 1983 26.7 percent of the population of the United States were aged under 18, while 11.7 percent were 65 or over. These two maps show the proportion of young people — under 18 years — and old people — 65 and over — in the different states.

There are wide variations between states. Utah, with 37.6 percent of its population under 18, stands out in the first map, along with Idaho (32.2 percent), Alaska (32.1), Wyoming (31.1), Mississippi (31.0), New Mexico (30.8), and Louisiana (30.6). Florida, with 23.0 percent aged under 18, has the lowest percentage of young people, followed by Rhode Island (23.8), and Massachusetts (23.9).

Florida shows the highest percentage of old people, 17.5 percent being aged 65 or more, followed by Arkansas, with 14.1 percent. Alaska, at the other extreme, has only 3 percent of people in this age group. Utah, with 7.6 percent, comes next.

Over the past few years, the age distribution for the United States as a whole has been shifting steadily toward the older age groups. In 1970, 9.8 percent of the population were aged 65 and over. In 1920, this percentage was only 4.6. The median age — the age at which exactly half the population is younger — has risen from 27.9 in 1970 to 30.9 in 1983.

These changes do not simply mean that people are living longer. The effect of the fall in fertility in the 1960s, which implied the fall in the numbers of young people later, is the major factor in the increase of the average age of the population.

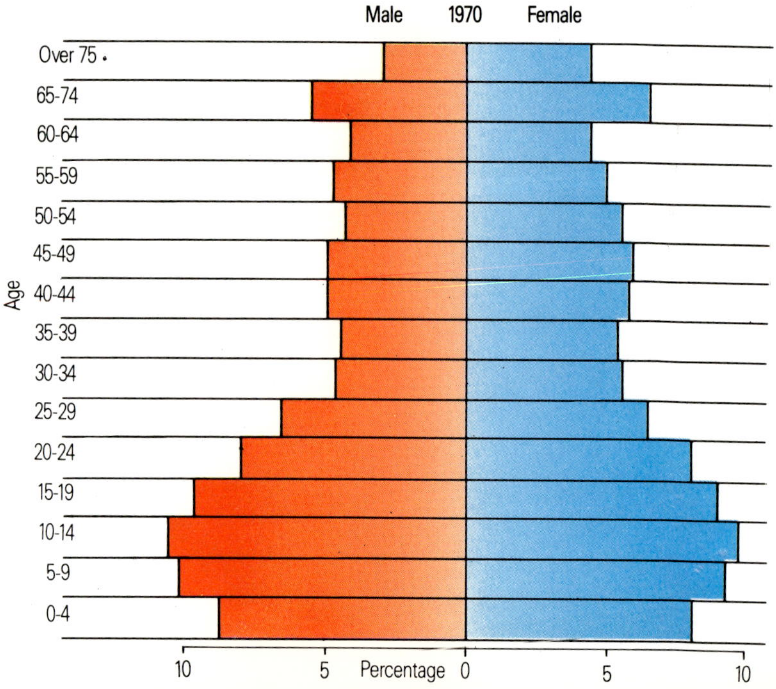

Diagram A: Age distributions, by sex, 1970, 1980, 1983

Earlier in this century, falls in death rates did not have as great an effect on the proportion of old people as might have been expected, because of the decrease in mortality among younger age groups. In the future, however, this may not be the case, and future falls in death rates will make a greater difference to the proportion of people in the older groups. Demographers forecast that, by the end of the century, there will be nearly as many people aged over 75 as between 65 and 75 years old.

Even more striking than the tendency of the population to get older is the widening difference between the age distributions of the sexes. Women tend to live longer than men, and the gap is widening. Diagram A represents the age distributions for men and women in 1970, 1980, and 1983. While the percentage of men in the "65 and over" group went up from 8.5 in 1970 to 9.6 in 1983, the corresponding percentage for women rose from 11.1 to 13.6.

The median age for men has increased from 26.6 in 1970 to 29.6 in 1983. But that for women was 29.2 in 1970 and 32.2 in 1983. The "75 years and over" group is larger than it used to be and shows even more striking changes. In 1970, 3.0 percent of men were in this group, and 4.4 percent of women. In 1983, these percentages had risen to 3.4 percent for men and 5.9 percent for women.

Diagram B graphs the marked decline in the ratio of men to women in the "65 and over" group during the course of this century. In 1910, there were slightly more men than women. The numbers evened out by the early 1930s. Then, the longer lifespan of women began to show its effect: by 1983, there were only 67.1 men for every 100 women in this age group.

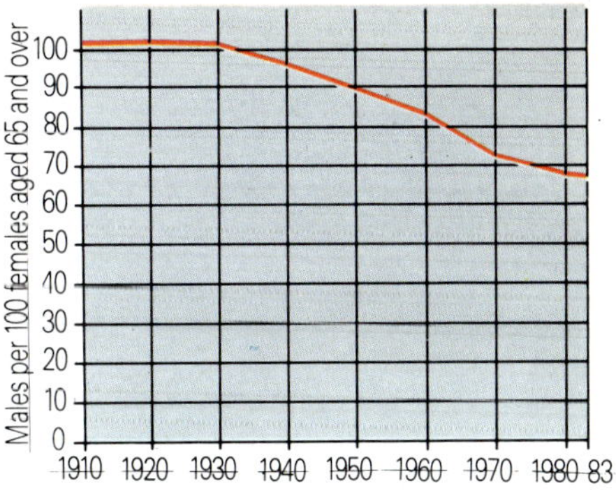

Diagram B: Number of men over 65 years old per 100 women over 65 years old, 1910-1983

Source: U.S. Bureau of the Census

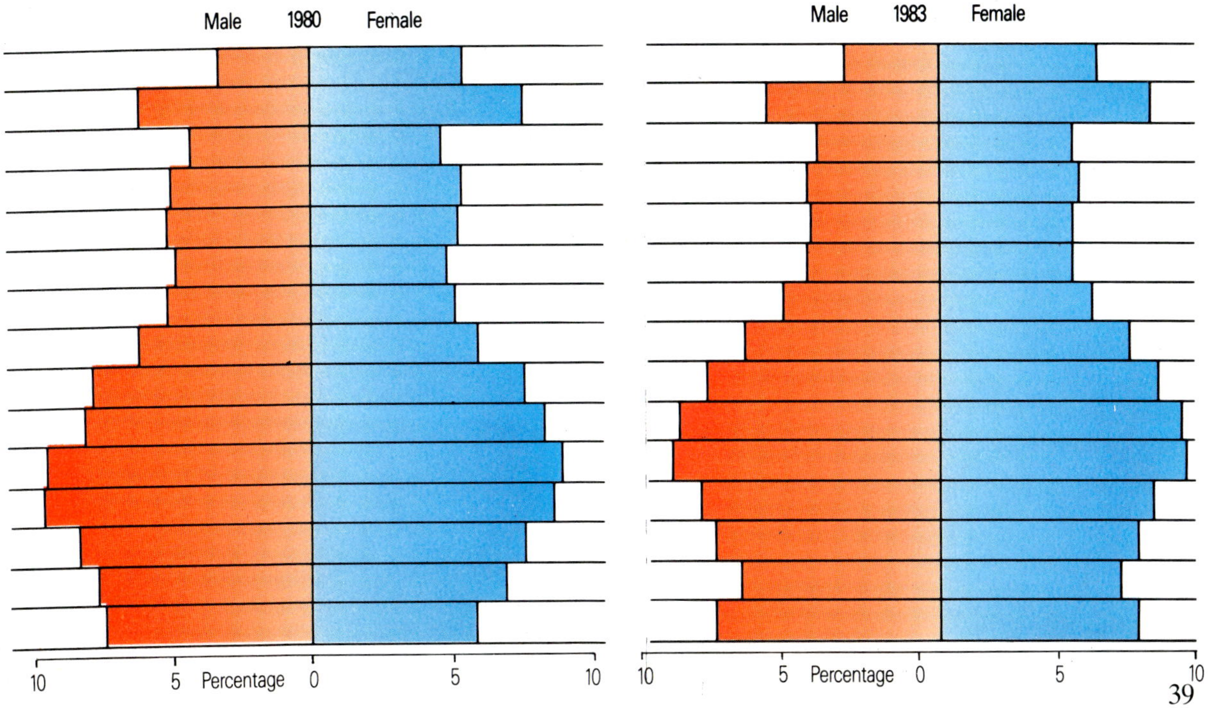

POPULATION DENSITY

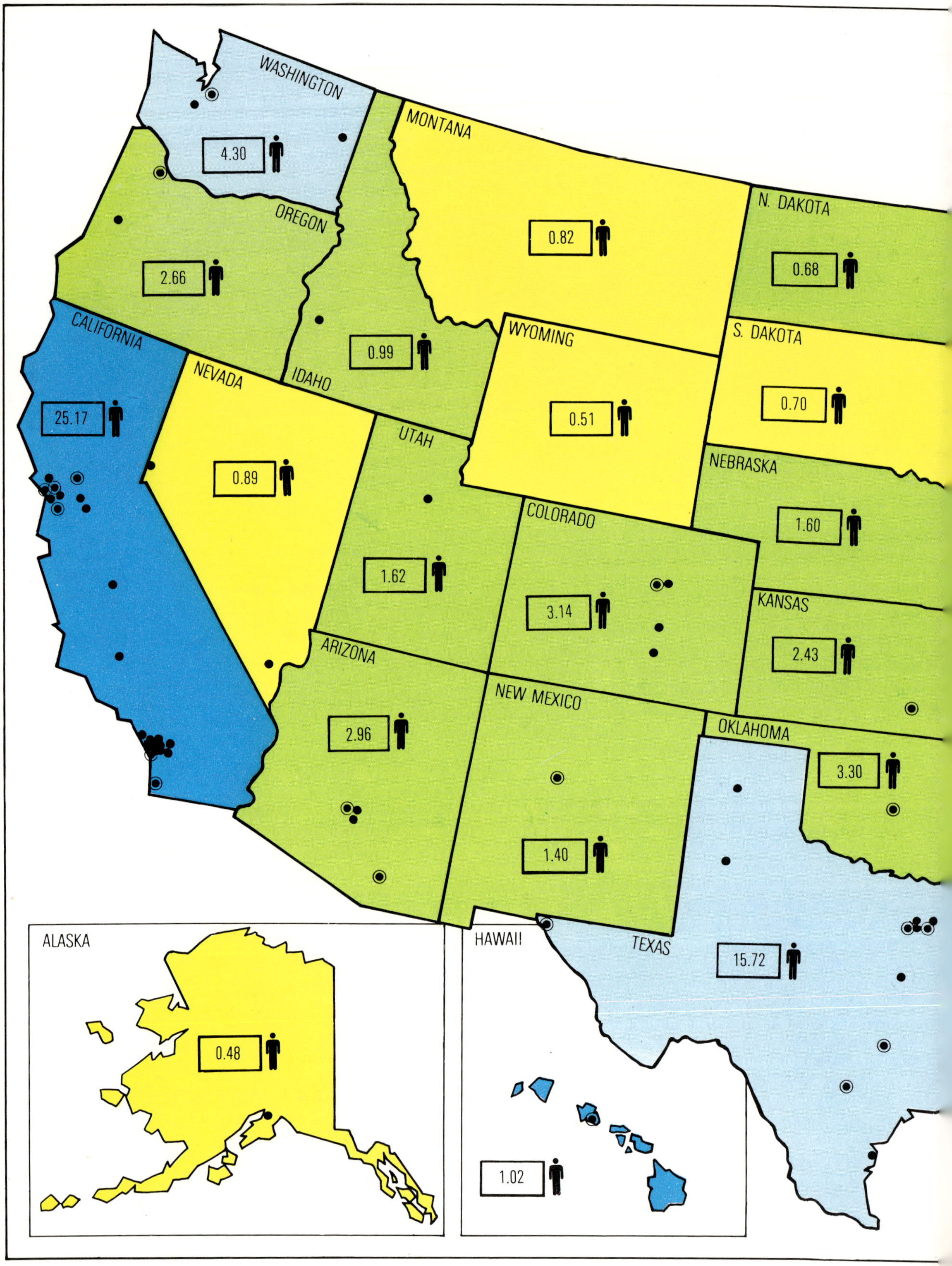

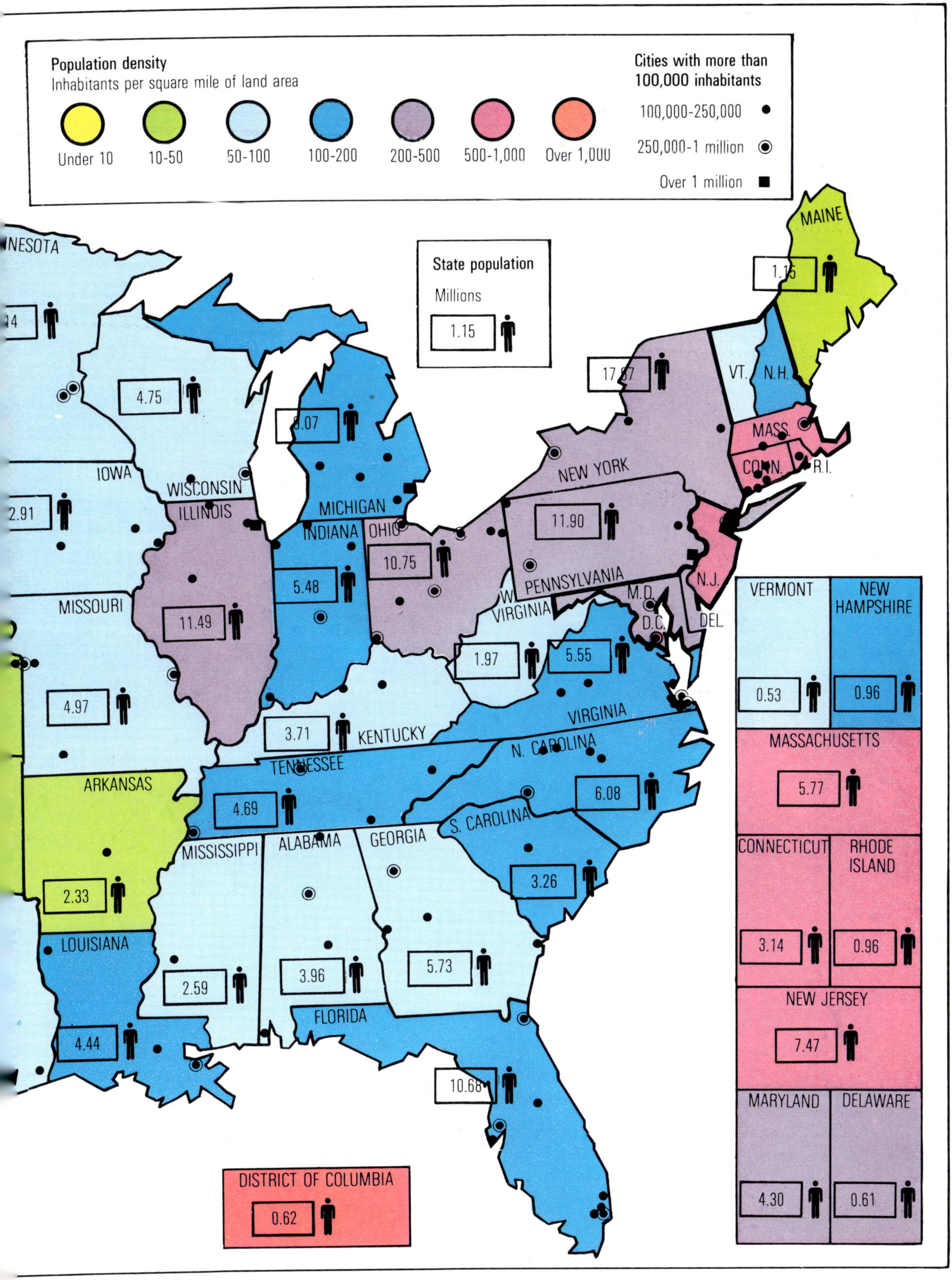

Population density
Inhabitants per square mile of land area
Under 10
10-50
50-100
100-200
200-500
500-1,000
Over 1,000
Cities with more than 100,000 inhabitants
100,000-250,000
250,000-1 million
Over 1 million
State population
Millions
1.15
MAINE
1.15
VT.
N.H.
MASS.
CONN.
R.I.
NEW YORK
17.57
PENNSYLVANIA
11.90
N.J.
DEL.
M.D.
D.C.
W. VIRGINIA
1.97
VIRGINIA
5.55
N. CAROLINA
6.08
S. CAROLINA
3.26
GEORGIA
5.73
FLORIDA
10.68
ALABAMA
3.96
MISSISSIPPI
2.59
LOUISIANA
4.44
ARKANSAS
2.33
TENNESSEE
4.69
KENTUCKY
3.71
OHIO
10.75
INDIANA
5.48
ILLINOIS
11.49
MICHIGAN
9.07
WISCONSIN
4.75
IOWA
2.91
MISSOURI
4.97
NESOTA
VERMONT
0.53
NEW HAMPSHIRE
0.96
MASSACHUSETTS
5.77
CONNECTICUT
3.14
RHODE ISLAND
0.96
NEW JERSEY
7.47
MARYLAND
4.30
DELAWARE
0.61
DISTRICT OF COLUMBIA
0.62

POPULATION DENSITY

POPULATION DENSITY
(people per square mile, 1983)

1	Washington D.C.	9,891
2	New Jersey	1,000
3	Rhode I.	906
4	Massachusetts	737
5	Connecticut	644
6	Maryland	437
7	New York	373
8	Delaware	314
9	Pennsylvania	265
10	Ohio	262
11	Illinois	206
12	Florida	197
13	California	161
14	Michigan	159
15	Hawaii	159
16	Indiana	152
17	Virginia	140
18	N. Carolina	125
19	Tennessee	114
20	S. Carolina	108
21	New Hampshire	107
22	Louisiana	100
23	Georgia	99
24	Kentucky	94
25	Wisconsin	87
26	W. Virginia	81
27	Alabama	78
28	Missouri	72
29	Washington	65
30	Texas	60
31	Vermont	57
32	Mississippi	55
33	Minnesota	52
34	Iowa	52
35	Oklahoma	48
36	Arkansas	45
37	Maine	37
38	Kansas	30
39	Colorado	30
40	Oregon	28
41	Arizona	26
42	Nebraska	21
43	Utah	20
44	New Mexico	12
45	Idaho	12
46	N. Dakota	10
47	S. Dakota	9
48	Nevada	8
49	Montana	6
50	Wyoming	5
51	Alaska	1

About 234 million Americans occupy a total land area of 3.6 million square miles. So, on average, there are about 65 people for each square mile. But as you can see from this map there are considerable differences between the states.

The table (left) gives the average population densities (1983) of the states, in people per square mile, in descending order. As usual, the District of Columbia is exceptional, packing 623,000 people into 63 square miles to give an average density of almost 10,000. Of the states New Jersey heads the list with 1,000 people per square mile, followed by Rhode Island (906). Down at the bottom of the list are Wyoming, with 5 people to each square mile, and, not surprisingly, Alaska, with only one.

Obviously there are even greater variations within each state, urban areas carrying a far higher density of population. The map marks these centres of population, showing cities with over 100,000 people grouped into three bands according to size. The map also indicates the population of each state. California, with more than 25 million people, has over 10 percent of the total U.S. population, well ahead of New York (17.67 million) and Texas (15.72 million).

The differences between population densities of cities are also considerable. Using the figures for 1980, we find 23,455 residents for each square mile of New York City, rising to 64,337 in the borough of Manhattan. In comparison, the 1.2 million inhabitants of Houston, Texas, occupied 556 square miles — a density of 2,158. In Los Angeles, California, the density of population in 1980 was 6,384, in Detroit, Michigan, 8,874, in Chicago, Illinois, 13,174 and in San Francisco, California, 14,633. At the other extreme, there were only 101 people for every square mile in Anchorage, Alaska.

Diagram A is a pie chart showing how the total U.S. population is distributed among the nine divisions of the country. The Atlantic Seaboard — East North Central, Middle Atlantic, and South Atlantic — accounts for about half of the total, each division being about one-sixth. The Pacific division approaches the same proportion. This leaves the remaining five divisions accounting for one-third of the total.

Diagram B shows how the population density of the United States has increased over the last 200 years as the country has gradually expanded its territory. The five small maps show the area occupied by the United States in 1790, 1840, 1890, 1940 and 1980. The area of the square beneath each map is proportional to the area shaded on the map. Each dot in a square represents one

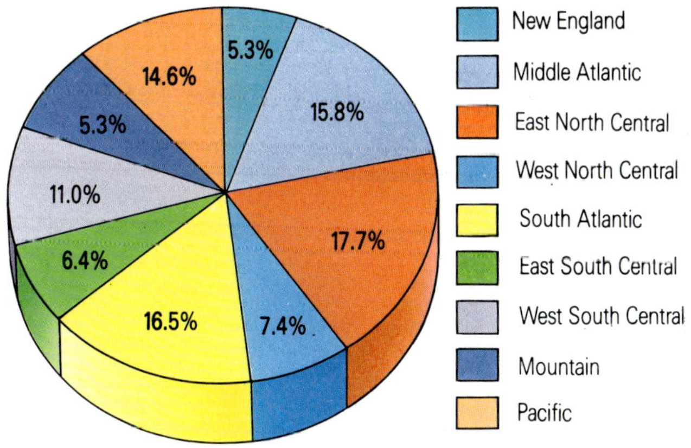

Diagram A: Distribution of total population by division

POPULATION DENSITY BY DIVISION

The average population densities of the divisions in 1980 were as follows:

New England	196
Middle Atlantic	369
East North Central	171
West North Central	34
South Atlantic	138
East South Central	82
West South Central	56
Mountain	13
Pacific	36

However, it is important to recognize that this pattern is changing. During the past half century, population densities in the Northeast and Midwest have risen by about 50 percent, and those in the South by 100 percent, but in the West they have risen by approximately 35 percent.

million people living in the area at the time. Below each square is the corresponding population density.

The first settlements on the Atlantic coast had grown by the time of the first census in 1790 to a density of 4.5 people per square mile. Between then and 1840 the area of settlement increased by almost 70 percent. Yet, despite this massive increase in territory, a major influx of immigrants in the early nineteenth century pushed the density up to 9.8. Again the territory expanded and again an even greater flood of immigrants in the middle of the century had more than doubled the density by 1890, to give 21.2 people per square mile. By the start of World War II the density had doubled once more, though this time the increase was not accompanied by an expansion of territory. By 1980, both Alaska and Hawaii had become states and the density had risen a further 70 percent.

Source: U.S. Bureau of the Census, 1980

Diagram B: Population density, 1790-1980. The area of each square is proportional to the area shaded on the small map above. Each dot represents one million people

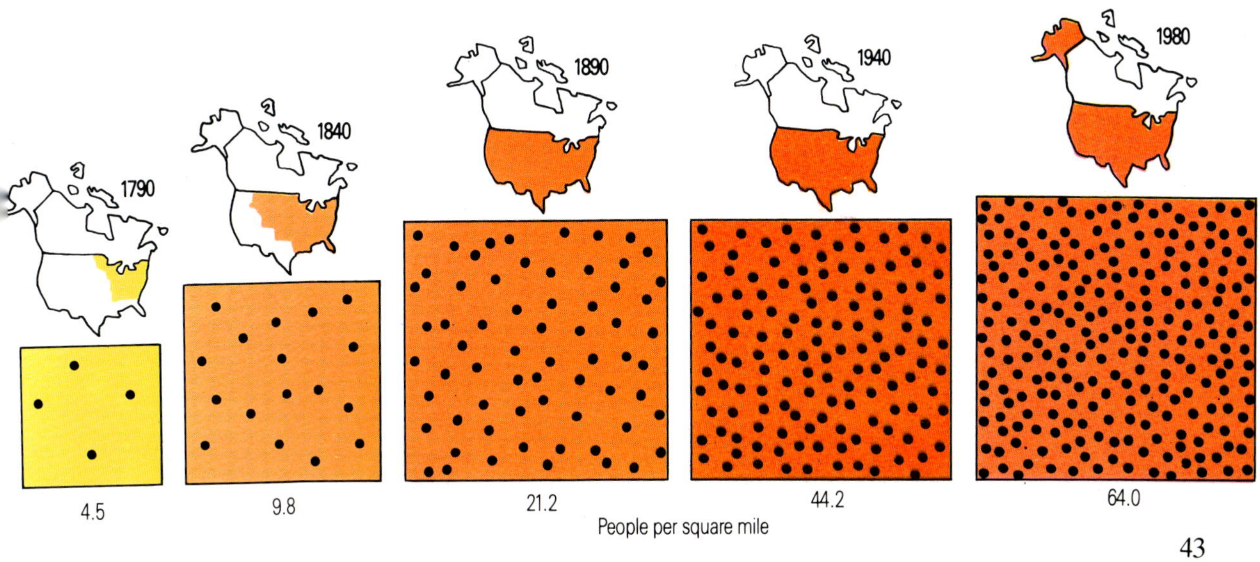

URBAN AND RURAL UNITED STATES

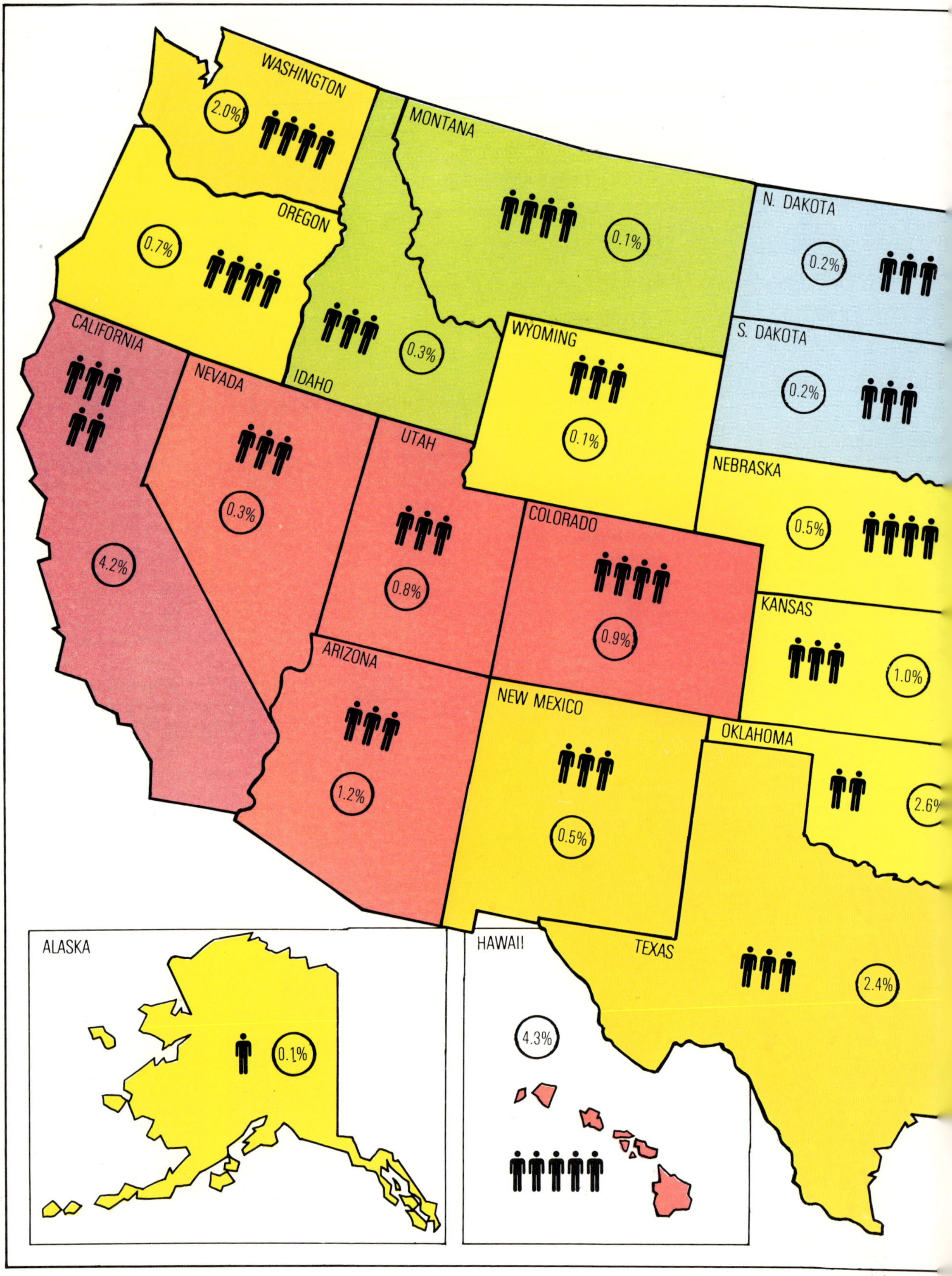

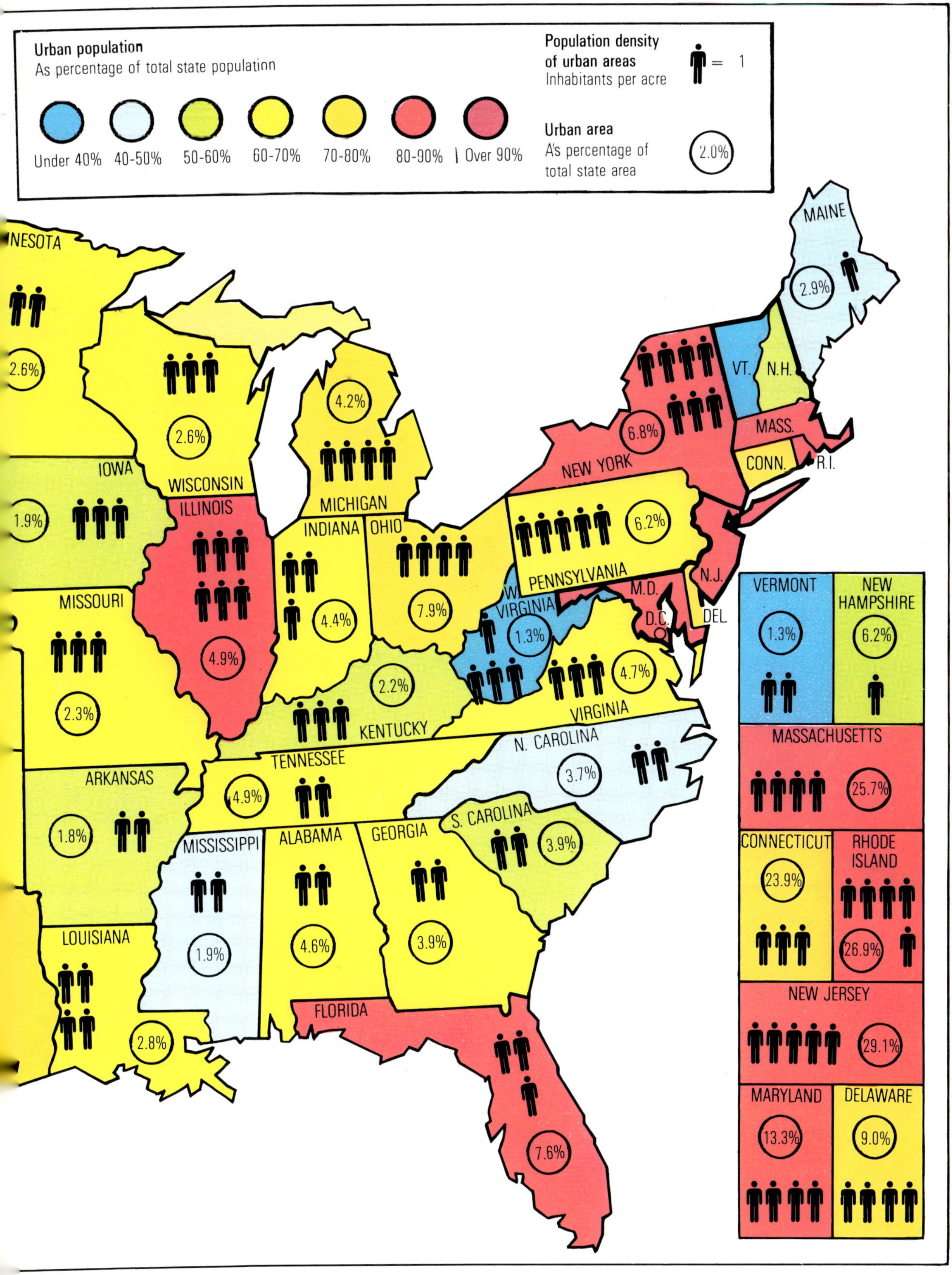
Urban population
As percentage of total state population
Under 40%
40-50%
50-60%
60-70%
70-80%
80-90%
Over 90%
Population density of urban areas
Inhabitants per acre
= 1
Urban area
As percentage of total state area
2.0%
MINNESOTA
2.6%
WISCONSIN
2.6%
MICHIGAN
4.2%
IOWA
1.9%
ILLINOIS
4.9%
INDIANA
4.4%
OHIO
7.9%
MISSOURI
2.3%
KENTUCKY
2.2%
W. VIRGINIA
1.3%
VIRGINIA
4.7%
PENNSYLVANIA
6.2%
NEW YORK
6.8%
MAINE
2.9%
VT.
N.H.
MASS.
CONN.
R.I.
N.J.
M.D.
D.C.
DEL
TENNESSEE
4.9%
N. CAROLINA
3.7%
S. CAROLINA
3.9%
ARKANSAS
1.8%
MISSISSIPPI
1.9%
ALABAMA
4.6%
GEORGIA
3.9%
LOUISIANA
2.8%
FLORIDA
7.6%
VERMONT
1.3%
NEW HAMPSHIRE
6.2%
MASSACHUSETTS
25.7%
CONNECTICUT
23.9%
RHODE ISLAND
26.9%
NEW JERSEY
29.1%
MARYLAND
13.3%
DELAWARE
9.0%

URBAN AND RURAL UNITED STATES

Nearly three-quarters of the population of the United States now live in urban areas. But, as the map shows, this proportion varies widely between different parts of the country. According to the 1980 census, while 9 out of 10 Californians live in urban areas, less than one-third of the people of Vermont do so.

The U.S. Bureau of the Census has a precise but involved definition of "urban". Basically, it includes (1) places with over 2,500 inhabitants, and (2) central cities that, together with "contiguous closely settled territory, have a total population of at least 50,000."

The map also indicates, for each state, the percentage of the area of the state considered to be urbanized. The Northeast region, as would be expected, shows the highest proportion of urban area, New Jersey heading the list with 29 percent. California also shows a fairly high proportion, with 4.2 percent of its area urbanized. Alaska, at the other extreme, has only 0.1 percent of its area classified as "urban." (The District of Columbia is not shown here, because it is classified as totally urban.)

It must be borne in mind that urbanized areas themselves will vary from small villages to massive industrialized regions. The map indicates this variation by showing the average density of population per acre in the urban areas of each state.

It is worth noting that in 1980, 28.4 million people — one-eighth of the population of the United States — lived in 22 cities of over 500,000 inhabitants. Since 1960, however, successive censuses have shown a decrease in the percentage of people who live in these large cities. In 1960, 16 percent lived in cities with over half a million

Diagram A: Distribution of urban population by division, 1980

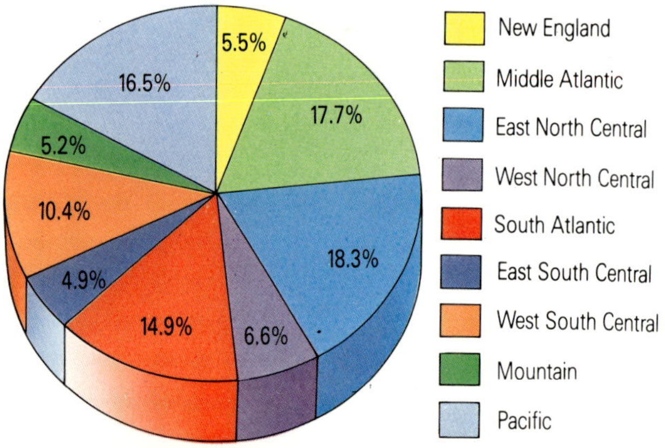

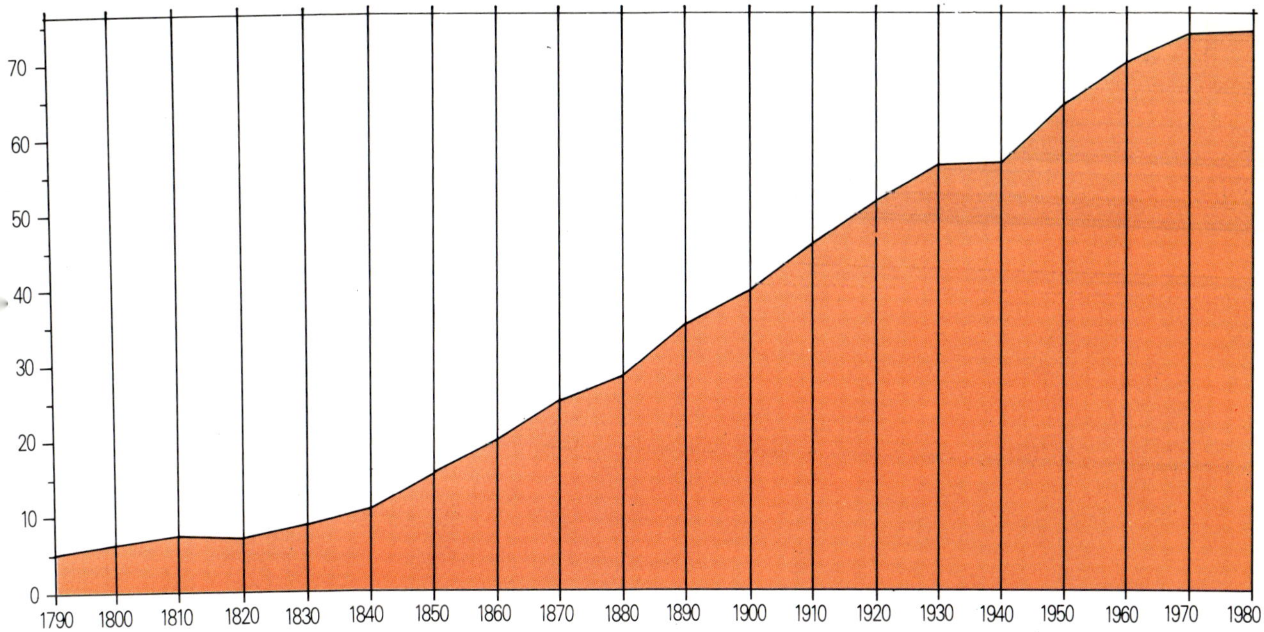

Diagram B: Percentage of total population living in urban areas, 1790-1980

inhabitants, in 1970 15 percent, and in 1980 12.5 percent. On the other hand, the proportion of the population living in places with under 10,000 inhabitants has increased, from 25 percent in 1960, to 29 percent in 1970, and 30 percent in 1980.

A related process is revealed by the census breakdown of urban population into those living in "central cities" and those in the "urban fringe." In 1970, 54.5 million people were in this latter group, comprising 26.8 percent of the total population. By 1980, this figure had risen to 72.1 million, or 31.8 percent. In addition, the percentage of the population recorded as living in rural areas, but within what the Bureau of the Census calls "Metropolitan Statistical Areas", rose from 8.1 to 10.6 between 1970 and 1980. (A Metropolitan Statistical Area is defined as a large population nucleus together with adjacent associated communities.)

Diagram A is a pie chart showing the urban population of the nine divisions of the United States at the time of the 1980 census. Half of the urban population live in three divisions — Middle Atlantic, East North Central and South Atlantic, with the Pacific division accounting for another sixth.

Of the 59.5 million people classified by the 1980 census as living in rural areas, nearly one-quarter live in the East North Central division, and slightly more than a quarter in the South Atlantic division.

The movement from the countryside into the cities has gone on since the first settlements were established. Diagram B shows this process by graphing the percentage of the population considered to be urbanized for each census since 1790.

Source: U.S. Bureau of the Census

AMERICANS ON THE MOVE

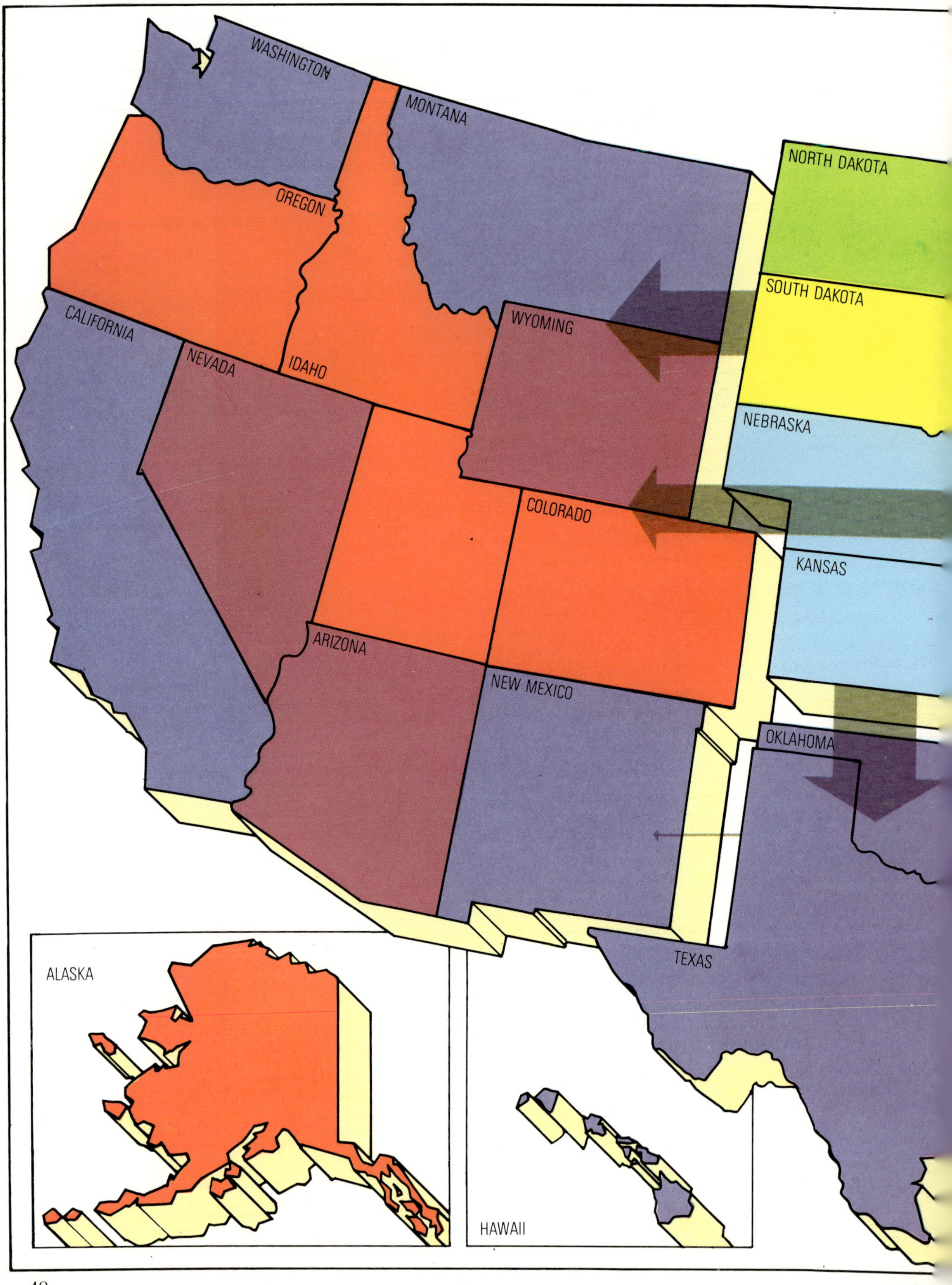

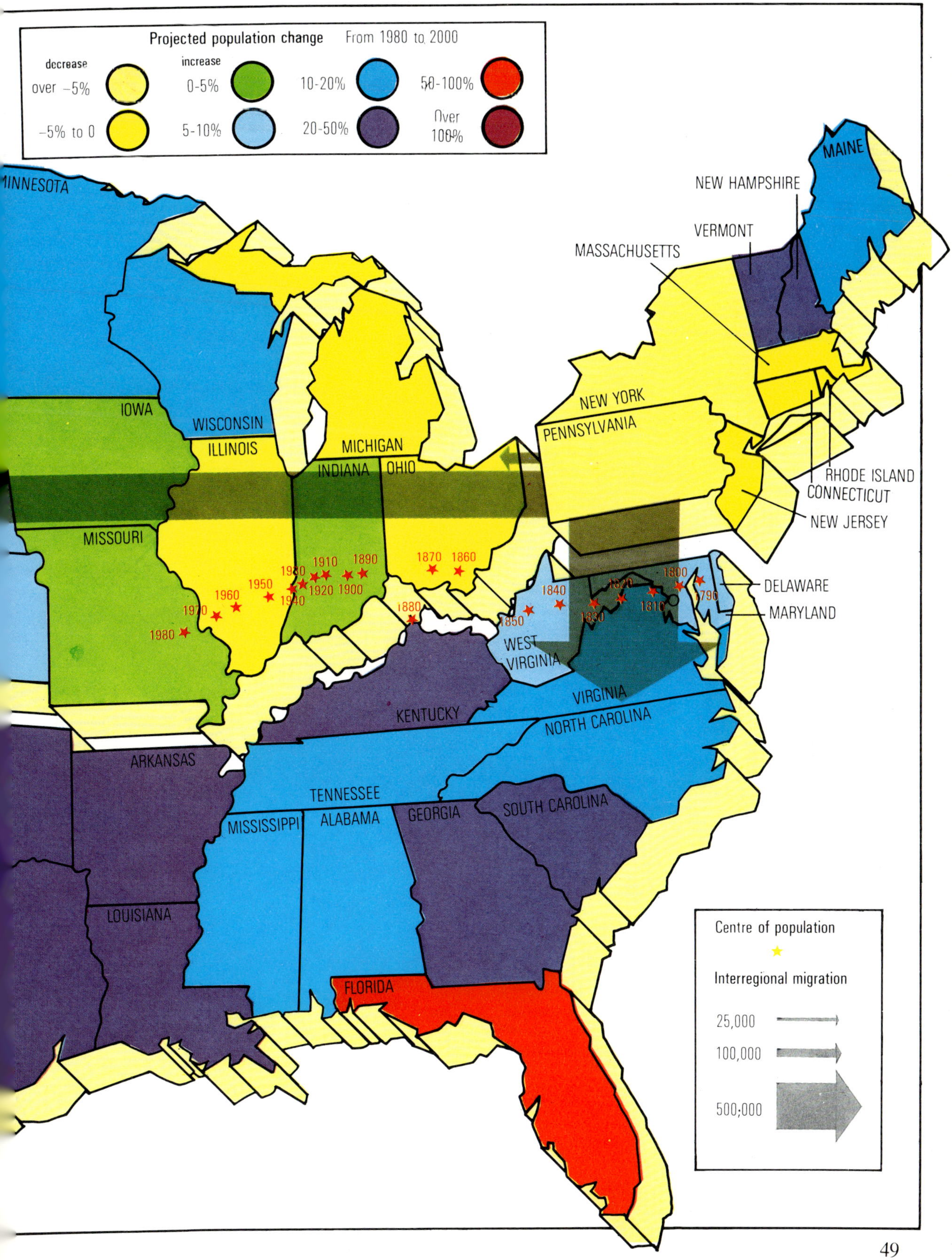
Projected population change From 1980 to 2000
decrease
over −5%
−5% to 0
increase
0-5%
5-10%
10-20%
20-50%
50-100%
Over 100%
MINNESOTA
IOWA
WISCONSIN
ILLINOIS
MICHIGAN
INDIANA
OHIO
MISSOURI
NEW YORK
PENNSYLVANIA
MAINE
NEW HAMPSHIRE
VERMONT
MASSACHUSETTS
RHODE ISLAND
CONNECTICUT
NEW JERSEY
DELAWARE
MARYLAND
WEST VIRGINIA
VIRGINIA
KENTUCKY
NORTH CAROLINA
ARKANSAS
TENNESSEE
MISSISSIPPI
ALABAMA
GEORGIA
SOUTH CAROLINA
LOUISIANA
FLORIDA
1790
1800
1810
1820
1830
1840
1850
1860
1870
1880
1890
1900
1910
1920
1930
1940
1950
1960
1970
1980
Centre of population
Interregional migration
25,000
100,000
500,000

AMERICANS ON THE MOVE

The migration of Americans has been from east to west. The map shows this tendency from several angles.

The Bureau of the Census has computed a "centre of population" for each census since the first in 1790. It describes this as follows: "'centre of population' is that point at which an imaginary flat, weightless, and rigid map of the United States would balance if weights of identical value were placed on it so that each weight represented the location of one person on the date of the census."

The map shows how this point has shifted from just east of Baltimore in 1790 to Jefferson County, Missouri, in 1980. Note how the rapid movement west after 1870 was followed by a much slower pace between 1890 and 1940, and then by a faster shift again during and after World War II.

The arrows on the map indicate net migration between the four regions, in the period 1975-1980. The main feature continued to be the movement out of the Northeast and Midwest, into the South and West.

Based on the results of the 1980 census, the Bureau of the Census worked out projections of population for the regions to the end of the century. The states are coloured according to the percentage changes projected for the period 1980-2000. Most of the differences between states can be attributed to migration.

As would be expected, the biggest projected losses in population are to be found in the Northeast, and the biggest gains in the South and West. The District of Columbia is an exception. By the year

Diagram A: Percentage of total population resident in the regions, 1950-1983

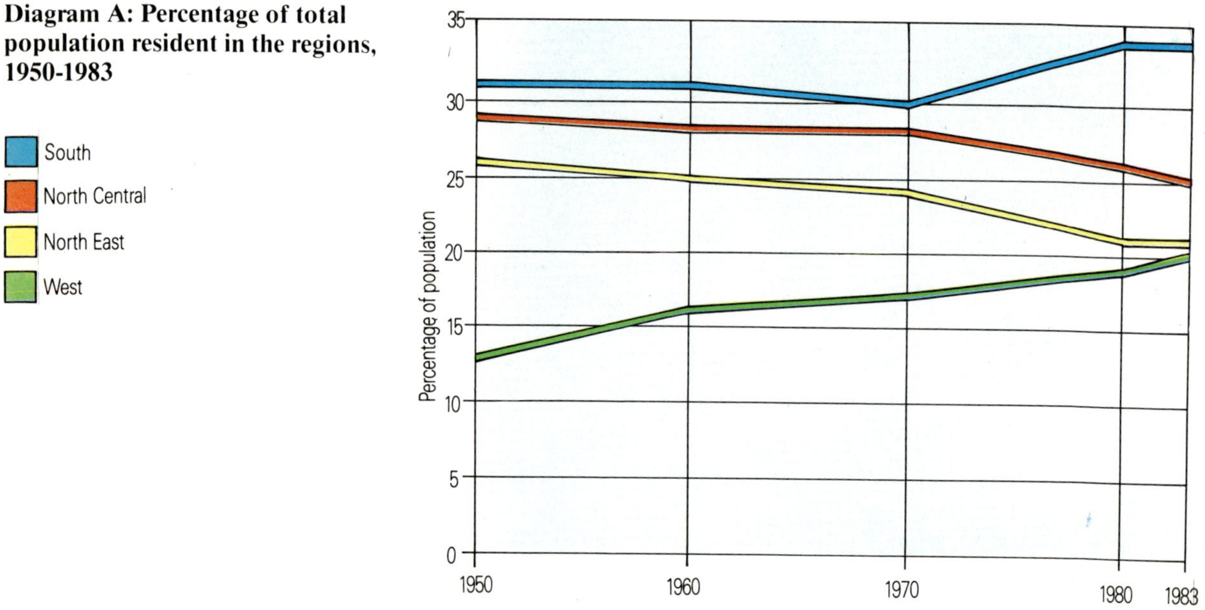

2000, its population is expected to fall to below 60 percent of its 1980 level. New York State comes next, with a projected drop of 14 percent.

Among the states with increasing populations, Nevada heads the list with an expected rise of 138 percent. It is followed by Wyoming with 113 percent, Arizona with 100 percent, and Florida with 75 percent. New Hampshire is the exception among the northeastern states, showing a projected rise in population of nearly 50 percent.

Diagram A traces the same process for the period 1950-1983, graphing the movement of regional populations, expressed as percentages of the total U.S. population. As will be seen, the West, which in 1950 held only one-eighth of the population, now accounts for one-fifth.

Diagram B gives a more detailed picture of movement. The 1980 census asked people where they had lived in 1975. The diagram ranks the states according to the percentage of those residents in 1980 who had lived in another state five years earlier. (This excludes those under five years old in 1980.) At the top we see that over 30 percent of Nevada residents in 1980 had moved there during the previous five years. At the bottom, we find that all but 4 percent of New York State residents in 1980 were already living there in 1975.

However, while all this information points to a continued trend of movement south and west, there are some indications that it has been slowing down. Some experts now think that the numbers of families moving out of the Northeast may have reached a peak around 1980, although the industrial Midwest is still losing people heavily.

During the 1970s the Northeast showed a net out migration averaging 289,000 per year. Between 1980 and 1983, however, this average dropped to about 85,000. The largest part of this change is accounted for by New York State, where an average loss due to migration of 182,000 per year in the 1970s was lowered to 45,000 in 1980-1983.

Source: U.S. Bureau of the Census

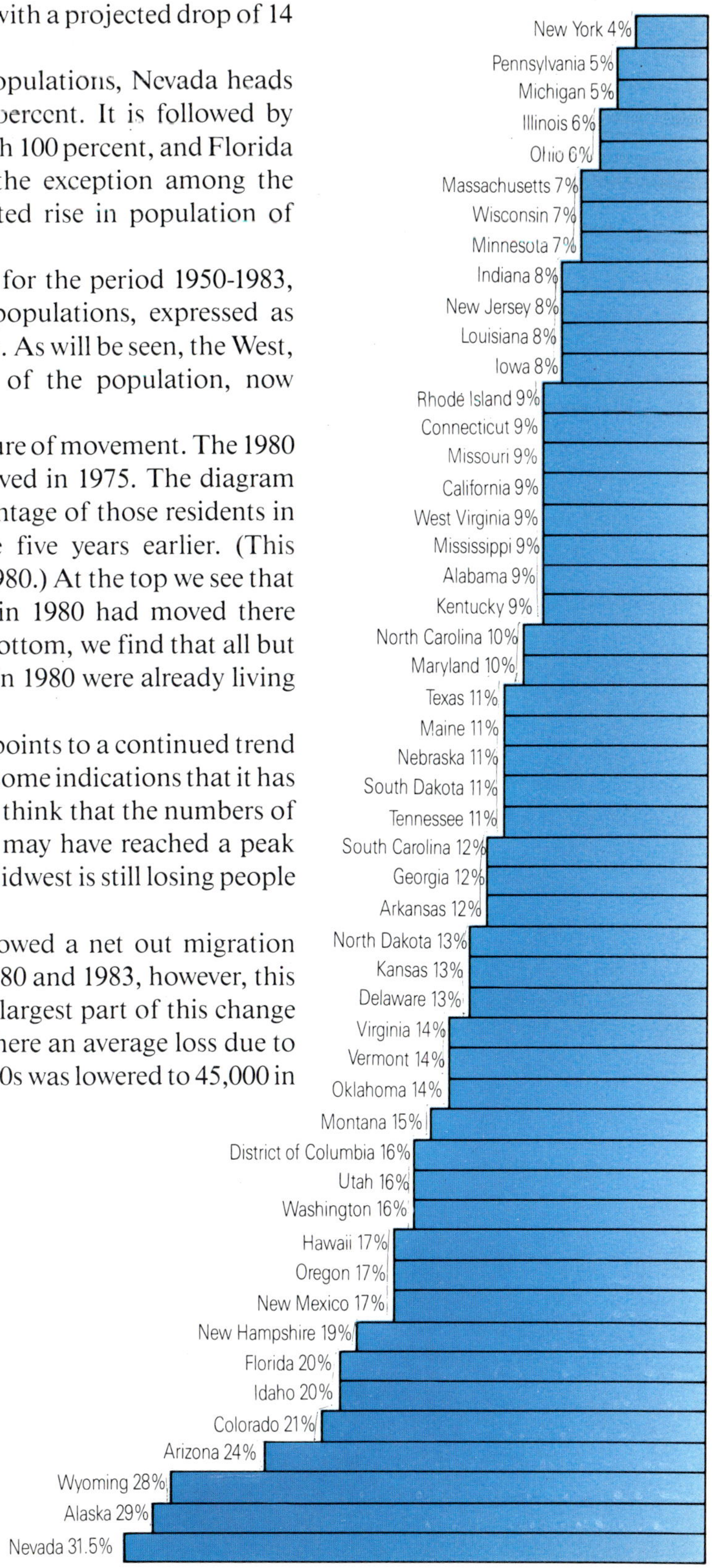

Diagram B: Percentage of 1980 resident population of each state (5 years of age and over) who lived in a different state in 1975

IMMIGRATION

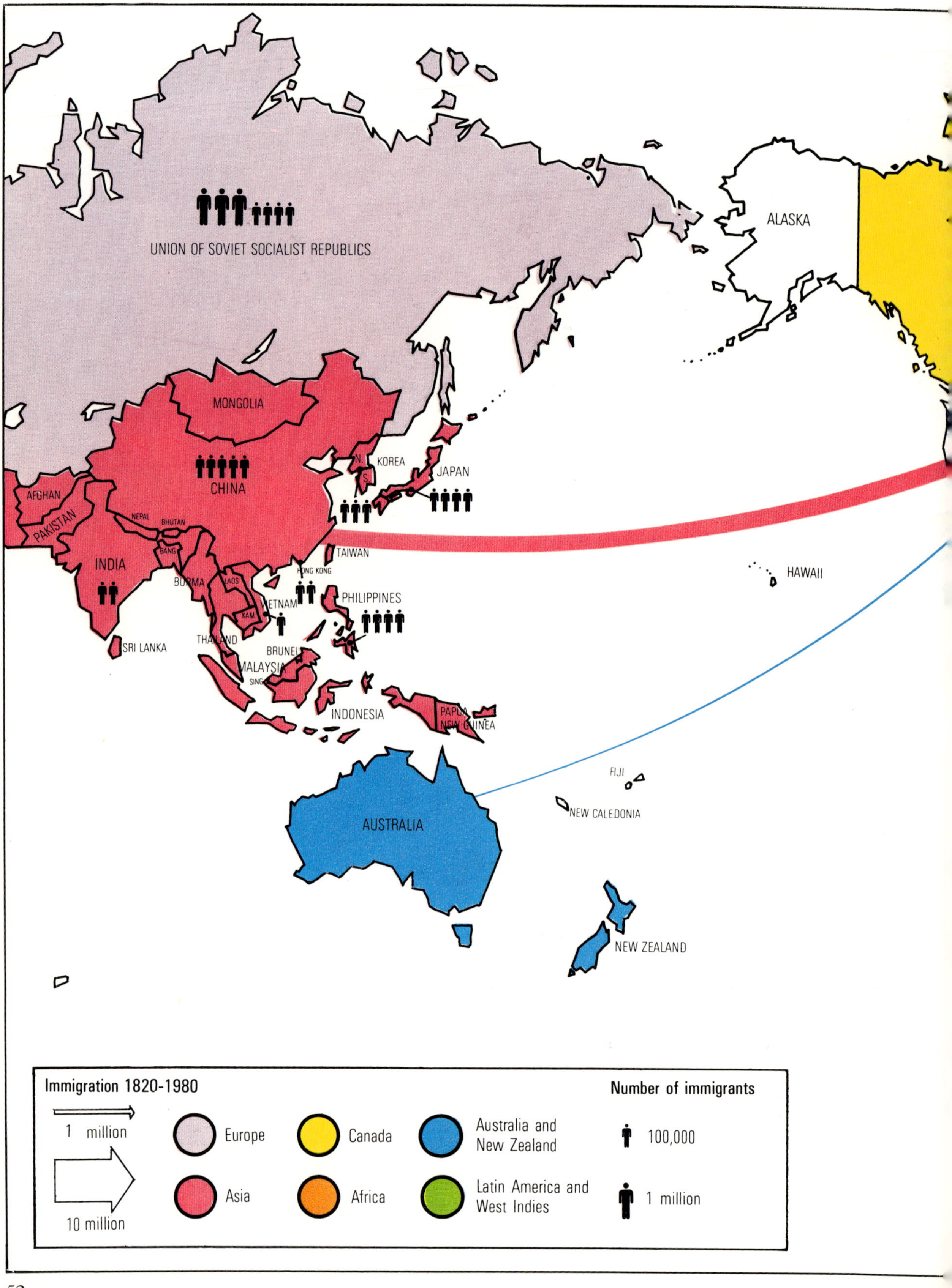

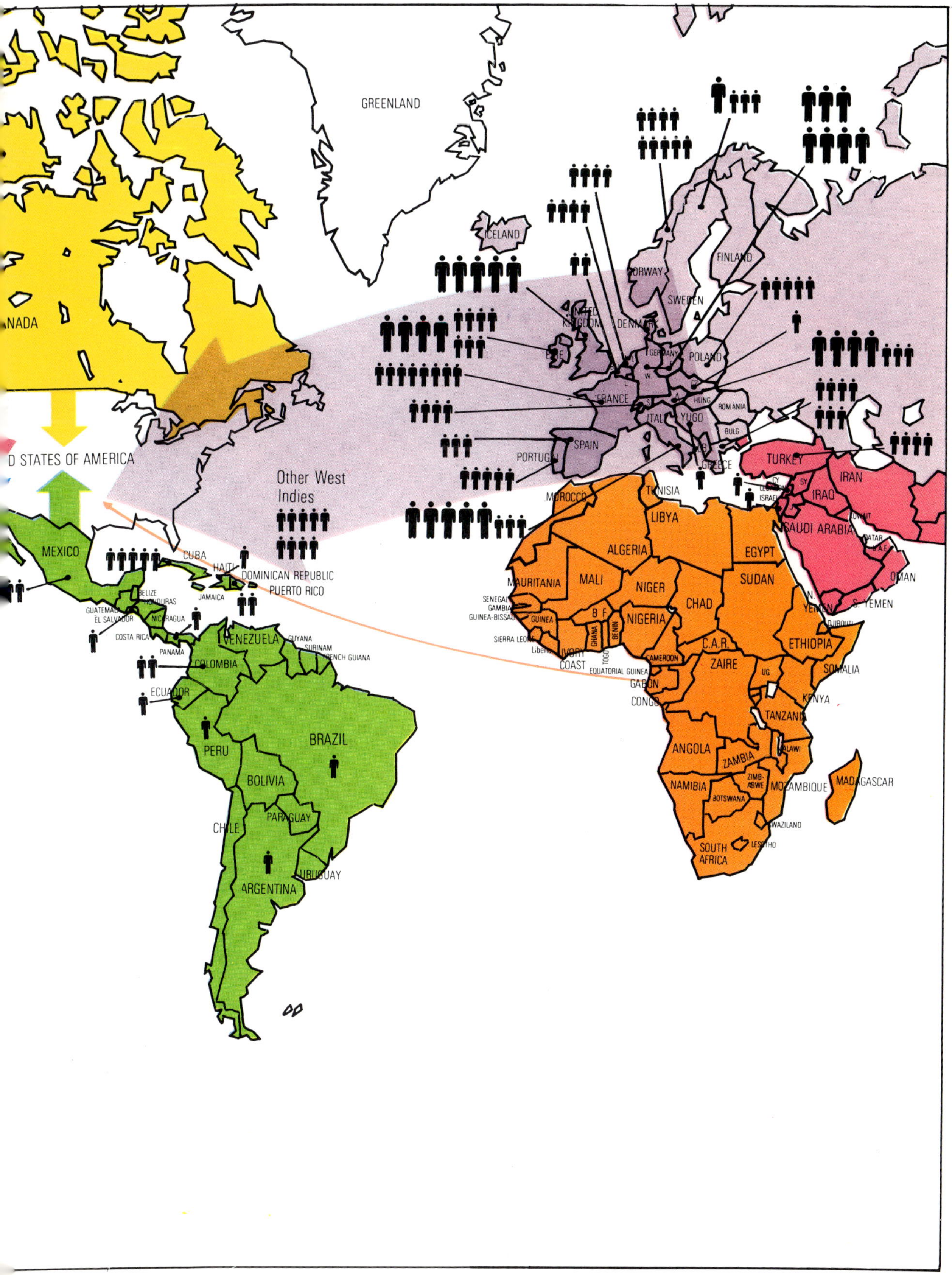

GREENLAND
ICELAND
NADA
D STATES OF AMERICA
MEXICO
CUBA
HAITI
DOMINICAN REPUBLIC
PUERTO RICO
JAMAICA
BELIZE
HONDURAS
GUATEMALA
EL SALVADOR
NICARAGUA
COSTA RICA
PANAMA
Other West Indies
VENEZUELA
GUYANA
SURINAM
FRENCH GUIANA
COLOMBIA
ECUADOR
PERU
BRAZIL
BOLIVIA
PARAGUAY
CHILE
URUGUAY
ARGENTINA
NORWAY
SWEDEN
FINLAND
UNITED KINGDOM
DENMARK
EIRE
GERMANY
POLAND
FRANCE
HUNG
ROMANIA
YUGO
ITALY
BULG
SPAIN
PORTUGAL
GREECE
TURKEY
IRAN
IRAQ
SY
ISRAEL
SAUDI ARABIA
KUWAIT
QATAR
U.A.E.
OMAN
N. YEMEN
S. YEMEN
MOROCCO
TUNISIA
LIBYA
ALGERIA
EGYPT
MAURITANIA
MALI
NIGER
CHAD
SUDAN
SENEGAL
GAMBIA
GUINEA-BISSAU
GUINEA
SIERRA LEONE
B F
GHANA
BENIN
NIGERIA
IVORY COAST
TOGO
CAMEROON
C.A.R.
ETHIOPIA
DJIBOUTI
SOMALIA
EQUATORIAL GUINEA
GABON
CONGO
ZAIRE
UG
KENYA
TANZANIA
ANGOLA
ZAMBIA
MALAWI
NAMIBIA
ZIMBABWE
MOZAMBIQUE
MADAGASCAR
BOTSWANA
SWAZILAND
LESOTHO
SOUTH AFRICA

IMMIGRATION

Since 1820, over 50 million people have come to the United States to settle, and this map shows where they came from. The thickness of the arrows indicates how many immigrants there were in the period1820-1980,the colours of the arrows corresponding to their continents of origin. The map also shows the numbers of immigrants from individual countries.

The earliest settlers on the northeastern coast were mainly from the British Isles, with a sprinkling of Germans and Dutch. In the eighteenth century, the largest influx consisted of people abducted from Africa as slaves — about half a million enforced "immigrants."

In the nineteenth century, however, many millions of immigrants arrived. Entry into the United States was almost entirely unrestricted at that time. It was only in 1819 that the numbers of immigrants even began to be recorded.

Diagram A graphs the annual rate of arrival since 1820. While immigration from Britain continued throughout the century, the steep rise in the total during the 1840s reflects two main factors. First, famine drove some 2 million Irish to make the Atlantic crossing. Second, after the political upheaval in Germany in 1848, many Germans immigrated to the United States, and they continued coming in great numbers until 1900.

During the Civil War, immigration fell off, but it resumed after 1865. The depression that began in 1872 also reduced the influx for a time, but it was followed by a rapid rise in immigration from southern and eastern Europe.

The tremendous expansion of U.S. industry then began to pull in huge masses of labour from Europe, with Italy and Russia making large contributions. In the 1880s, it was estimated that 28 percent of immigrants were German-speaking, while in 1901-1910, 23 percent were Italian-speaking.

Diagram A: Total annual immigration into the United States, 1820-1983

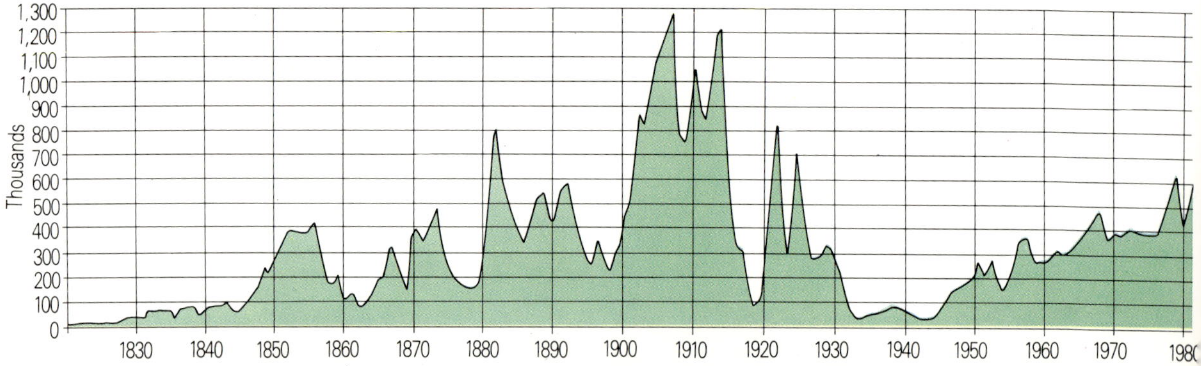

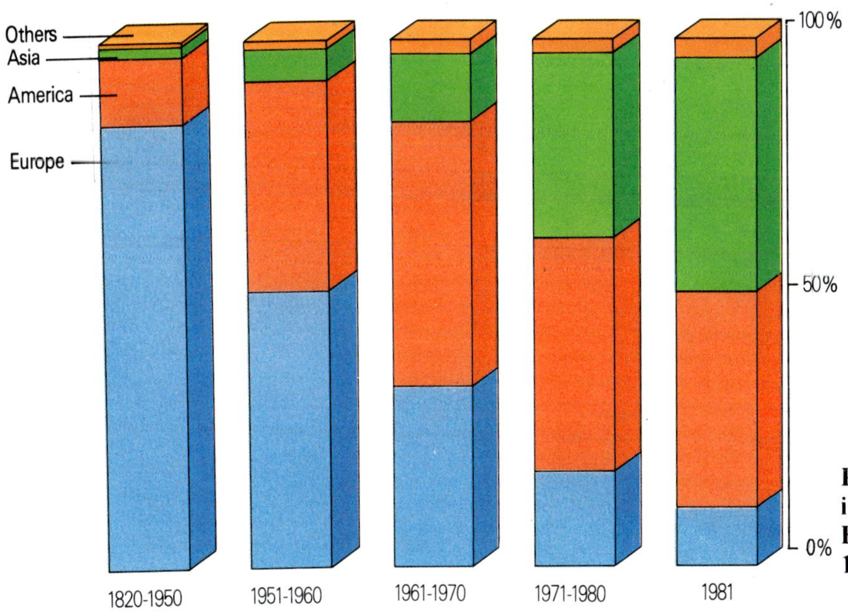

Diagram B: Percentage of immigrants from Asia, America, Europe and other countries, 1820-1981

Despite the first beginnings of legal restrictions on immigration, the curve moved up to record heights at the turn of the century. The all-time annual peak was reached in 1907, when nearly 1.3 million immigrants arrived in the United States.

After the disruption caused by World War I, the influx resumed, but it was now regulated by the Immigration Quota Acts of 1921 and 1924. The immigration of people from Asia had already been controlled under laws passed in 1882, 1907, and 1917. Now European immigration was also controlled, specific quotas being fixed for each country of origin. (This system continued until 1965.) The Great Depression of 1929-1934 brought the numbers of immigrants down to a fraction of their former levels. Then the war reduced the influx to a minimum.

Postwar immigration followed quite a different pattern from that of the previous century. Diagram B contrasts the proportions of immigrants from different parts of the world in the last few decades with the predominantly European origin of the earlier immigrations. It shows how Asia and Latin America have accounted for higher and higher proportions since World War II. In the 1960s and 1970s, about 30 percent of immigrants were from Spanish-speaking countries.

The social characteristics of the postwar immigrants are also quite different from those of their predecessors. In the 1820-1940 period, the typical immigrant was under 30 years old and from a peasant or laboring background. After World War II, many of the immigrants had professional or technical skills.

Sources: U.S. Immigration and Naturalization Service;
U.S. Bureau of the Census

TERRITORIAL EXPANSION

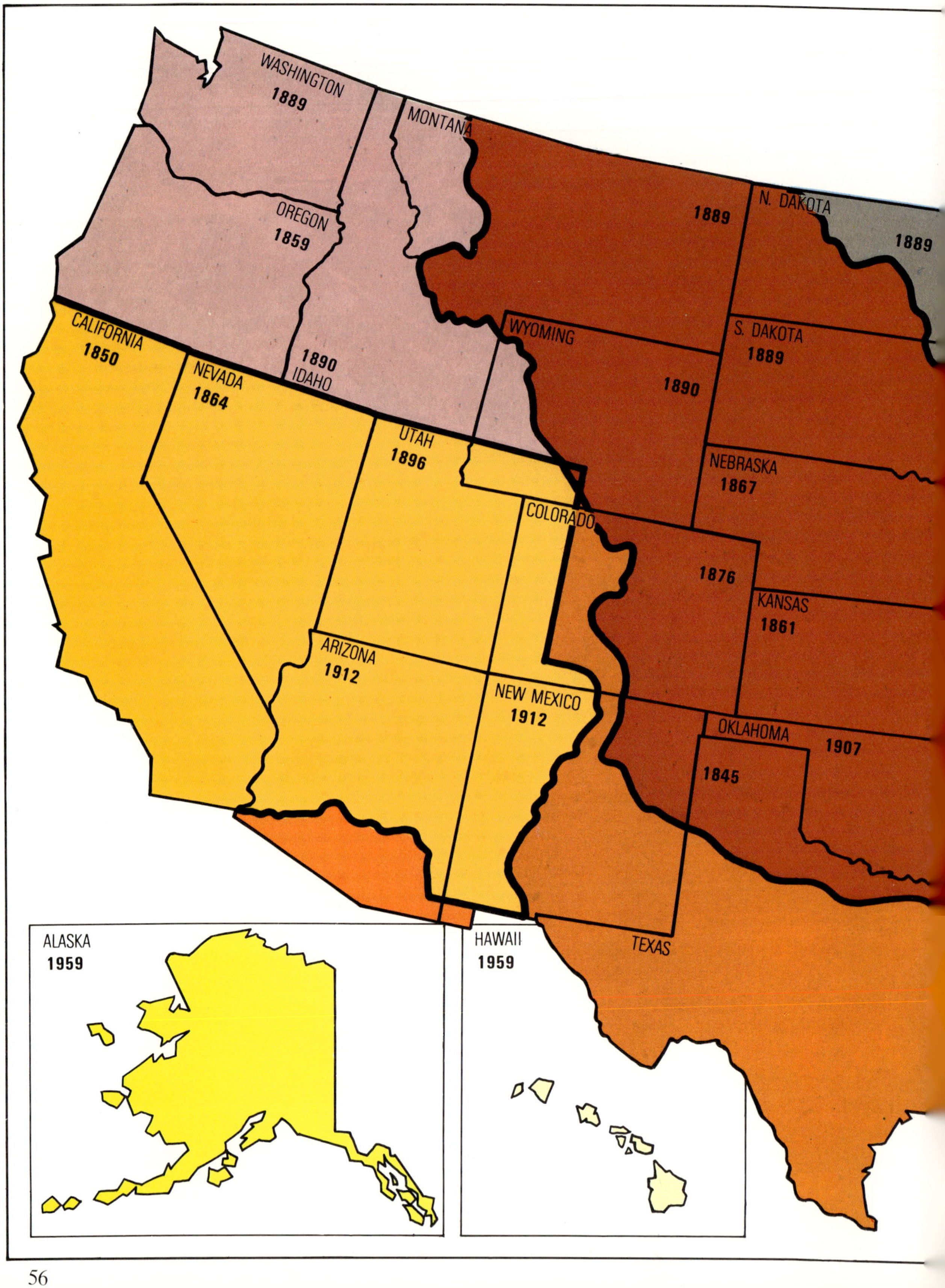

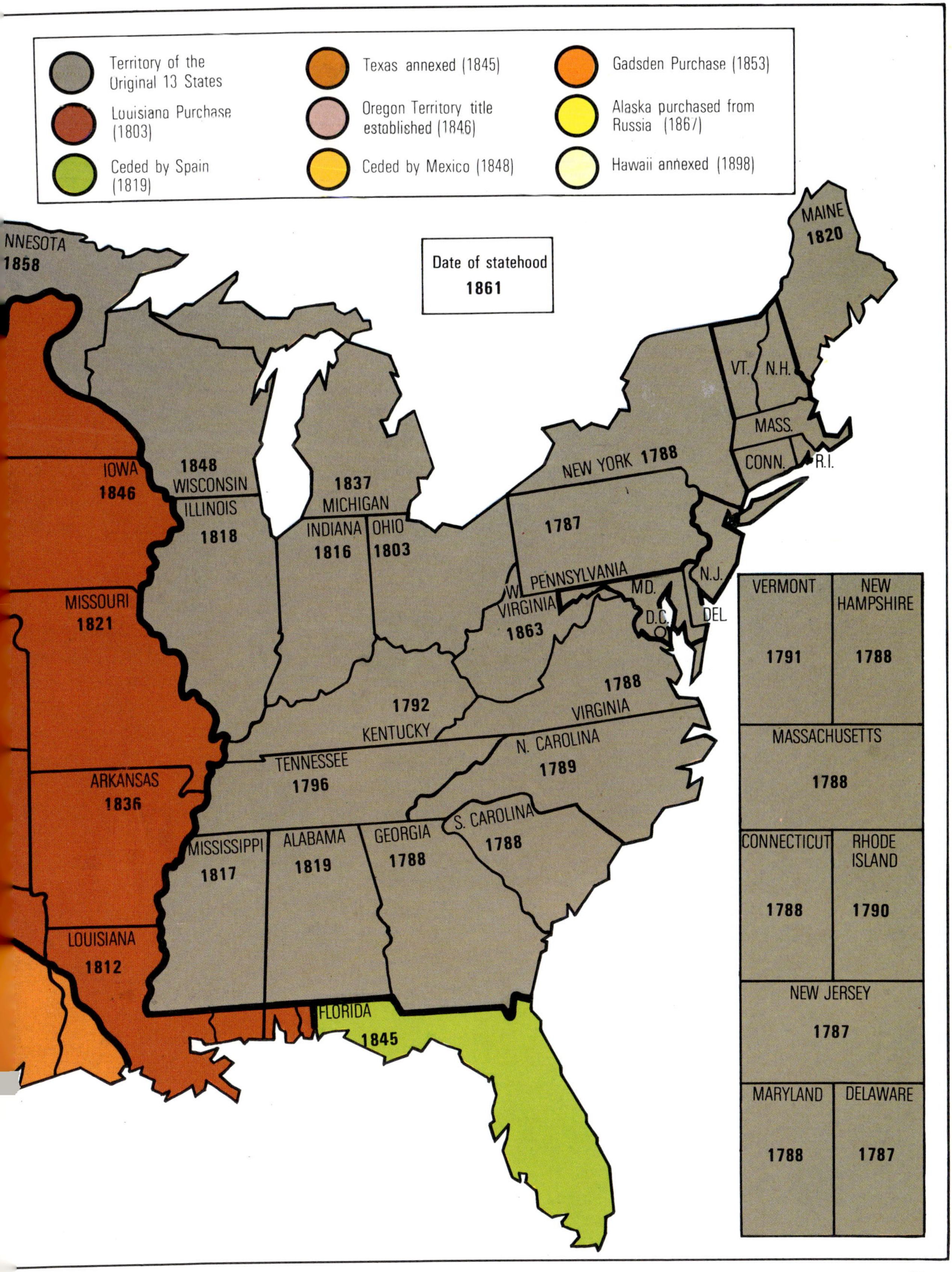

Territory of the Original 13 States
Louisiana Purchase (1803)
Ceded by Spain (1819)
Texas annexed (1845)
Oregon Territory title established (1846)
Ceded by Mexico (1848)
Gadsden Purchase (1853)
Alaska purchased from Russia (1867)
Hawaii annexed (1898)
Date of statehood 1861
NNESOTA 1858
MAINE 1820
VT.
N.H.
MASS.
CONN.
R.I.
NEW YORK 1788
1848 WISCONSIN
1837 MICHIGAN
IOWA 1846
ILLINOIS 1818
INDIANA 1816
OHIO 1803
1787 PENNSYLVANIA
N.J.
MD.
D.C.
DEL
W. VIRGINIA 1863
MISSOURI 1821
1792 KENTUCKY
1788 VIRGINIA
TENNESSEE 1796
N. CAROLINA 1789
ARKANSAS 1836
S. CAROLINA 1788
MISSISSIPPI 1817
ALABAMA 1819
GEORGIA 1788
LOUISIANA 1812
FLORIDA 1845
VERMONT 1791
NEW HAMPSHIRE 1788
MASSACHUSETTS 1788
CONNECTICUT 1788
RHODE ISLAND 1790
NEW JERSEY 1787
MARYLAND 1788
DELAWARE 1787

TERRITORIAL EXPANSION

This map shows the territory of the United States of America, as it grew from the treaty of 1783 to the annexation of Hawaii in 1898. The map also shows the boundaries of each state, and the date on which it was admitted to the Union.

The territory of the "Original Thirteen" states, bounded by Canada in the north and Spanish-held Florida in the south, stretched from the Atlantic coast westward to the Mississippi River. It comprised 891,364 square miles, though many areas were subject to rival claims by France and Spain.

The Louisiana Purchase in 1803 was the most important territorial acquisition during the transcontinental development of the United States. Bought from France for $15 million, it almost doubled the area of the United States at one stroke and contained most of what is now the west-central section of the country. The Louisiana Purchase ensured the free navigation of the Mississippi River, and the elimination of France in the struggle for North America.

In 1819 Secretary of State John Quincy Adams succeeded in purchasing Florida from Spain for $5 million in return for abandoning U.S. claims to Texas. The same treaty (the Transcontinental Treaty) also recognized a U.S. boundary extending westward to the Pacific at the 42nd parallel. This strengthened the U.S. claim to the Pacific coast north of the 42nd parallel, an area which, by an 1818 agreement between the United States and Britain, was subject to joint occupation by the two countries.

At that time the only settlement in the region was a British Hudson's Bay Company post at Port Vancouver, but American settlers flocked to Oregon in the late 1830s and were soon petitioning for entry to the Union. In 1846 Britain acceded to U.S. claims in a treaty that continued the 49th parallel westward to the Pacific as a boundary between the two countries.

Diagram A: Growth of cities from 1790-1980. For each successive date shown, the size of city indicated on the map increases, from cities with over 10,000 inhabitants in 1790 to those with over half a million in 1980. Regions shaded blue indicate the extent of the contiguous United States at each date

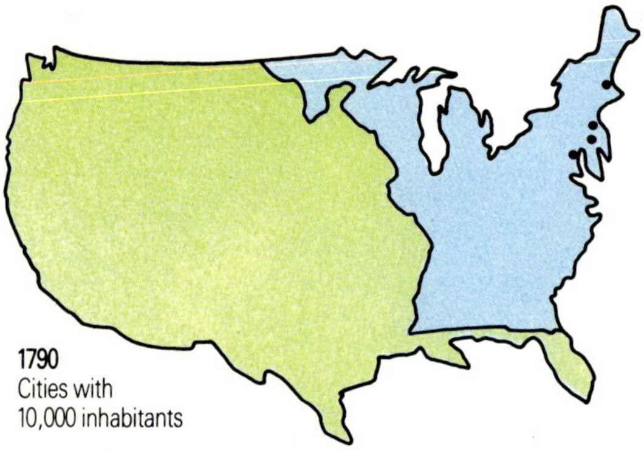

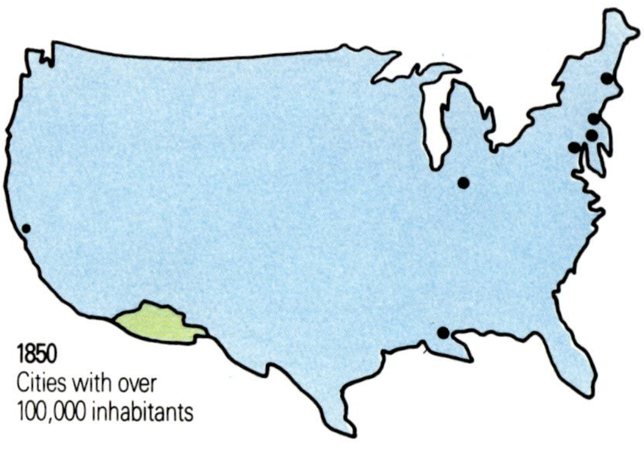

TOP TEN: LARGEST U.S. CITIES

1790	1850	1900	1980
New York	New York	New York	New York
Philadelphia	Baltimore	Chicago	Chicago
Boston	Boston	Philadelphia	Los Angeles
Baltimore	Philadelphia	St Louis	Philadelphia
Richmond	New Orleans	Boston	Houston
Norfolk	Cincinnati	Baltimore	Detroit
Lexington-Fayette	St Louis	Cleveland	Dallas
Louisville	Pittsburgh	Buffalo	San Diego
——	Louisville	San Francisco	Phoenix
——	Buffalo	Cincinnati	Baltimore

In 1836 Texas declared its independence from Mexico and nine years later was annexed by the United States. This action worsened already bad relations between Mexico and the United States; and a boundary dispute in 1846 led to war between the two countries. The war was ended by treaty in 1848 in which Mexico ceded present-day Utah, Nevada, California, Arizona, Colorado, and New Mexico to the United States for $15 million. The border between the United States and Mexico was revised by the Gadsden Purchase of 1853.

In 1867 Alaska was purchased from Russia by Secretary of State William H Seward. The price was $7.2 million, about 2 cents per acre. Although many called this "Seward's Folly," the large natural resources and strategic location of "the last frontier" more than justified it. With 591,000 square miles, Alaska is one-fifth of the total area of the rest of the United States.

A brief war with Spain in 1898 gave the United States an overseas empire including Cuba, the Philippine Islands, Puerto Rico, and Guam. The first two later became independent nations but the latter two remain U.S. territories. During the war the United States annexed Hawaii.

Source: U.S. Bureau of the Census

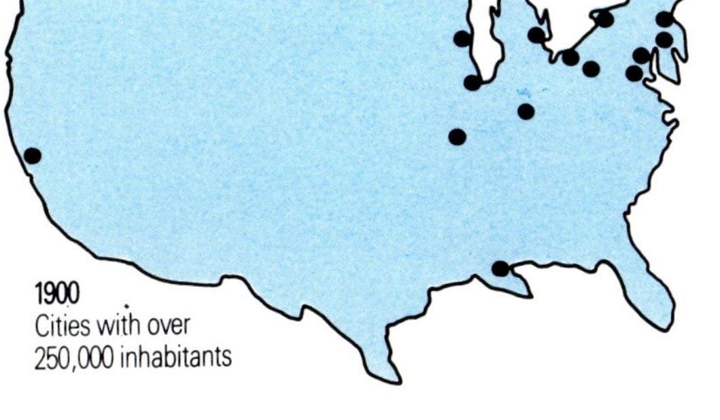

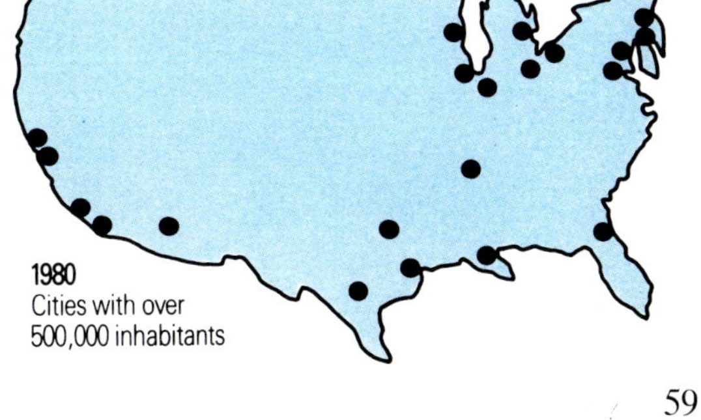

FARMLANDS

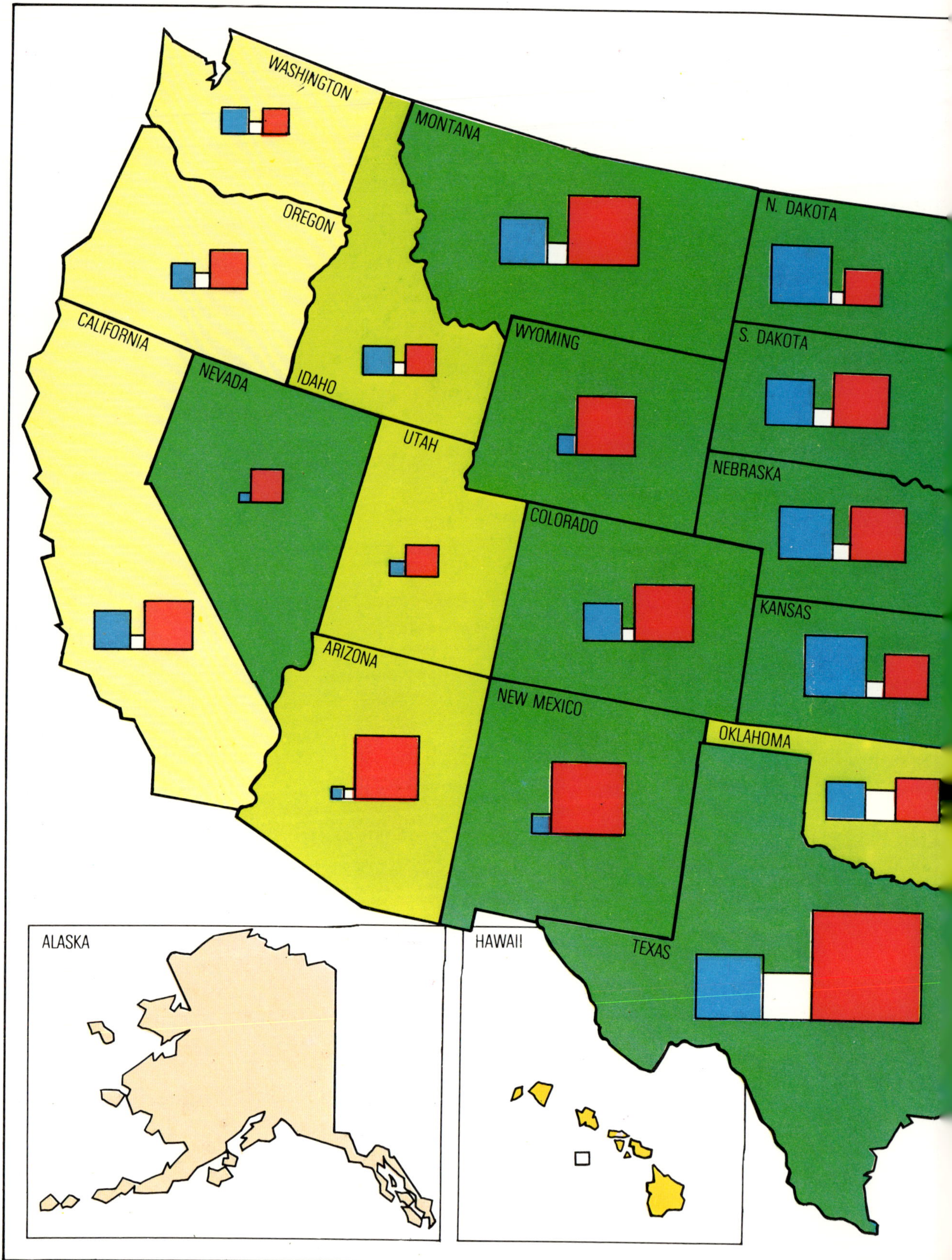

WASHINGTON
MONTANA
N. DAKOTA
OREGON
IDAHO
WYOMING
S. DAKOTA
CALIFORNIA
NEVADA
UTAH
NEBRASKA
COLORADO
KANSAS
ARIZONA
NEW MEXICO
OKLAHOMA
TEXAS
ALASKA
HAWAII

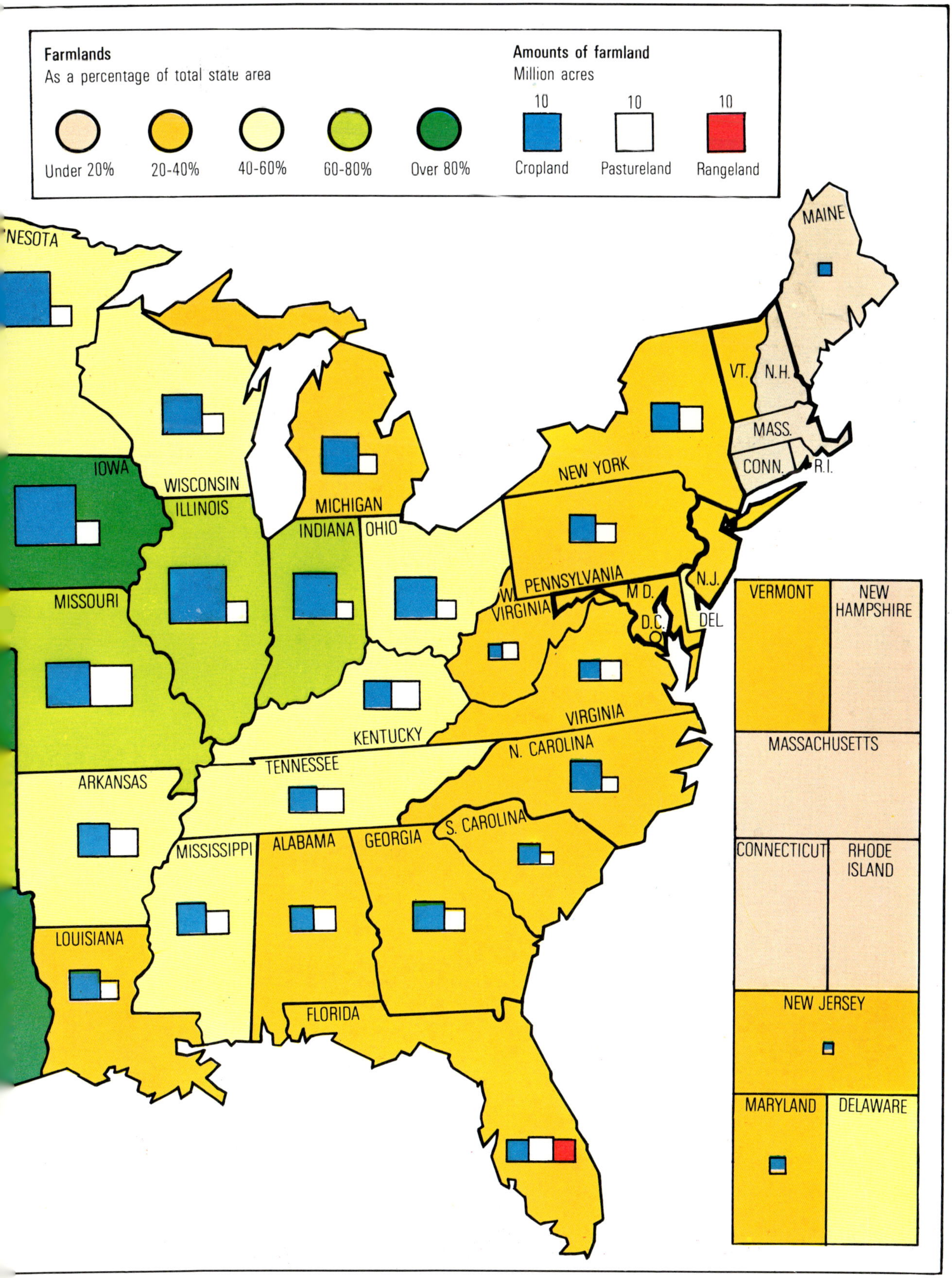
Farmlands
As a percentage of total state area
Under 20%
20-40%
40-60%
60-80%
Over 80%
Amounts of farmland
Million acres
10
10
10
Cropland
Pastureland
Rangeland
NESOTA
MAINE
VT.
N.H.
MASS.
CONN.
R.I.
NEW YORK
PENNSYLVANIA
N.J.
MD.
D.C.
DEL.
W. VIRGINIA
VIRGINIA
N. CAROLINA
S. CAROLINA
GEORGIA
FLORIDA
ALABAMA
MISSISSIPPI
LOUISIANA
ARKANSAS
TENNESSEE
KENTUCKY
OHIO
INDIANA
ILLINOIS
MICHIGAN
WISCONSIN
IOWA
MISSOURI
VERMONT
NEW HAMPSHIRE
MASSACHUSETTS
CONNECTICUT
RHODE ISLAND
NEW JERSEY
MARYLAND
DELAWARE

FARMLANDS

As in other industrial countries, the number of people working on farms and the relative contribution of agriculture to the national income have declined in recent decades. This does not mean that agriculture is less important in the economic sector generally. If anything, it has become more important. U.S. farmers must satisfy a growing population demanding a greater variety of food. They have succeeded to such an extent that the main problem of agriculture in the United States is not shortages but surpluses, which require government intervention to regulate prices and buy up superfluous product.

Farmland in the contiguous United States amounts to about 64 percent of the total area, excluding federally-owned land. The map shows the area of farmland as a proportion of the total area in each state. It also shows the amount of farmland in each state divided into three types: cropland, pasture, and rangeland. (Areas of less than 1 million acres have been omitted.) Rangeland is confined almost entirely to the western half of the country, whereas pasture and cropland are more evenly spread, with only a few of the most arid western states failing to register in all three categories.

The absence of symbols for some small northeastern states means that none of the categories of farmland attains an area of 1 million acres.

Diagram A: Number of farmworkers, 1820-1983. Pie charts show farmworkers as a percentage of population

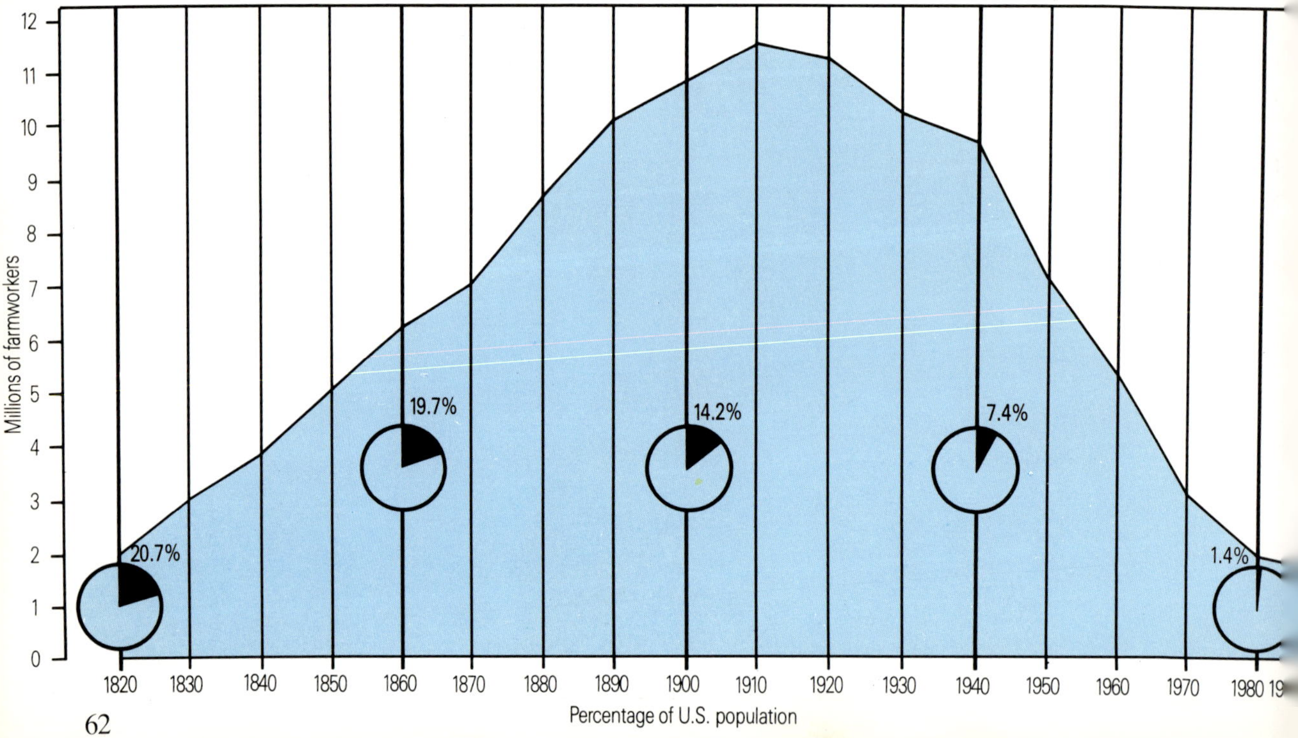

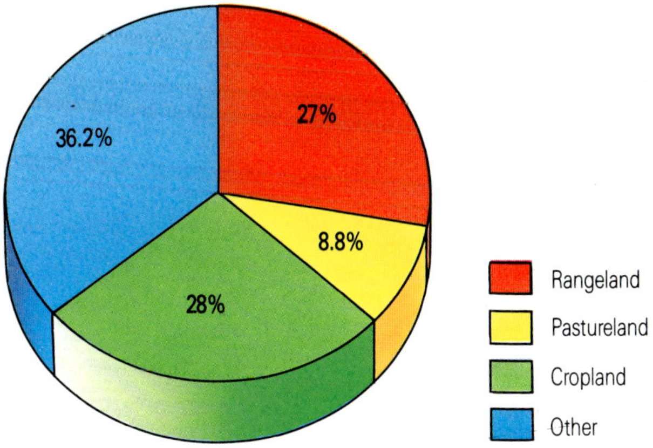

Diagram B: Farmland by type as a percentage of total non-federally owned land, 1982

The decline in the number of workers employed on farms (see Diagram A) has been rapid since World War II. Agrarian economists have referred to "a new agriculture" in this period, in which, despite the sharp decline in farmworkers, output increased at a rate faster than demand from an ever-growing population.

In terms of productivity, this is a remarkable success story, based mainly on the effects of applying science and technology to agricultural functions. The total area of cropland did not change significantly in the period 1950-1980, though there were marked regional variations (for example, cropland in the South declined by 46 percent between 1939 and 1974). But with capital, in the shape of machines, chemicals, etc., replacing labour in food production, today's farms are generally much larger while employing far fewer workers.

An associated feature is the rise of "agribusiness," a term implying an industrial-type operation that manages every stage of food production, "from seed to supermarket."

Between 1940 and 1980 the number of farms fell from 6.4 million to 2.4 million, and the average size increased from 167 acres to 430 acres. Large farms are characteristic of the West rather than the East or South, but the trend toward fewer and larger farms, involving the rise of farming corporations and the decline of family farms, is nationwide.

Sources: U.S. Dept. of Agriculture;
U.S. Bureau of Labor Statistics

CROP PRODUCTION

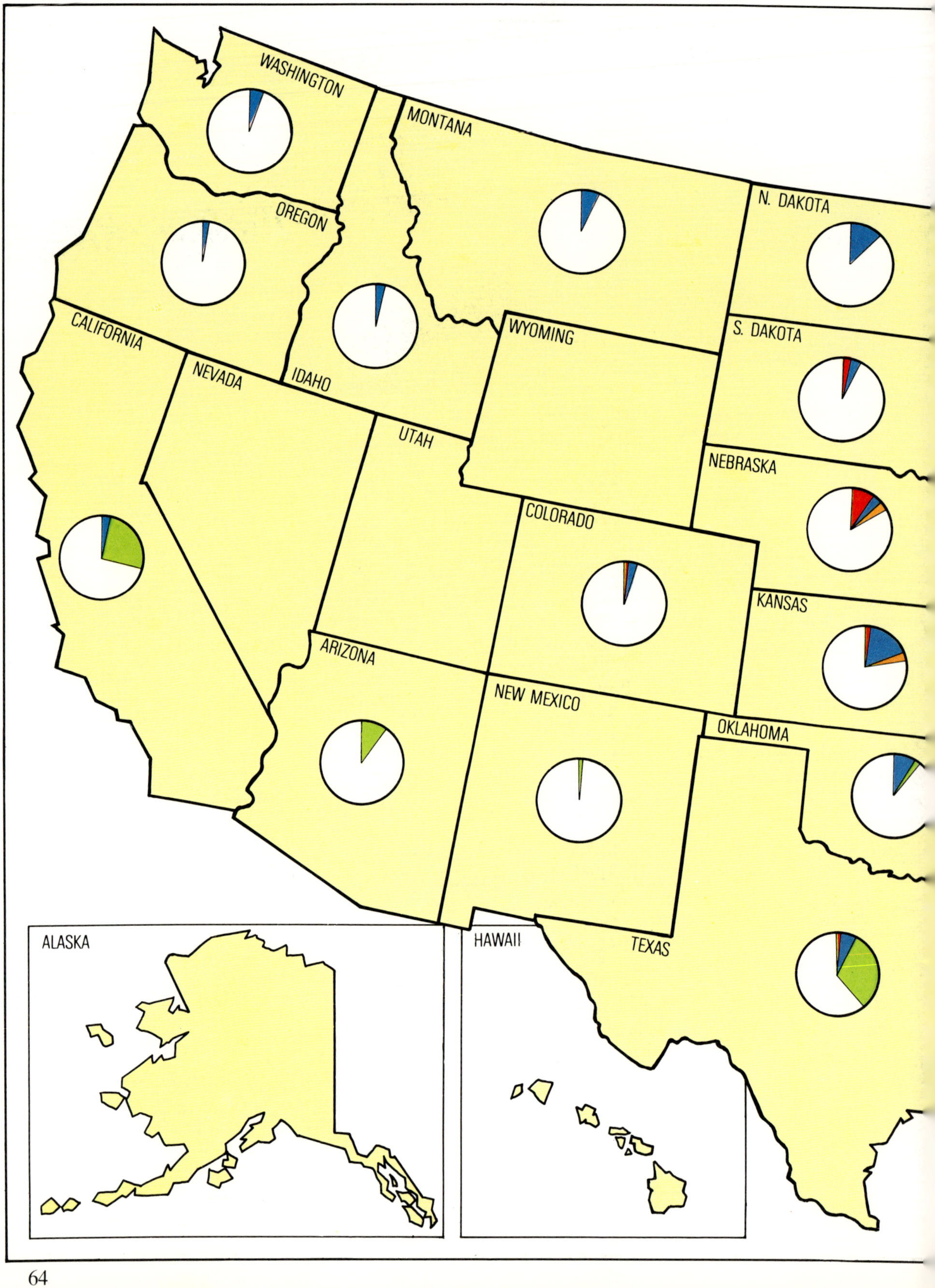

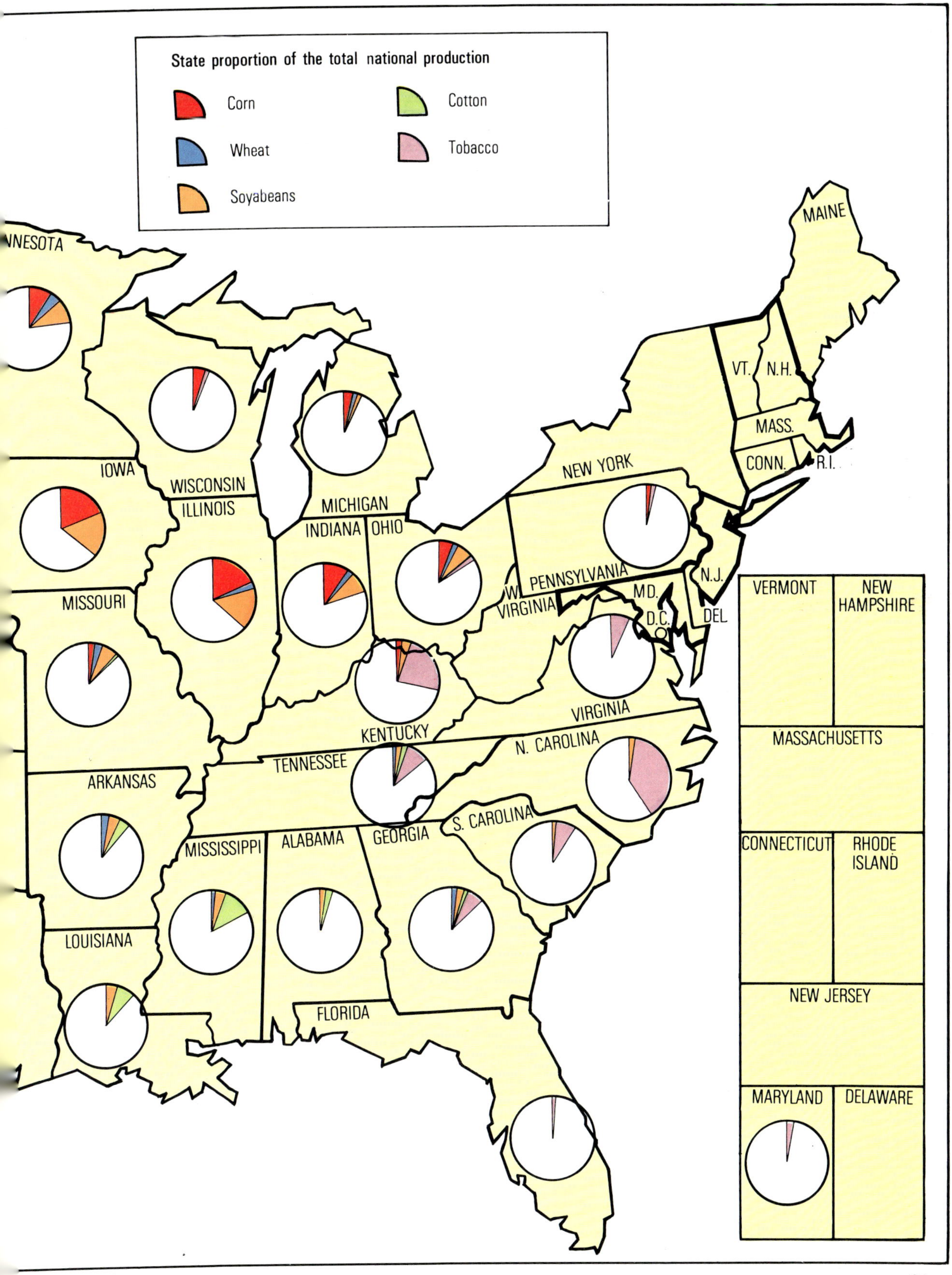
State proportion of the total national production
Corn
Wheat
Soyabeans
Cotton
Tobacco
MINNESOTA
IOWA
WISCONSIN
ILLINOIS
MICHIGAN
INDIANA
OHIO
MISSOURI
NEW YORK
PENNSYLVANIA
N.J.
MD.
D.C.
DEL
W. VIRGINIA
VIRGINIA
KENTUCKY
TENNESSEE
N. CAROLINA
S. CAROLINA
ARKANSAS
MISSISSIPPI
ALABAMA
GEORGIA
LOUISIANA
FLORIDA
MAINE
VT.
N.H.
MASS.
CONN.
R.I.
VERMONT
NEW HAMPSHIRE
MASSACHUSETTS
CONNECTICUT
RHODE ISLAND
NEW JERSEY
MARYLAND
DELAWARE

CROP PRODUCTION

The United States is not only self-sufficient in most crops (though not tropical produce), it is a net exporter of many, notably of grains and cereals. This fact is of more than economic importance. Grain exports may be used as an instrument of foreign policy, as President Carter demonstrated when he imposed a grain embargo on the Soviet Union in 1979.

The map shows the production in each state of the five largest U.S. crops expressed as a proportion of the national total. Where the total state production of any crop is less than 1 percent of the national total, it has been omitted. These minor producers contribute to the national total as follows: corn 9.5 percent; wheat 6.4 percent; soyabeans 3.6 percent; tobacco 1.7 percent; cotton 1.1 percent.

The map is based on production figures for 1983. For most crops, notably corn and cotton but also many lesser crops such as sorghum, rice, oats, and sugar beets, 1983 production was low by comparison with the annual average during the preceding decade (see Diagram B). Nevertheless, production far outweighed domestic consumption, and exports, even of corn and cotton, were larger than in the previous year.

Diagram A: Principal crops by value, 1983, in billions of dollars

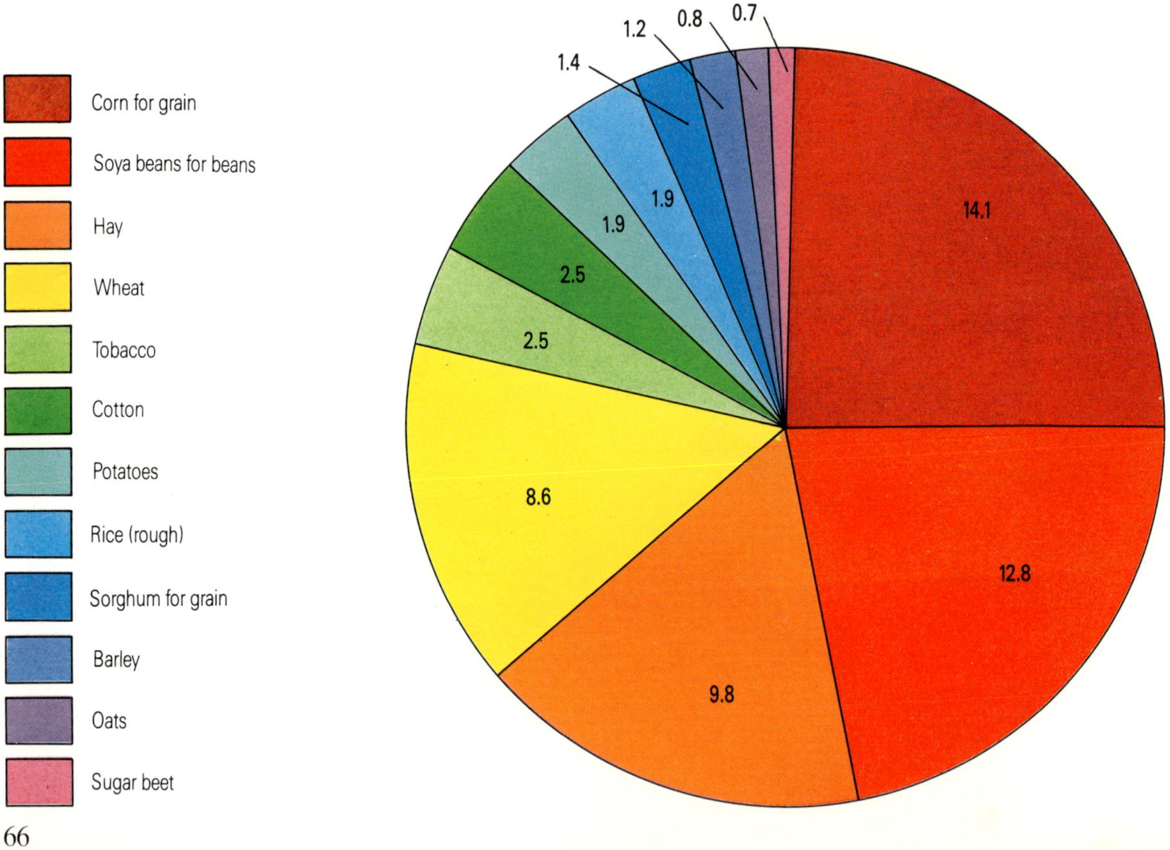

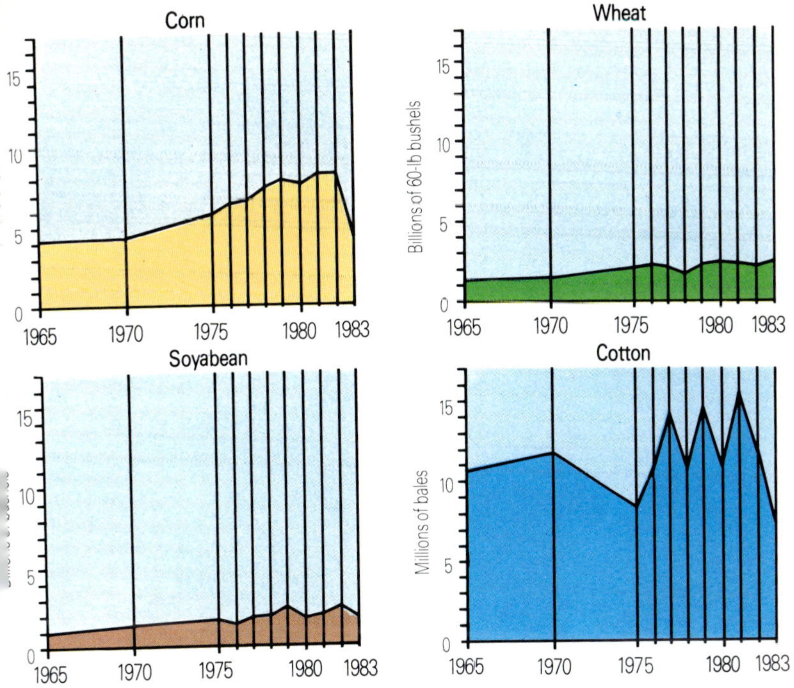

Diagram B: Production of leading crops, 1965-1983

The map reflects the traditional regional pattern of U.S. agriculture: the massive grain harvests of the corn belt, which stretches from Ohio to Nebraska and from Minnesota to Missouri, and the cotton belt of the South, which stretches from South Carolina to Texas. It also reflects the substantial changes in crop distribution that have occurred in recent years.

The increase in soyabeans, corn, wheat and rice and the reduction in the area under tobacco, cotton, oats, and hay have changed the character of the main crop-producing regions. Cotton has moved increasingly to the Southwest, with Texas and California together producing more than half the national total — much of it under irrigation.

Among the major crops, output of cotton and tobacco decreased slightly between 1960 and 1980. By contrast, output of food grains increased by 80 percent. Wheat production roughly doubled, while the increase for corn was about 60 percent. These production figures are all the more remarkable considering that the area of cropland in use increased by less than 10 percent during the same period.

Increased productivity is largely the result of new strains of plants and new fertilizers, pesticides, etc. Between 1950 and 1980, the use of agricultural chemicals increased by a factor of six. Machines such as harvesters, balers, etc., did not increase significantly in number, but they did increase considerably in individual size and performance. In addition, irrigation has been a major factor in the Southwest, a region highly favorable to agriculture save for its natural aridity.

Source: U.S. Dept. of Agriculture

LIVESTOCK PRODUCTION

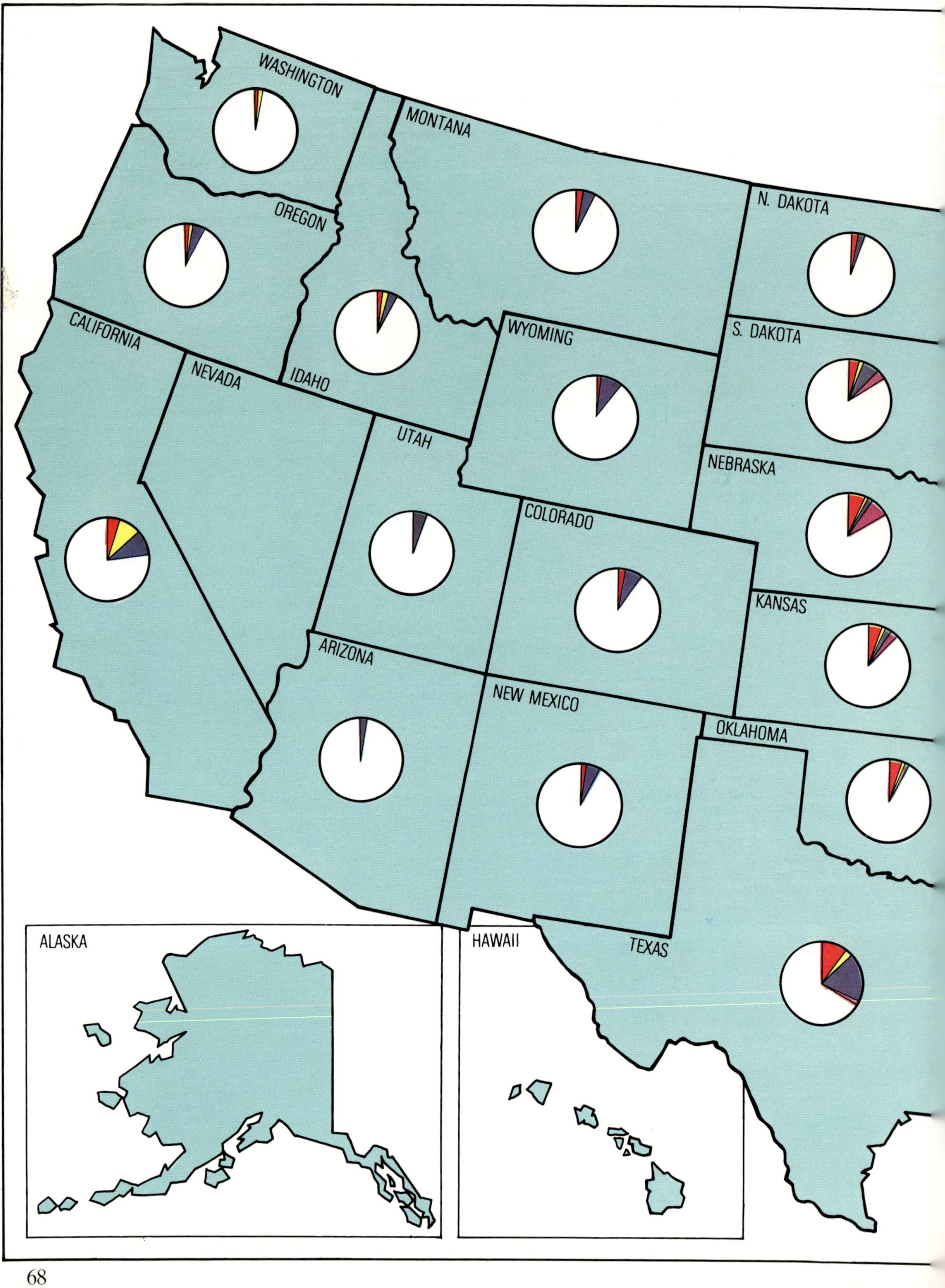

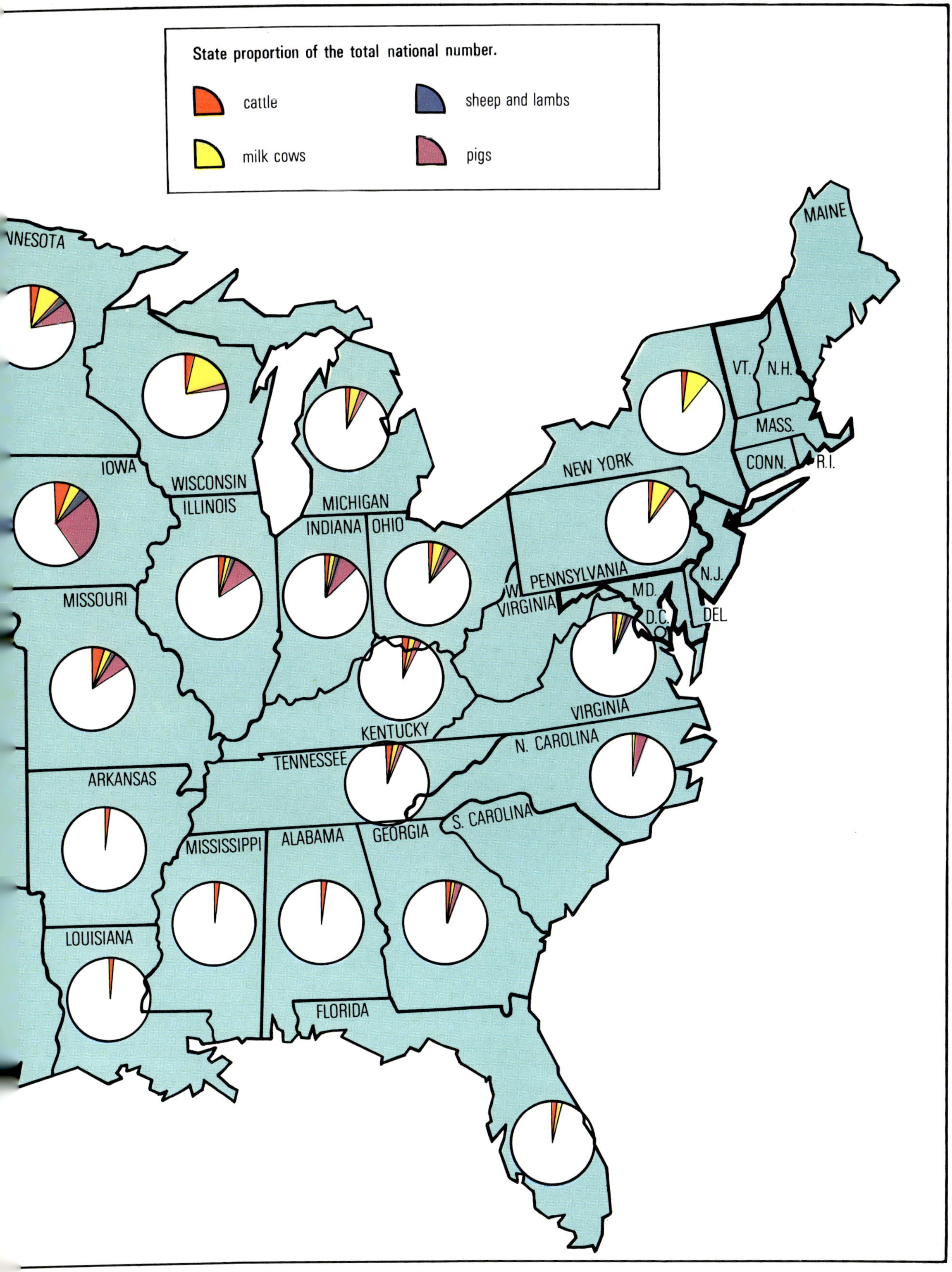
State proportion of the total national number.
cattle
sheep and lambs
milk cows
pigs
NNESOTA
MAINE
WISCONSIN
MICHIGAN
IOWA
ILLINOIS
INDIANA
OHIO
NEW YORK
VT.
N.H.
MASS.
CONN.
R.I.
PENNSYLVANIA
N.J.
MD.
DEL
D.C.
W. VIRGINIA
MISSOURI
KENTUCKY
VIRGINIA
TENNESSEE
N. CAROLINA
ARKANSAS
S. CAROLINA
MISSISSIPPI
ALABAMA
GEORGIA
LOUISIANA
FLORIDA

LIVESTOCK PRODUCTION

The remarkable increase in productivity that has characterized U.S. agriculture since World War II is no less evident in livestock than in crop production. All categories increased, though by varying proportions. The growth in poultry and egg output was especially notable.

The map shows the number of cattle, milk cows, sheep and pigs in each state expressed as a proportion of the national total. Where the state proportion is less than 1 percent of the national total it has been omitted.

It can be seen from the map that the traditional, regional pattern of livestock farming still holds, despite the changes of recent years. Dairy farming predominates in the Northeast, and dairy products contribute the largest share of cash receipts of farms in New England and in states such as New York, Pennsylvania, and Wisconsin.

The map also confirms that the corn belt is a misleading term for that rich agricultural area of the Midwest, where farm prosperity has always rested on a wider basis. A considerable proportion of the crop is fed to livestock which is subsequently marketed in the form of top-quality beef and pork. Livestock sales generally contribute a larger share than corn to farmers' incomes in this region.

In any state-oriented study, it is easy to be misled by scale. California and Texas are the leading states in terms of total farm products, but that is largely a result of their size; figures adjusted to take account of this would show more clearly the contribution of the corn/meat belt states of Iowa, Illinois, Indiana, and Ohio. Moreover, in terms of the value of farm sales per acre, neither Texas, which is more remarkable for sheer acreage than productivity, nor California feature prominently: the leading state, due to its intensive poultry farming, is Delaware. Yet Delaware does not appear among the leading states for poultry production simply because it is so small.

The poultry production figures show that production of chickens (and eggs) is spread relatively evenly across the country by comparison with broilers (young birds bred exclusively for meat) and turkeys. The figures relate to chickens and turkeys produced during 1983. The *total number* of birds on farms is of course considerably higher.

The table shows the leading states in livestock production at the end of 1983. As on the map, "cattle" means all cattle on farms;

TOP TEN: STATES WITH GREATEST NUMBER OF LIVESTOCK, 1983

Cattle

		(Thousands)
1	Texas	15,000
2	Nebraska	7,200
3	Iowa	6,450
4	Kansas	5,750
5	Missouri	5,500
6	Oklahoma	5,350
7	California	4,900
8	Wisconsin	4,400
9	South Dakota	4,060
10	Minnesota	3,610

Milk cows

		(Thousands)
1	Wisconsin	1,840
2	California	940
3	New York	935
4	Minnesota	890
5	Pennsylvania	738
6	Michigan	400
7	Ohio	393
8	Iowa	386
9	Texas	385
10	Missouri	252

Sheep

		(Thousands)
1	Texas	2,225
2	California	1,115
3	Wyoming	1,060
4	Colorado	750
5	South Dakota	680
6	New Mexico	610
7	Utah	590
8	Montana	560
9	Oregon	515
10	Iowa	457

Pigs

		(Thousands)
1	Iowa	14,800
2	Illinois	5,400
3	Minnesota	4,270
4	Indiana	4,200
5	Nebraska	3,900
6	Missouri	3,550
7	North Carolina	2,300
8	Ohio	2,100
9	South Dakota	1,650
10	Kansas	1,600

"milk cows" represents cows and heifers that have calved and are kept for milk; "sheep" includes lambs.

In most cases, it is not a very close race at the top of the table. For instance, Texas has more than twice as many sheep and nearly twice as many cattle as its nearest rivals (California and Nebraska respectively). Wisconsin has twice as many milk cows as the second state, California. Most remarkable of all, the state of Iowa contains three times as many pigs as Illinois (second in the table), and more than one-quarter of the national total. Iowa is also the only state to feature in the "top ten" of all four main livestock categories.

Source: U.S. Dept. of Agriculture

FARM ECONOMICS

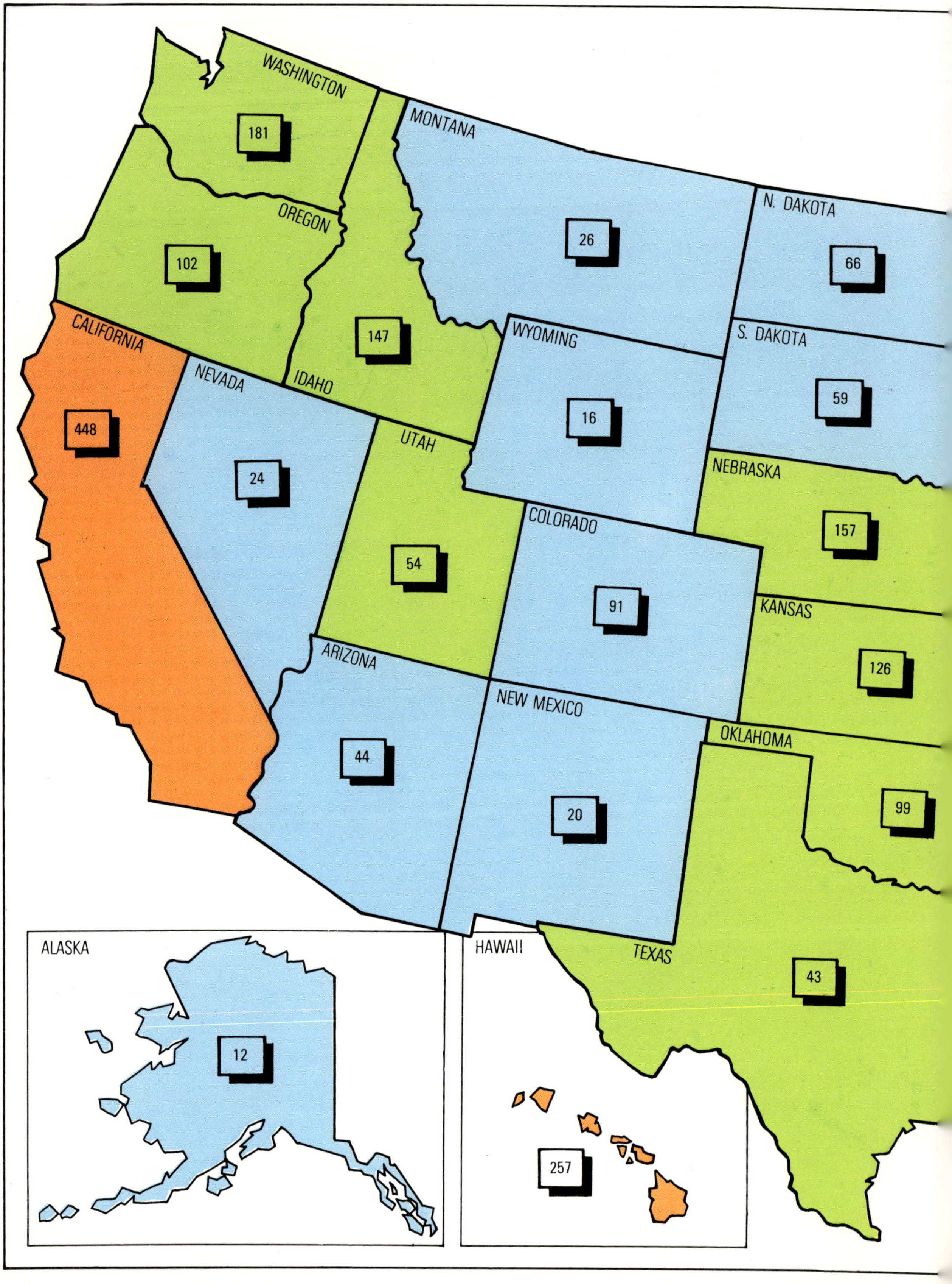

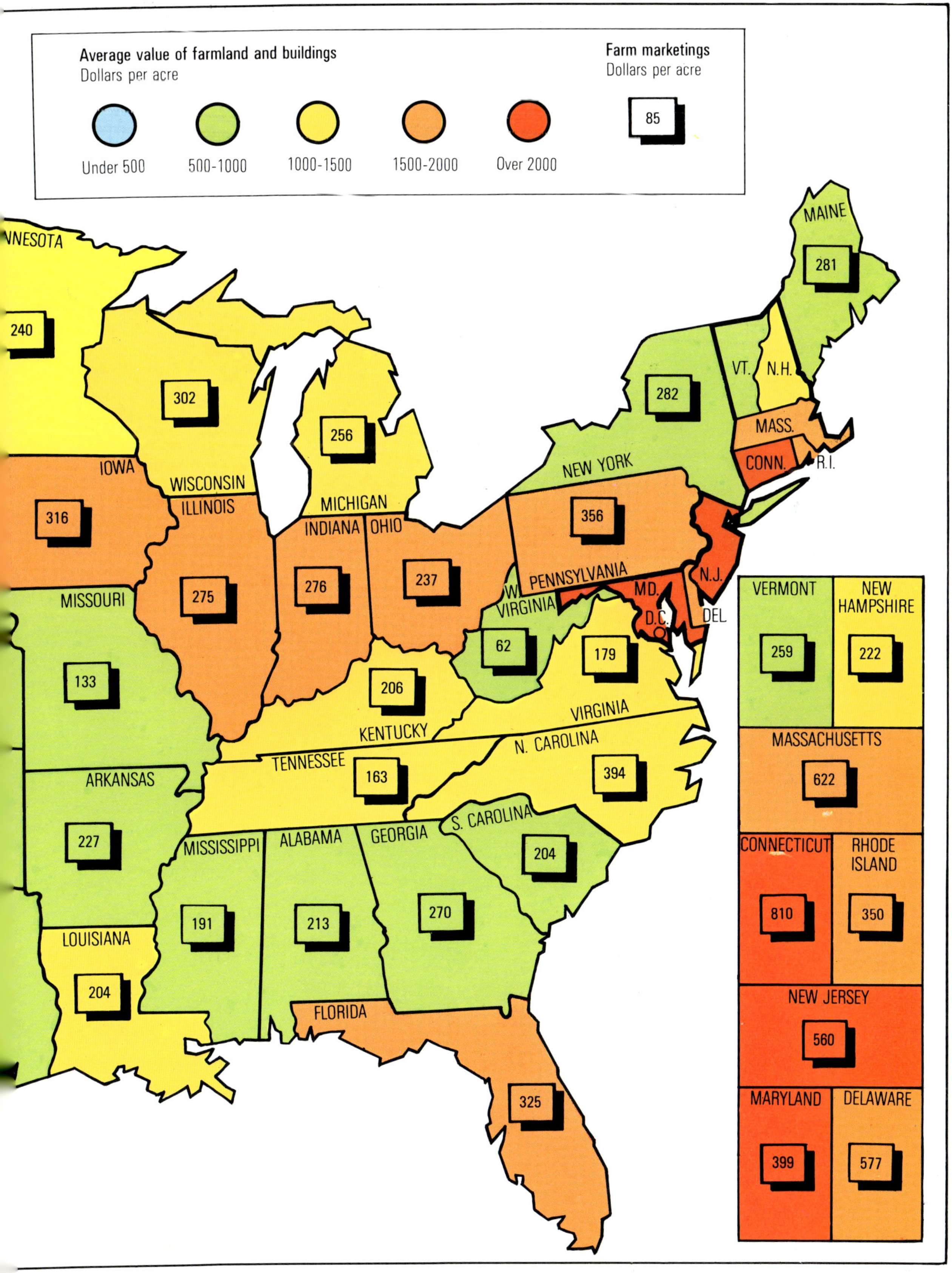

Average value of farmland and buildings
Dollars per acre
Under 500
500-1000
1000-1500
1500-2000
Over 2000
Farm marketings
Dollars per acre
85
MINNESOTA
240
WISCONSIN
302
MICHIGAN
256
IOWA
316
ILLINOIS
275
INDIANA
276
OHIO
237
MISSOURI
133
KENTUCKY
206
W. VIRGINIA
62
VIRGINIA
179
PENNSYLVANIA
356
NEW YORK
282
MAINE
281
VT.
N.H.
MASS.
CONN.
R.I.
N.J.
MD.
D.C.
DEL
TENNESSEE
163
N. CAROLINA
394
S. CAROLINA
204
ARKANSAS
227
MISSISSIPPI
191
ALABAMA
213
GEORGIA
270
LOUISIANA
204
FLORIDA
325
VERMONT
259
NEW HAMPSHIRE
222
MASSACHUSETTS
622
CONNECTICUT
810
RHODE ISLAND
350
NEW JERSEY
560
MARYLAND
399
DELAWARE
577

FARM ECONOMICS

The map shows the average value of farmland and farm buildings by state in 1984. New Jersey leads, with an average of $3,148 per acre, followed by Rhode Island at $3,046. However, it should be pointed out that neither of these states has a great deal of farmland. Wyoming has the lowest value per acre, $165. The average for the whole of the United States is $739.

The map also shows the average value of farm marketings in 1983, in dollars per acre. On average, U.S. farm marketings were worth $137 per acre. State averages varied from $622 per acre in Massachusetts, down to $16 in Wyoming, and $12 in Alaska.

Diagram A shows the decline in the number of U.S. farms since 1950, and Diagram B the corresponding rise in the average size of a farm. In 1950, there were 5.65 million farms in the United States. By 1982, the number had halved. By 1983, it had fallen to 2.37 million. The 1984 figure was 2.33 million.

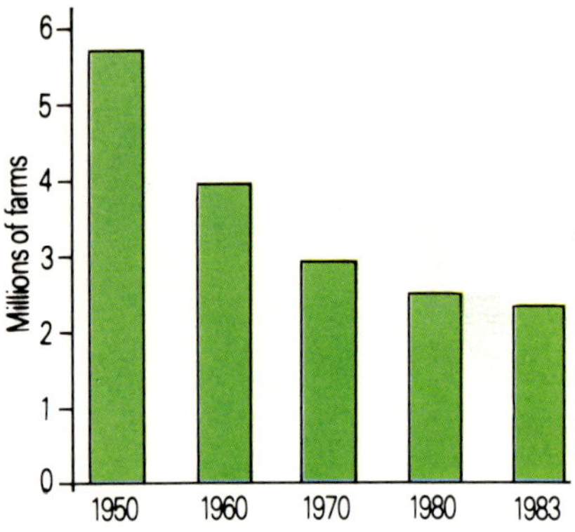

Diagram A: Numbers of U.S. farms, 1950-1983

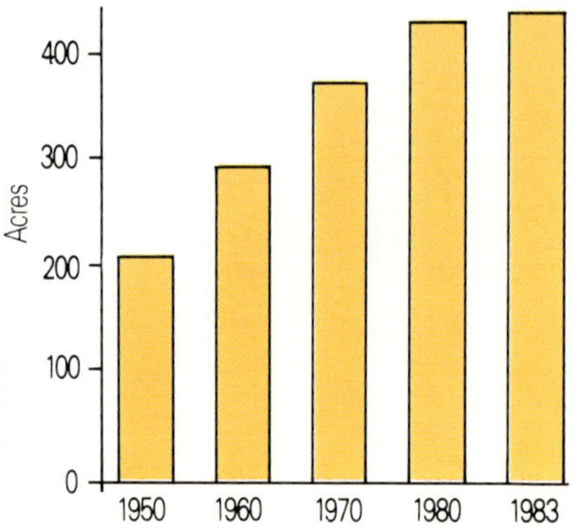

Diagram B: Average farm size, 1950-1983

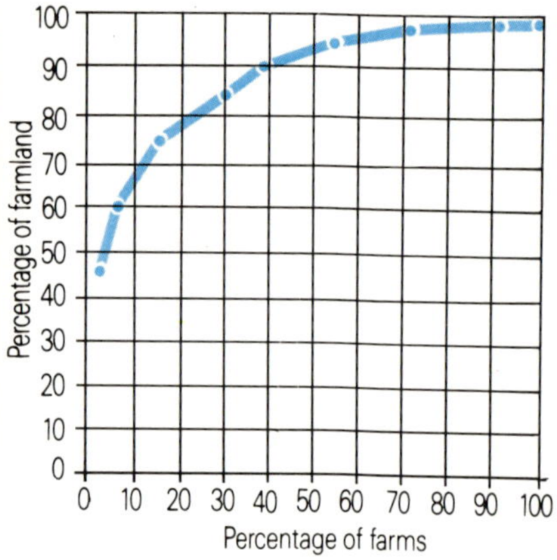

Diagram C: Concentration of U.S. farmland, 1982

Over the same period, the total acreage of farms fell only slightly, from 1,202 million acres, to 1,020 million acres. So the average farm size has more than doubled, from 213 acres in 1950, to 432 acres in 1983. (By 1984, it was 437.)

This concentration of farmland into large farms is illustrated in Diagram C, where it can be seen that the leading 3 percent of farms in terms of size contain almost half the total farmland, while the leading 17 percent account for over 75 percent of the total.

The economic results of the decrease in the number of farms and the increase in size are even more dramatic.

In 1983 the 25 farms whose sales valued $500,000 or over made up 1 percent of the total number of U.S. farms. They accounted for 10 percent of the total assets of farms and earned between them 48 percent of the total net income. At the opposite end of the scale, farms whose sales amounted to less than $20,000 made up 60 percent of all farms and together registered a net *loss* of $500 million in 1983.

Another consequence of large-scale farming is the increased use of machinery. This can be measured by the value of machinery per man-hour of labour employed. Diagram D graphs this indicator between 1960 and 1983. In 1960 it stood at $2.30 per man-hour of labour employed; by 1970 it had risen to $5.50; and in 1983 it reached $30.

Diagram E graphs the net income of farm operators from farming, expressed in constant (1967) dollars. This reached an all-time peak of $34.4 billion in current dollars in 1973. By 1983 it had fallen to $16.1 billion in current dollars. Taking account of inflation, the graph illustrates how large a decline this reflects in real terms.

In 1970, the per capita disposable income of the farm population was estimated to be $2,421, compared with $3,439 for the nonfarm population. In 1973, these figures were $4,401 for the farm population, and $4,311 for the rest. In 1983, the position had changed drastically: farm population, $6,917; non-farm, $10,057.

Sources: U.S. Bureau of the Census; U.S. Dept. of Agriculture, Economic Research Service

Diagram D: Capital intensity of U.S. farms by value of machinery in dollars per hour of labour, 1960-1983

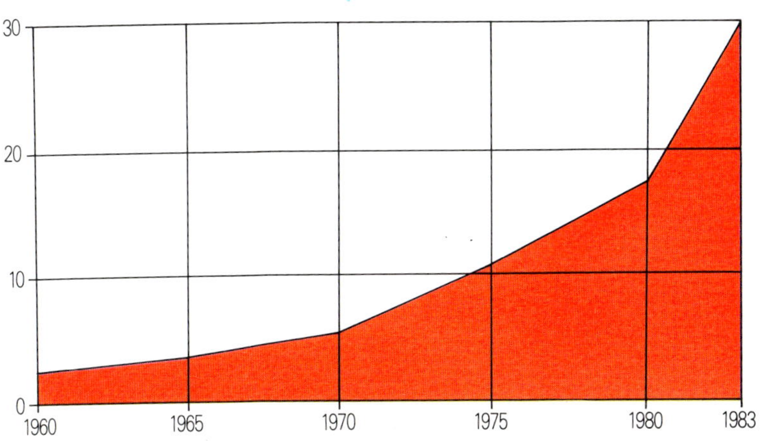

Diagram E: Net income of farm operators from farming, in constant (1967) dollars, 1970-1983

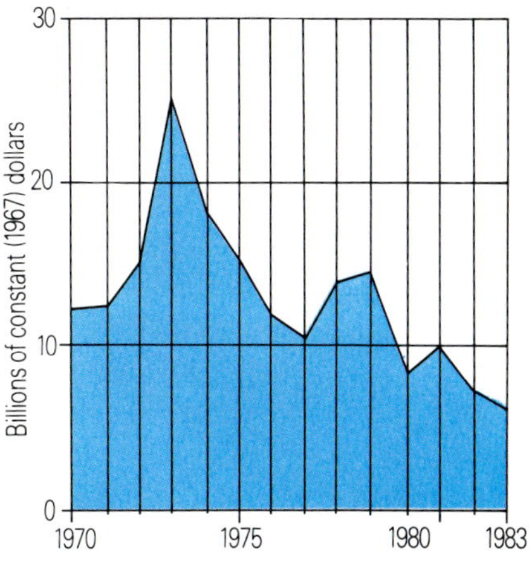

FORESTRY

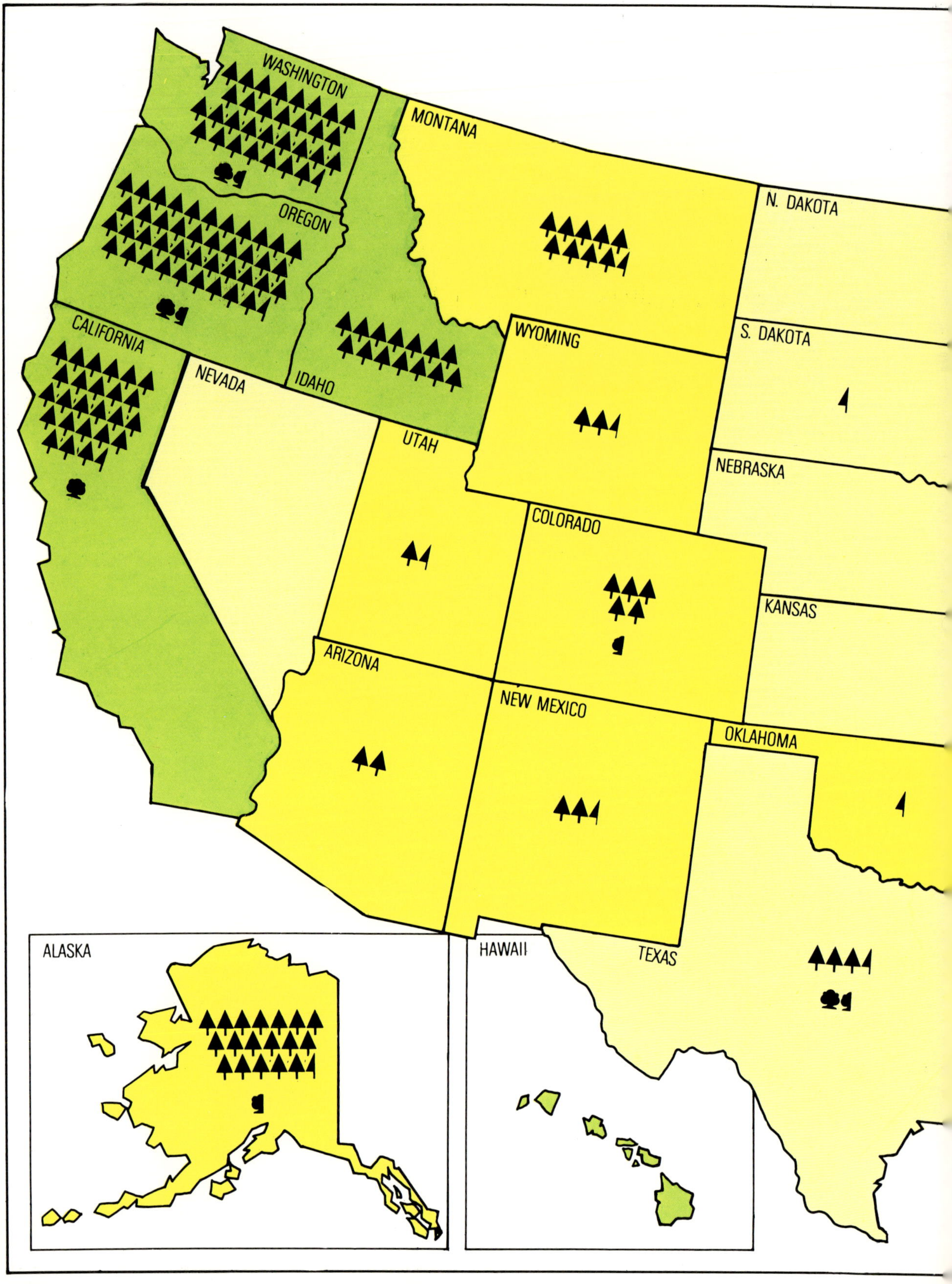
WASHINGTON
MONTANA
N. DAKOTA
OREGON
CALIFORNIA
IDAHO
WYOMING
S. DAKOTA
NEVADA
UTAH
NEBRASKA
COLORADO
KANSAS
ARIZONA
NEW MEXICO
OKLAHOMA
TEXAS
ALASKA
HAWAII

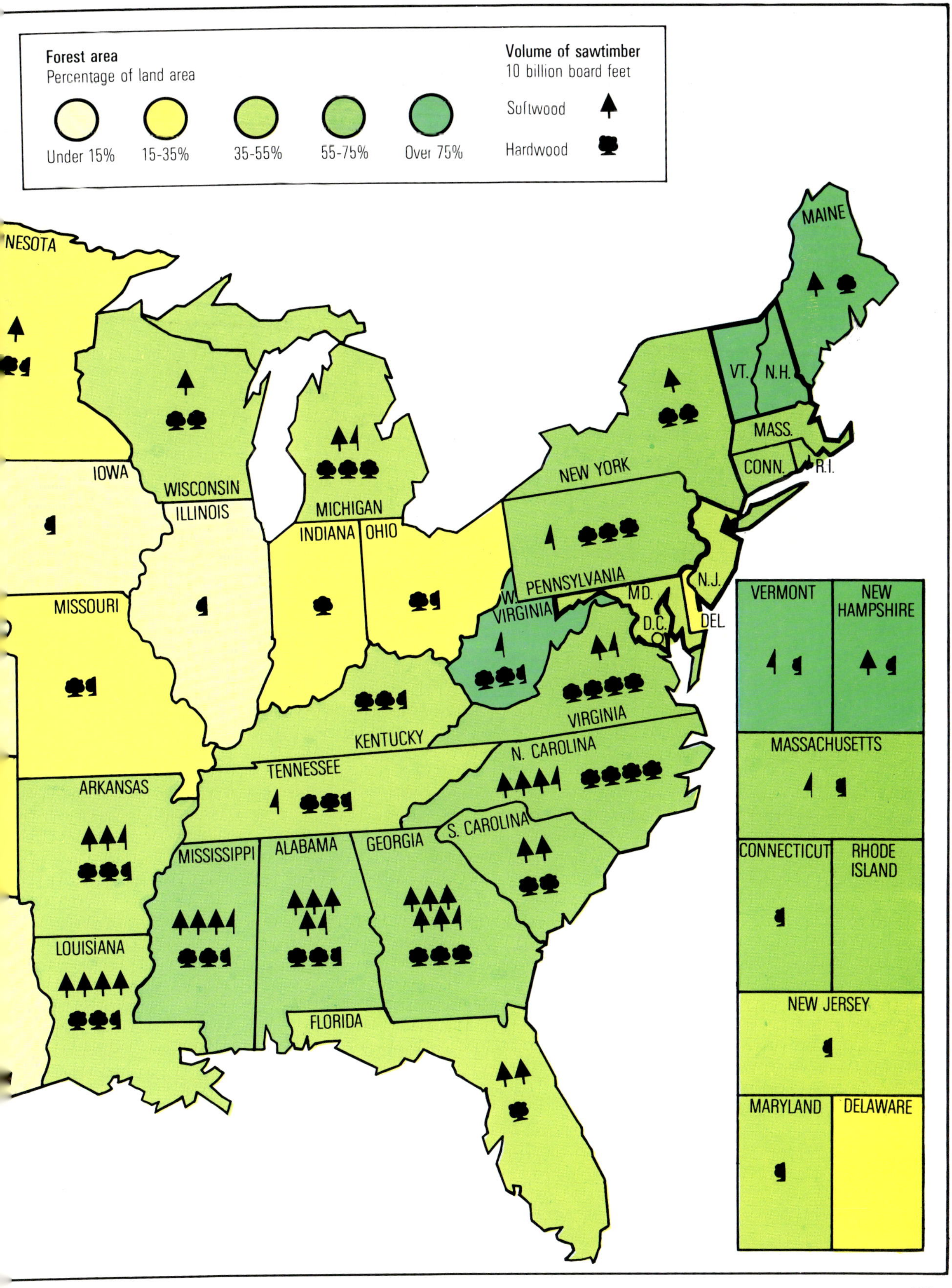

Forest area
Percentage of land area
Under 15%
15-35%
35-55%
55-75%
Over 75%
Volume of sawtimber
10 billion board feet
Softwood
Hardwood
NESOTA
IOWA
WISCONSIN
ILLINOIS
MICHIGAN
INDIANA
OHIO
MISSOURI
NEW YORK
PENNSYLVANIA
MAINE
VT.
N.H.
MASS.
CONN.
R.I.
N.J.
MD.
D.C.
DEL
W. VIRGINIA
VIRGINIA
KENTUCKY
TENNESSEE
N. CAROLINA
S. CAROLINA
ARKANSAS
MISSISSIPPI
ALABAMA
GEORGIA
LOUISIANA
FLORIDA
VERMONT
NEW HAMPSHIRE
MASSACHUSETTS
CONNECTICUT
RHODE ISLAND
NEW JERSEY
MARYLAND
DELAWARE

FORESTRY

TABLE A

TOP TEN: STATES WITH GREATEST PROPORTION OF FORESTLAND

1	Maine
2	New Hampshire
3	Vermont
4	West Virginia
5	Georgia
6	Alabama
7	Virginia
8	North Carolina
9	South Carolina
10	Rhode Island

TOP TEN: STATES WITH GREATEST VOLUME OF SAWTIMBER

1	Oregon
2	Washington
3	California
4	Alaska
5	Idaho
6	Montana
7	Georgia
8	North Carolina
9	Alabama
10	Louisiana

Approximately one-third of the total land area of the United States is forested. This is a small area compared with the unending virgin forests that confronted the first European settlers, but it is still substantial.

Of the total forested land, about 65 percent is classed as commercial timberland, and this area contains, according to the estimate of the U.S. Forest Service, approximately 2.6 trillion board feet of sawtimber, which is enough to rehouse the entire population.

Nevertheless, it is barely sufficient to meet the total current demands for timber and timber products. The balance between annual estimated growth and annual volume cut is a delicate one, and, although there has been a small growth in supply since about 1975, consumption has consistently exceeded production, and imports of timber and timber products such as newsprint have risen.

The map illustrates the highly regional nature of the timber industry. Production of softwood, which represents about 80 percent of total timber production, is concentrated in the states of the Pacific Northwest. Four states (Alaska, California, Oregon, and Washington) contain 56 percent of all commercially available softwood, and if Idaho and Montana are included the contribution of the Northwest rises to 67 percent.

In Oregon, which contains the largest body of standing timber in the United States, lumbering is the state's largest industry, and timber products make up more than half the total value of manufactures.

The plains of the Midwest have relatively few trees, but Texas has about 23 million acres of forest, about half of which grows commercial timber.

The main timber-producing region after the Northwest is the South. Here hardwood, insignificant in the Northwest, forms a high proportion of total timber resources. Just over half the national stock of hardwood grows in the southern states.

It is in the East that the virgin forest has been most severely depleted. The demands of agriculture, housing, industry and transport have reduced the forests by an estimated 75 percent. Nevertheless, considerable forestland remains, especially in the northeastern corner. Table A shows that this is still the most heavily forested region of the country, with Maine heading the list.

Diagram A reveals the enormous potential, in terms of volume of sawtimber, in the quick-growing forests of Oregon compared with those of Maine. Of course, a direct comparison is almost meaningless, as the nature of the industry is entirely different in those two states. For example, Maine's timber resources include a high proportion of hardwood.

Diagram B shows the main types of commercial timber currently grown. Douglas fir and southern yellow pine together provide a high percentage of the standing sawtimber in the United States. The Douglas fir is predominant in Washington and Oregon, where it grows to a height of 200 feet, with a trunk diameter of up to six feet. Symmetrical saplings are often sold as Christmas trees.

Southern yellow pine, as the name suggests, is cut primarily in the South, especially in Alabama, Georgia, Louisiana, and Mississippi. Ponderosa pine is second only to Douglas fir in the Northwest. Eastern white pine, which was the chief lumber-producing tree in the nineteenth century, is now of far less significance.

The United States contains nearly 100 species of oak, but only about one-quarter of these are of commercial significance. Together, they form by far the largest source of hardwood.

Sources: U.S. Forest Service; U.S. Bureau of the Census

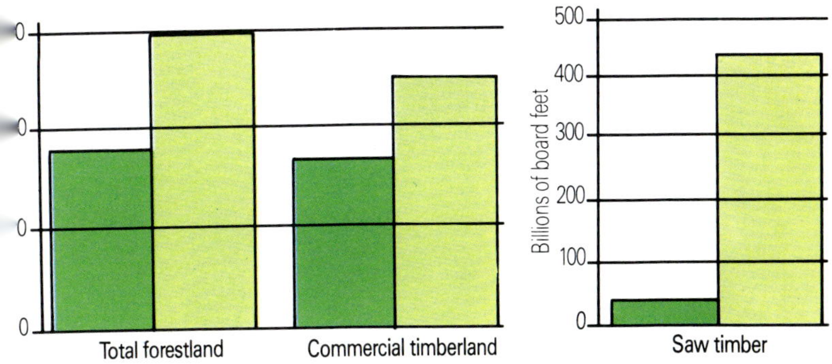

Diagram A: Comparison of total forestland and volume of sawtimber in Maine and Oregon

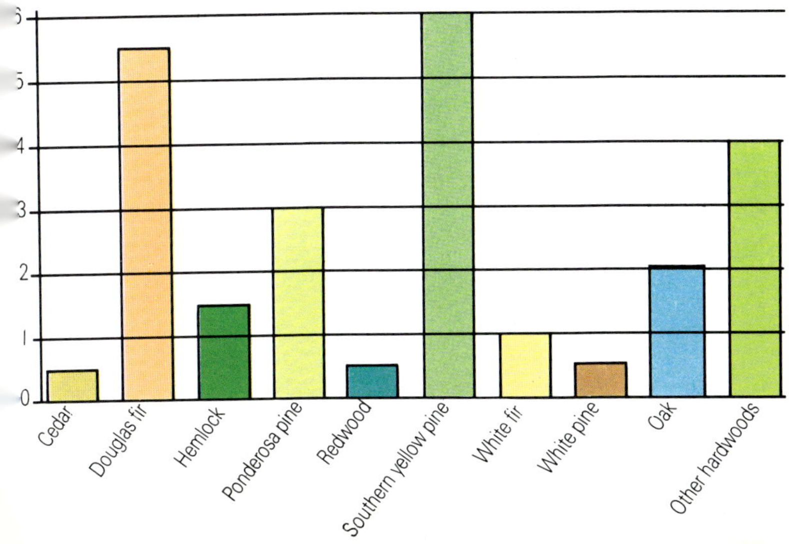

Diagram B: Lumber production by type of wood, 1981

MINERAL RESOURCES

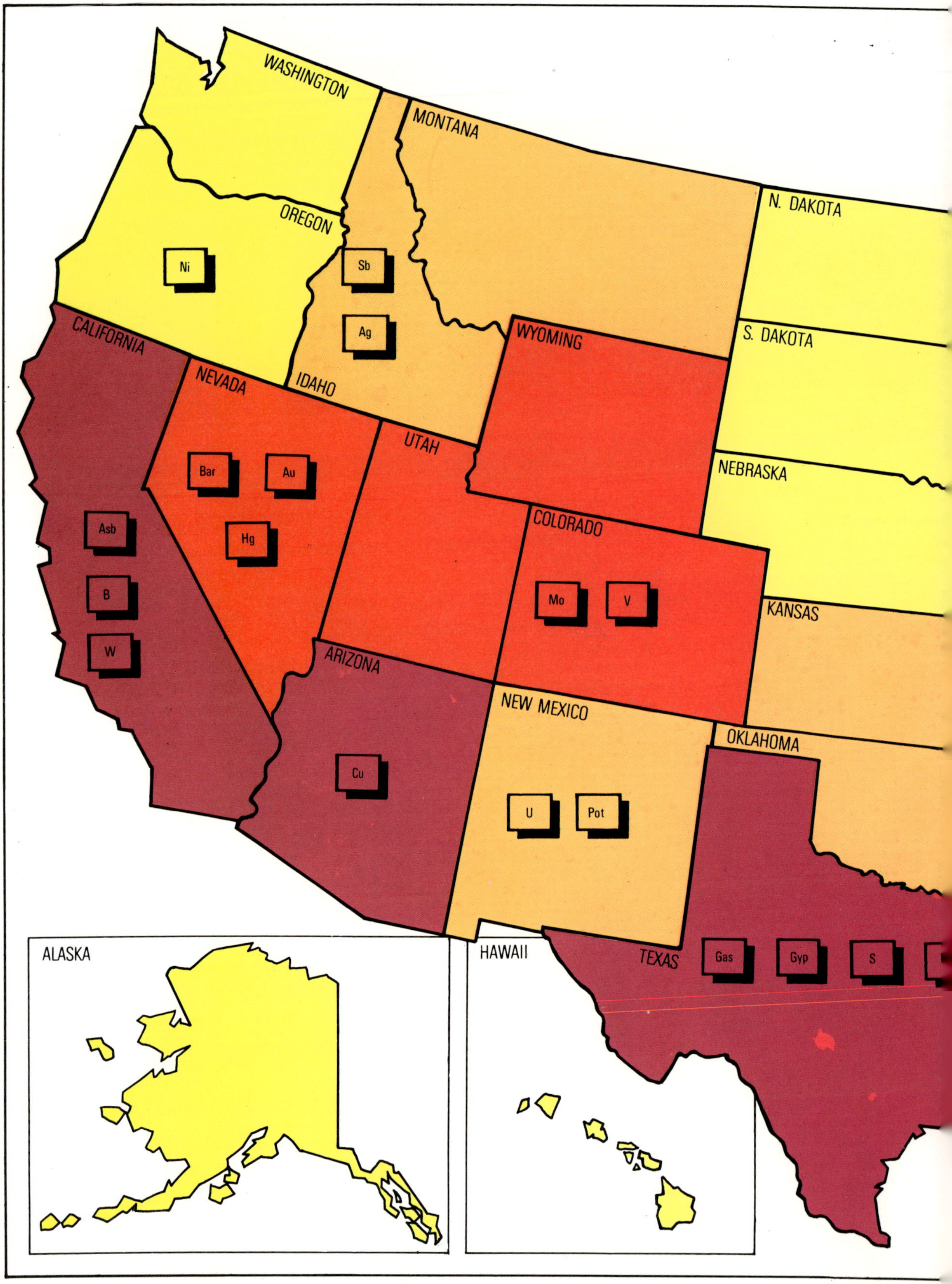

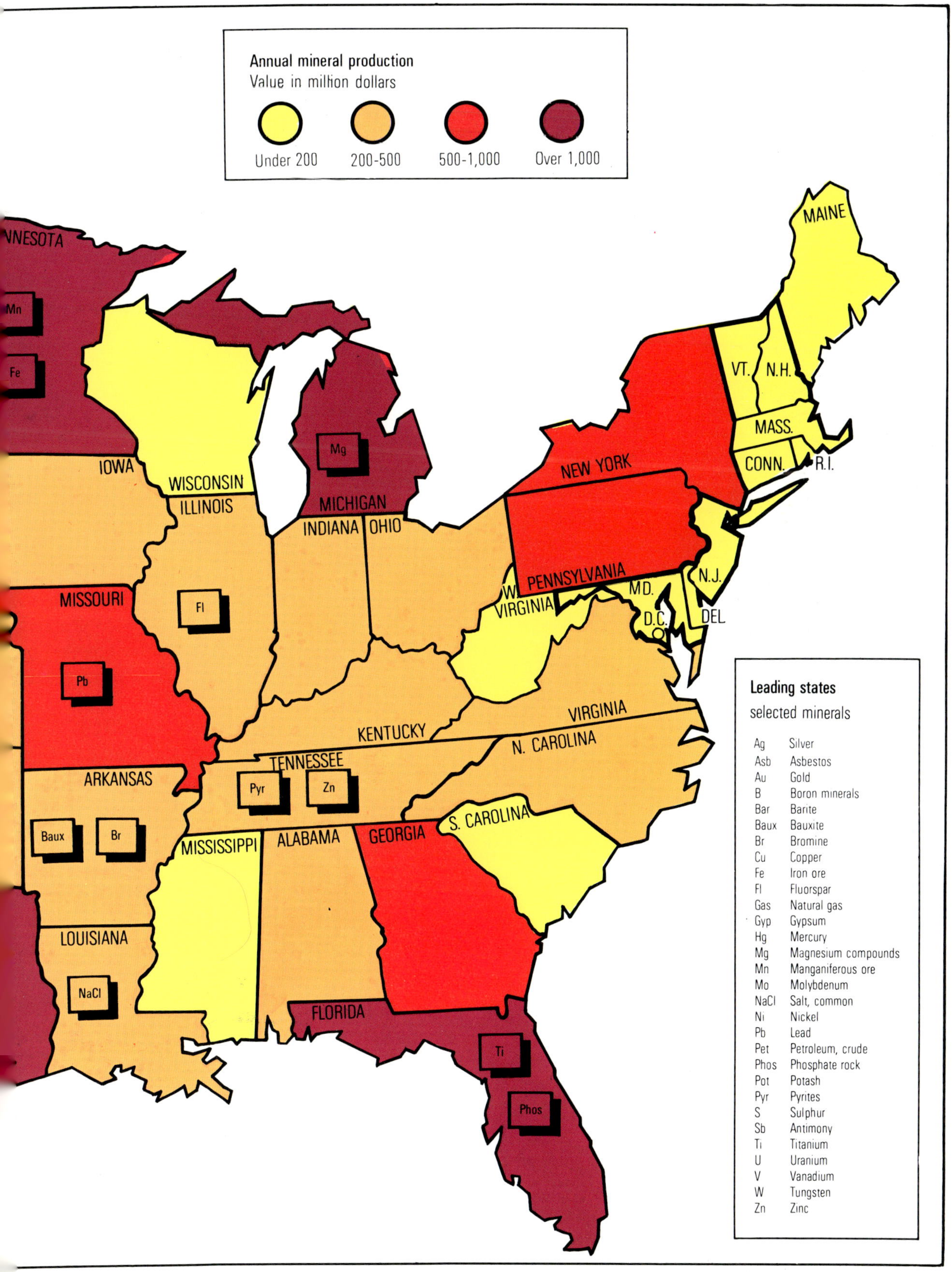
Annual mineral production
Value in million dollars
Under 200
200-500
500-1,000
Over 1,000
NNESOTA
Mn
Fe
WISCONSIN
MICHIGAN
Mg
IOWA
ILLINOIS
Fl
INDIANA
OHIO
MISSOURI
Pb
KENTUCKY
TENNESSEE
Pyr
Zn
ARKANSAS
Baux
Br
MISSISSIPPI
ALABAMA
GEORGIA
S. CAROLINA
N. CAROLINA
VIRGINIA
W. VIRGINIA
PENNSYLVANIA
NEW YORK
MD.
D.C.
DEL
N.J.
CONN.
R.I.
MASS.
VT.
N.H.
MAINE
LOUISIANA
NaCl
FLORIDA
Ti
Phos
Leading states
selected minerals
Ag Silver
Asb Asbestos
Au Gold
B Boron minerals
Bar Barite
Baux Bauxite
Br Bromine
Cu Copper
Fe Iron ore
Fl Fluorspar
Gas Natural gas
Gyp Gypsum
Hg Mercury
Mg Magnesium compounds
Mn Manganiferous ore
Mo Molybdenum
NaCl Salt, common
Ni Nickel
Pb Lead
Pet Petroleum, crude
Phos Phosphate rock
Pot Potash
Pyr Pyrites
S Sulphur
Sb Antimony
Ti Titanium
U Uranium
V Vanadium
W Tungsten
Zn Zinc

MINERAL RESOURCES

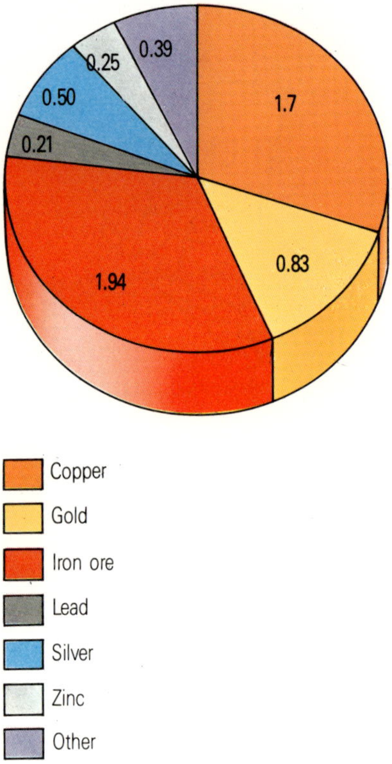

Diagram A: Value of U.S. production of metallic minerals (recoverable content of ore), 1983 in billions of dollars

The United States was richly endowed by nature with mineral resources, but high rates of production and the efforts of two world wars made severe inroads into that inheritance. After World War II, the United States became an importer of many metallic minerals that it had formerly exported.

Supplies of nearly 90 percent of the most essential minerals in use in the 1980s depended in part on imports. Some minerals, such as manganese ore and chromite (both vital in the steel industry), were wholly imported. The dependence on other nations, sometimes nations of doubtful political stability, for supplies of vital raw materials has been a cause of concern for the U.S. government in recent years. (The main suppliers of chromite are South Africa and the Soviet Union.)

One result of the rapid depletion of traditional mineral resources has been a concern to explore and exploit new resources. The oceans, which have already proved a fruitful provider of fossil fuels, also contain vast mineral supplies. Several U.S. enterprises have shown interest in developing techniques to recover in particular manganese nodules, which also contain copper, nickel and cobalt, from the ocean floor.

The map shows the value of total annual mineral production by state (including fossil fuels), together with the leading state producers of important minerals.

Mining altogether contributes less than 2 percent of the national income, and if oil, gas, and coal extraction are subtracted, the figure slumps to about 0.2 percent. Nevertheless, metallic minerals alone represent approximately $5.5 billion. Moreover, the fundamental, historical importance of the exploitation of natural resources in the development of industrial prosperity has given the mining industry in general a special significance as an indicator of the material wellbeing of the nation.

After fossil fuels — petroleum, natural gas, and coal — which are considered separately on the next page, the most valuable group are the nonmetallic, nonfuel minerals. These include the materials used primarily in the construction industry — stone, sand, and gravel, which are the most valuable mineral resources in a majority of the states — as well as gypsum, clays, sulphur, fluorspar, phosphate rock (for fertilizers), potassium salts, asbestos, and common salt. Most of these, especially the products of the stone and gravel quarries, are widely available. Production of others is more localized; for instance, sulphur comes from the coastal region of Louisiana and Texas. But supplies are large: U.S. production of sulphur is about 20 percent of annual world production.

Metals are the third most valuable group of mineral resources. The map displays the predominance of the West in the production of metallic minerals, while Diagram A illustrates the main components of the group on a national basis.

The main exception to western predominance is iron ore, which is the leading metallic mineral in terms of both volume and value. Historically, the main centre of iron ore production has been the Great Lakes region, but by the 1980s these supplies had been severely depleted. Although Minnesota and Michigan remain the chief producers, third and fourth places are occupied by California and Wyoming.

Mining of copper, second in importance to iron, has also declined in the Lakes region, having ceased almost completely in Michigan. The main copper producers in the early 1980s were Arizona, Montana, Nevada, New Mexico, and Utah.

Bauxite, the main ore of aluminium, is an example of a metallic ore of which production (mainly in Arkansas) has dwindled to relatively insignificant amounts within recent years. As a result, it is one of the leading imported minerals (see Diagram B).

Lead and zinc are reasonably widespread in the East, Midwest, and Rocky Mountain regions. In recent years, mines in southern Missouri have maintained national production figures, especially of lead.

Sources: U.S. Bureau of Economic Analysis; U.S. Bureau of Mines

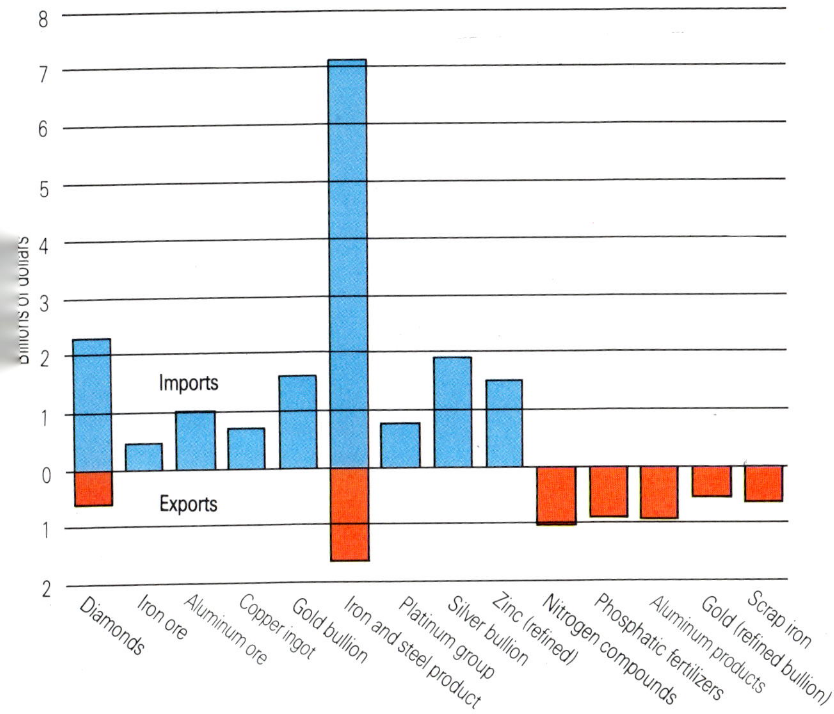

Diagram B: U.S. imports and exports of selected minerals, 1983

FOSSIL FUELS

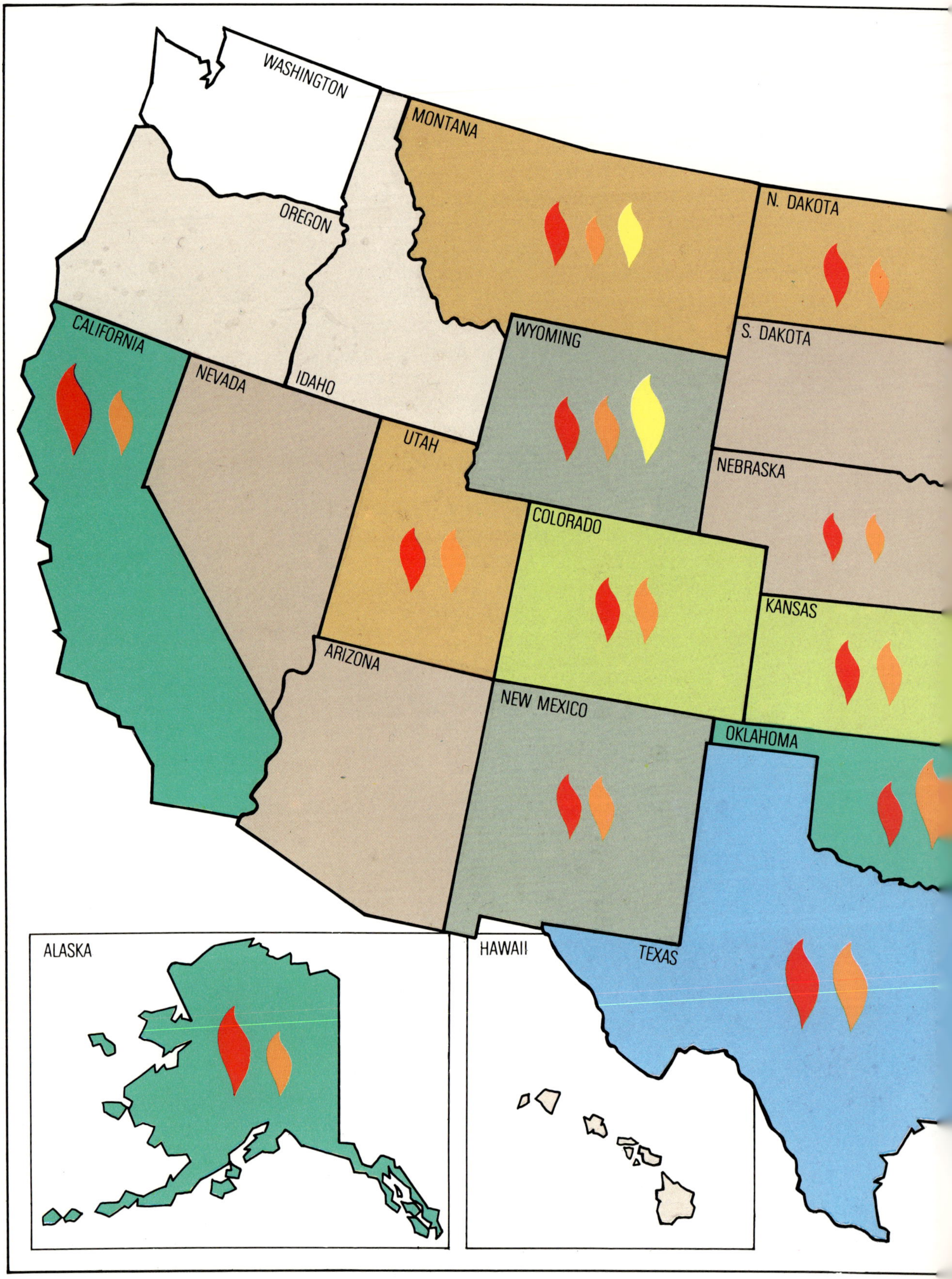

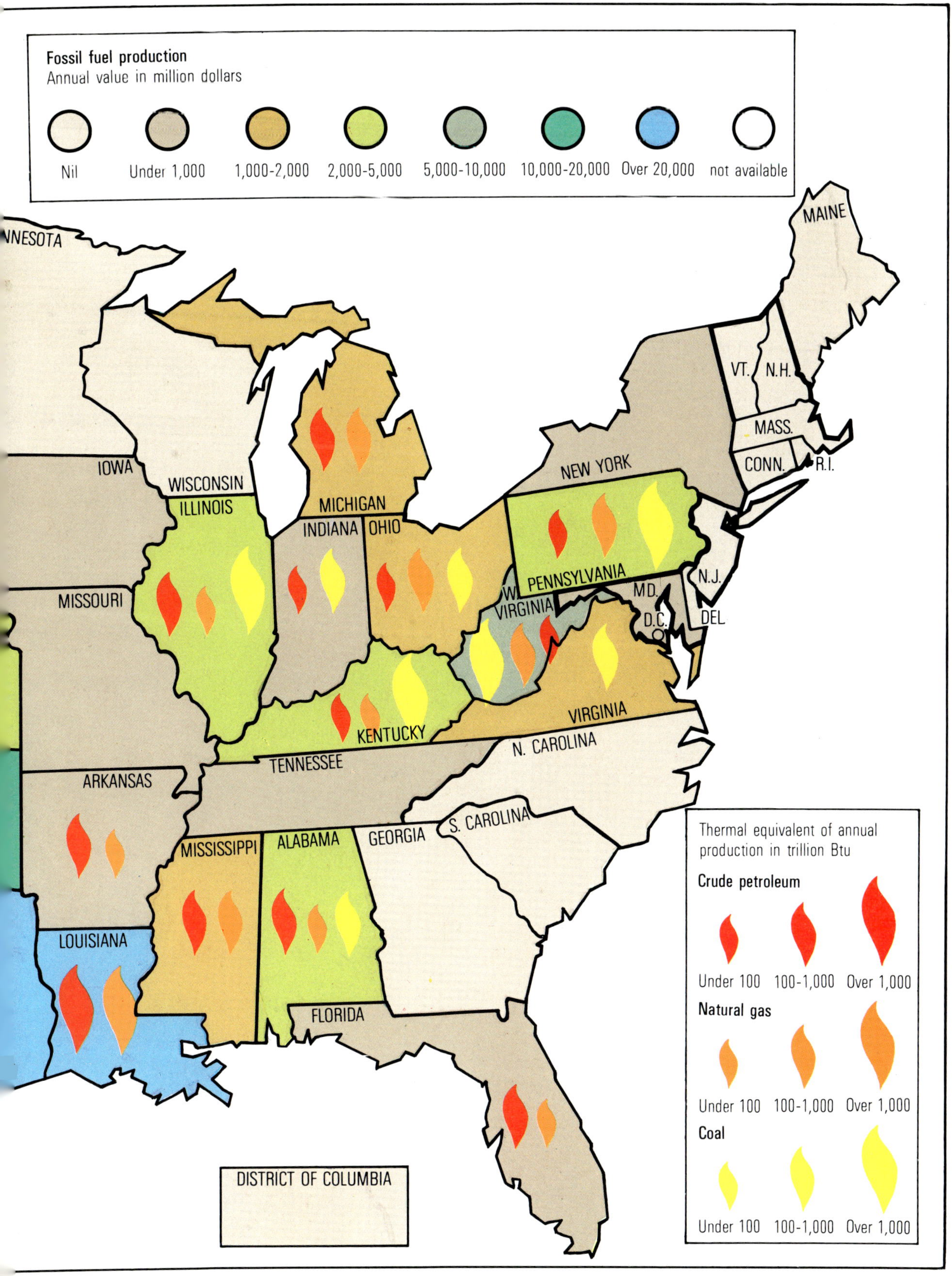
Fossil fuel production
Annual value in million dollars
Nil
Under 1,000
1,000-2,000
2,000-5,000
5,000-10,000
10,000-20,000
Over 20,000
not available
MAINE
VT.
N.H.
MASS.
CONN.
R.I.
NEW YORK
N.J.
PENNSYLVANIA
MD.
D.C.
DEL
W. VIRGINIA
VIRGINIA
N. CAROLINA
S. CAROLINA
GEORGIA
FLORIDA
ALABAMA
MISSISSIPPI
TENNESSEE
KENTUCKY
OHIO
INDIANA
MICHIGAN
ILLINOIS
WISCONSIN
IOWA
MINNESOTA
MISSOURI
ARKANSAS
LOUISIANA
DISTRICT OF COLUMBIA
Thermal equivalent of annual production in trillion Btu
Crude petroleum
Under 100
100-1,000
Over 1,000
Natural gas
Under 100
100-1,000
Over 1,000
Coal
Under 100
100-1,000
Over 1,000

FOSSIL FUELS

When the Arab nations imposed an embargo on oil exports to the United States in 1973, many people were surprised to discover that the country is not self-sufficient in fossil fuels (coal, oil, and natural gas). Moreover, as Diagram A illustrates, imports of crude petroleum increased dramatically during the 1970s.

The map shows total production of fossil fuels by states. The most productive region for oil and natural gas is the Gulf — mainly the offshore wells of Louisiana and Texas — and the inshore fields of Texas, Oklahoma, and California. Lesser amounts are produced in many other states, especially in the South and West.

The main addition to these resources in recent years has come from Alaska, where oil production began in 1959. By 1961 oil was already the state's most important mineral, with over 6 million barrels produced that year. By 1984 annual production had reached 630 million barrels, making Alaska the largest oil producer after Texas. Natural gas exceeded 260 billion cubic feet, and the combined value of the two fuels represented the majority of state revenue. Nevertheless, while the Alaska pipeline greatly improved national oil production figures, total supplies still fell far short of total consumption.

The intense public concern over diminishing supplies of fossil fuels — particularly oil — in the 1970s abated considerably during the early 1980s, when an economic recession combined with widespread energy conservation led to a decline in the import of

Diagram A: Total petroleum output compared with imports of crude oil and refined petroleum products, 1950-1983

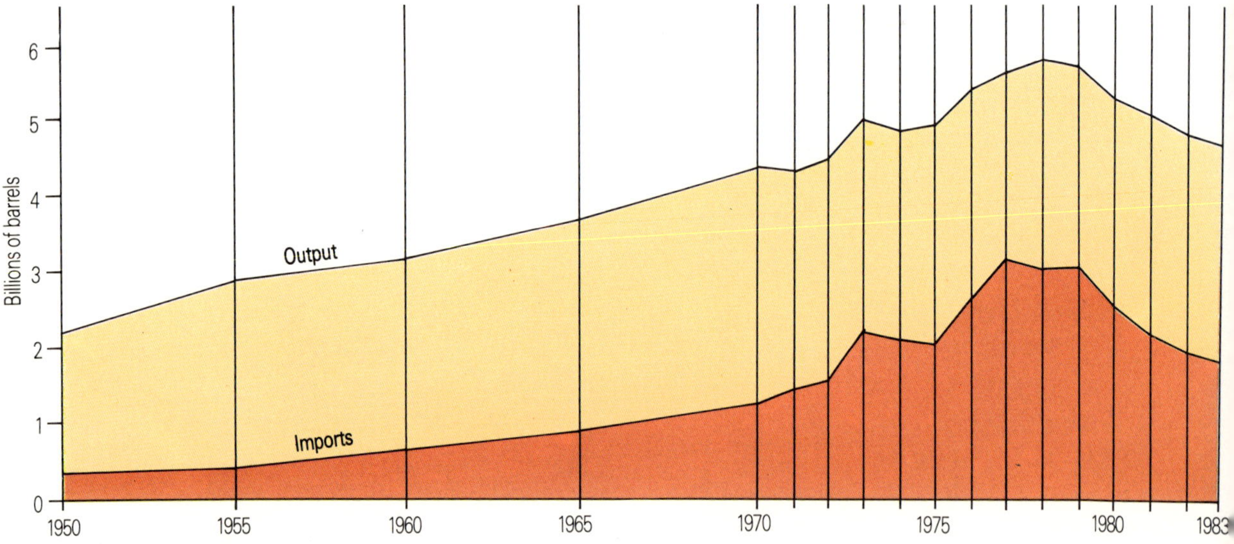

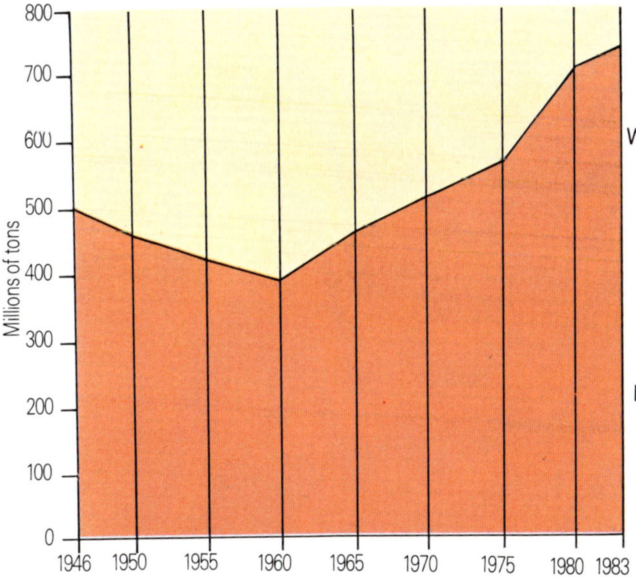

Diagram B: U.S. coal consumption, 1946-1983

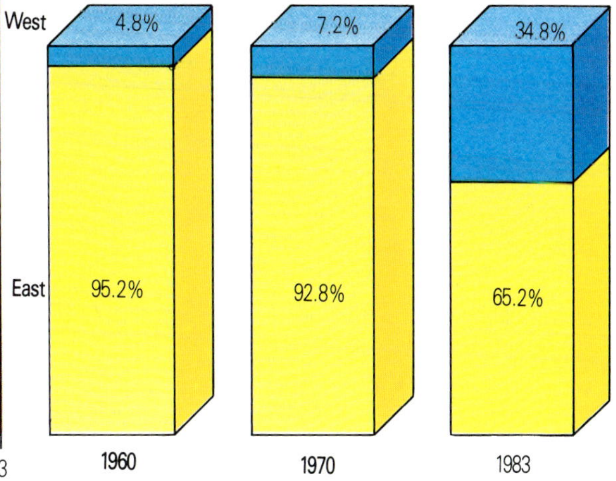

Diagram C: Regional change in coal production, 1960-1983

crude petroleum. But, with total consumption of oil and natural gas outstripping total discoveries each year, proved reserves continue to fall. They are currently equivalent to about 10 years' production.

By contrast, there is no worry about running out of coal. There is enough coal in the ground to last, at current rates of consumption, for several hundred years.

Coal consumption entered a period of decline after World War II, but experienced a revival during the 1960s, and accelerated in the following decade as a result of the oil crisis — and consequent rising oil prices (see Diagram B).

In 1960, nearly all coal mining was in the East (see Diagram C), particularly Appalachia. Eastern coal, however, is high in sulphur and thus environmentally objectionable. The rise in production of western coal, which has a low sulphur content, was also assisted in the 1970s by the rising price, which helped to compensate for high transportation costs.

The main coal-mining state in the West is Wyoming, where production — negligible before the 1970s — rose to nearly 15 percent of the national total by 1980. Wyoming is also a major producer of crude petroleum and natural gas. Its total output of fossil fuels reached $6.0 billion in 1984.

Sources: U.S. Bureau of Mines;
U.S. Energy Information Administration

Note: Various energy sources are converted from original units (e.g., short tons, cubic feet, barrels, kilowatt-hours) to the thermal equivalent using British thermal units (Btu). A Btu is the amount of energy required to raise the temperature of 1 pound of water 1 degree Fahrenheit at or near 39.2 degrees F.

ENERGY

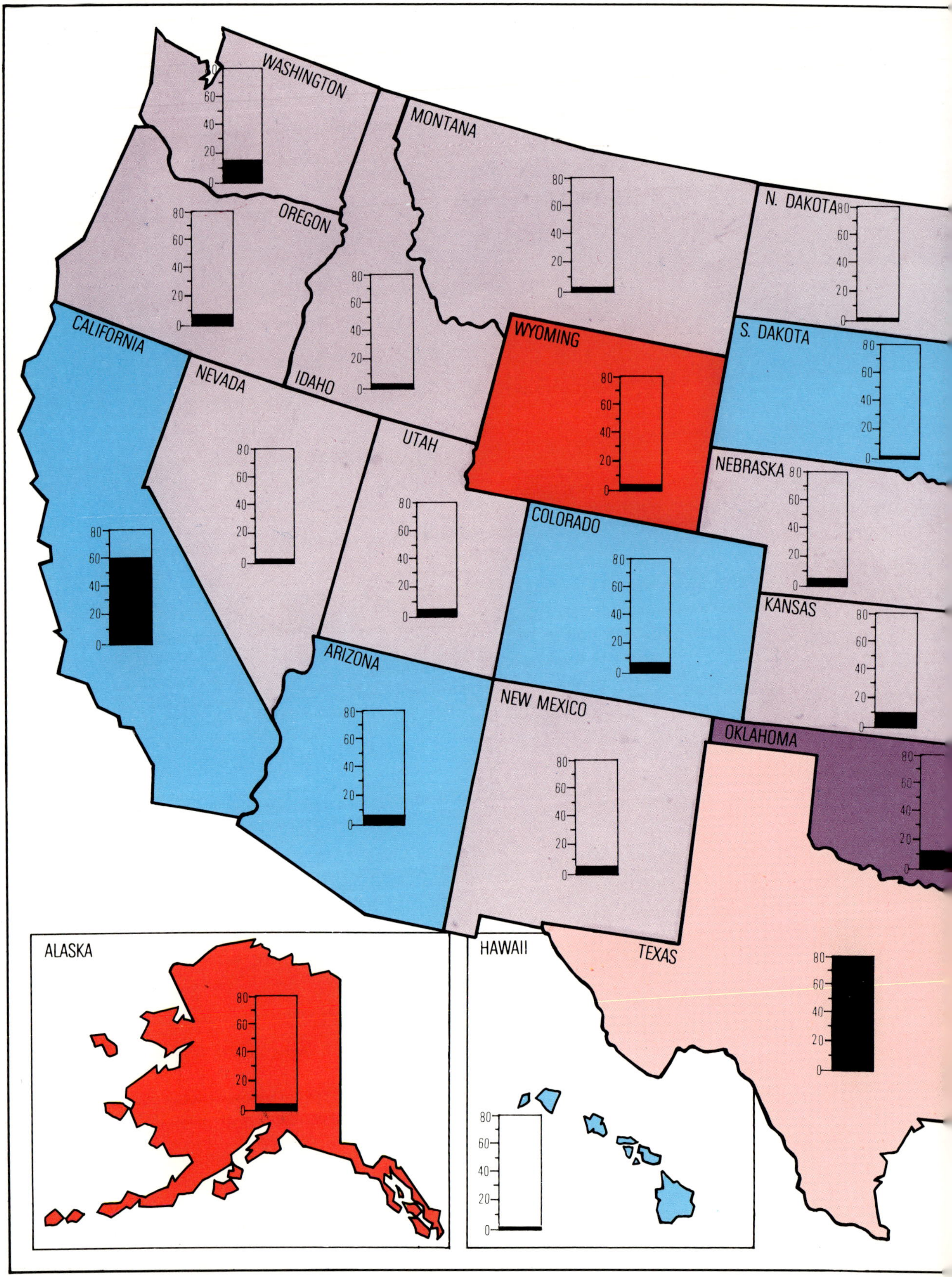

WASHINGTON
OREGON
MONTANA
N. DAKOTA
IDAHO
WYOMING
S. DAKOTA
CALIFORNIA
NEVADA
UTAH
NEBRASKA
COLORADO
KANSAS
ARIZONA
NEW MEXICO
OKLAHOMA
TEXAS
ALASKA
HAWAII
0
20
40
60
80

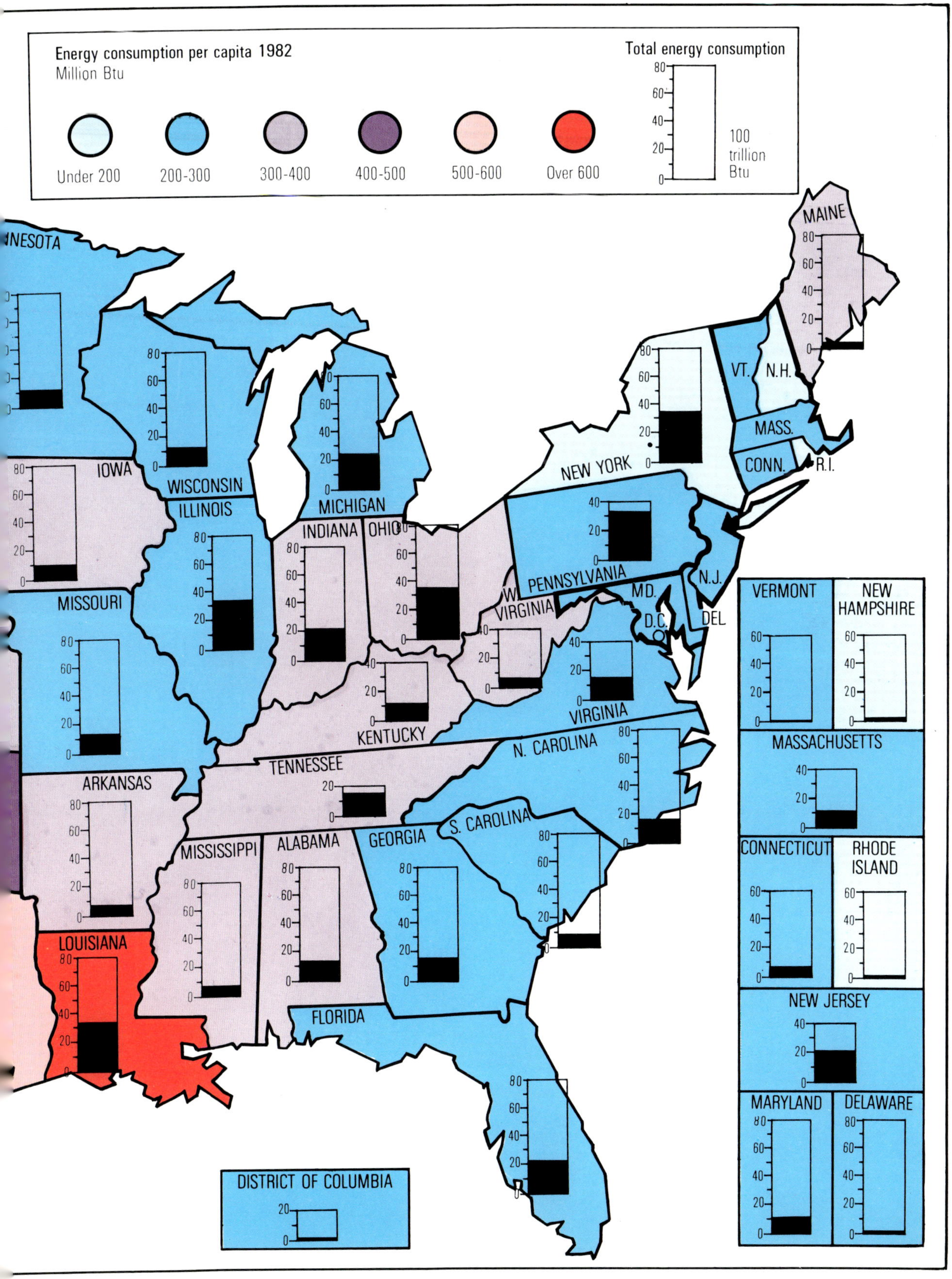
Energy consumption per capita 1982
Million Btu
Under 200
200-300
300-400
400-500
500-600
Over 600
Total energy consumption
100 trillion Btu
MAINE
VT.
N.H.
MASS.
CONN.
R.I.
NEW YORK
PENNSYLVANIA
N.J.
MD.
D.C.
DEL
W. VIRGINIA
VIRGINIA
N. CAROLINA
S. CAROLINA
GEORGIA
FLORIDA
ALABAMA
MISSISSIPPI
TENNESSEE
KENTUCKY
OHIO
INDIANA
MICHIGAN
ILLINOIS
WISCONSIN
IOWA
MISSOURI
ARKANSAS
LOUISIANA
VERMONT
NEW HAMPSHIRE
MASSACHUSETTS
CONNECTICUT
RHODE ISLAND
NEW JERSEY
MARYLAND
DELAWARE
DISTRICT OF COLUMBIA

ENERGY

The subject of energy consumption might not have featured in an atlas of the United States twenty years ago, but since the oil crisis of the 1970s it has become a subject of major importance.

The map illustrates the consumption of energy by state, in two aspects: (1) consumption per capita, and (2) total energy consumption. The figures are given in Btu (British thermal units). This is a useful overall indication of energy consumption, which avoids the difficulty of comparison between (for example) a barrel of petroleum, a ton of coal, and a cubic foot of gas. One Btu is the amount of energy required to raise the temperature of one pound of water by one degree Fahrenheit at its maximum density. Sample conversions are as follows:

1 barrel of petroleum	=	5.41 million Btu
1 cubic foot of natural gas	=	1.03 thousand Btu
1 short ton of coal	=	21.55 million Btu

There is in general no significant relationship between total energy consumption and consumption per capita; the crucial sector is not the domestic but the industrial sector. Nationwide, the industrial sector accounts for more than one-third of total consumption, which can be broken down as follows:

Industrial	37 percent
Transportation	27 percent
Residential	21 percent
Commercial	15 percent

Diagram A: Major sources of energy consumption

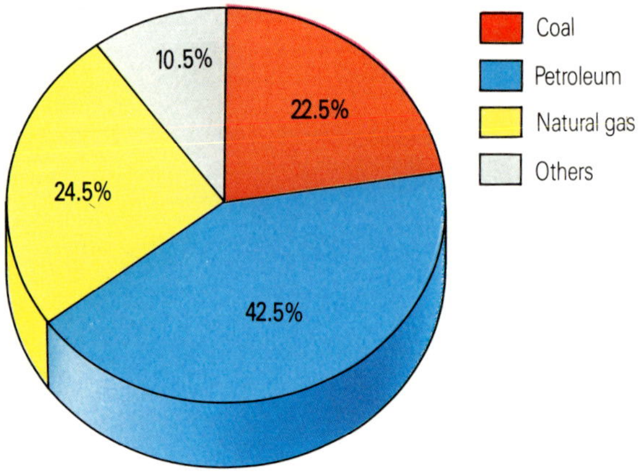

In a highly industrialized state such as Ohio, industrial consumption is over 42 percent of the total, whereas in Arizona, industry accounts for less than 27 percent of total energy consumption.

The predominance of petroleum as a source of energy is shown in Diagram A. Natural gas and coal are the other main sources. The smallest slice of the pie, "Others," includes hydropower, nuclear power, and geothermal power, as well as such statistically insignificant contributors as windmills.

Considerable changes have taken place in the composition of energy supply since World War II. Between 1950 and 1960, the contribution of coal declined from 38 percent of the national total to 22 percent. It continued to decline, though at a slower rate, until the oil crisis of the early 1970s. By 1983 coal consumption had regained the level of 1960. Petroleum and natural gas production increased during the same period, although since the 1950s the United States has become steadily more dependent on oil imports.

The energy crisis of the 1970s is shown in the movement of fossil fuel prices in Diagram B. The figures represent prices in real terms (based on 1972 values). During the decade 1960-1970, prices were more or less steady (discounting inflation), and the sharp increase between 1970 and 1975 reflects the rocketing international price of oil. That affected other fuels, and indeed prices generally. The trend continued until halted in 1980-1981 by a combination of reduced demand and increased supplies.

Source: U.S. Energy Information Administration

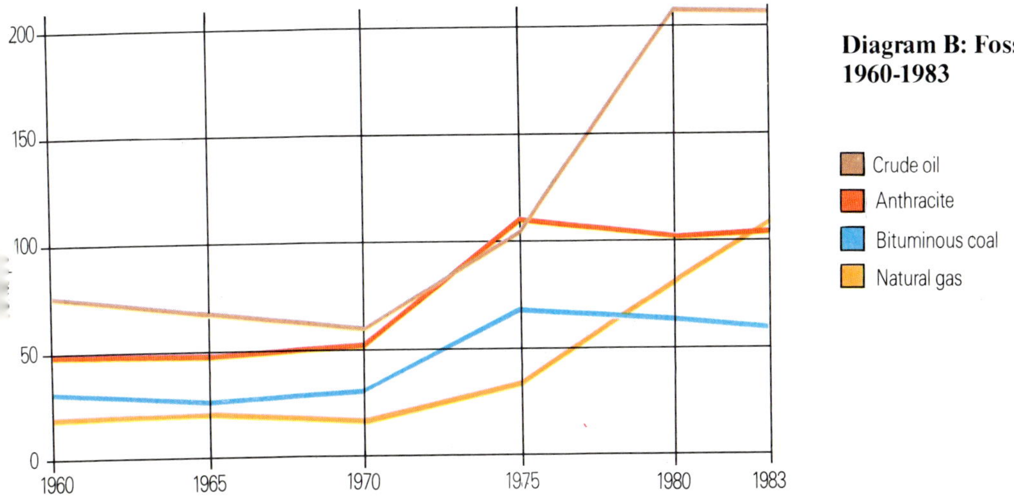

Diagram B: Fossil fuel prices, 1960-1983

MANUFACTURING

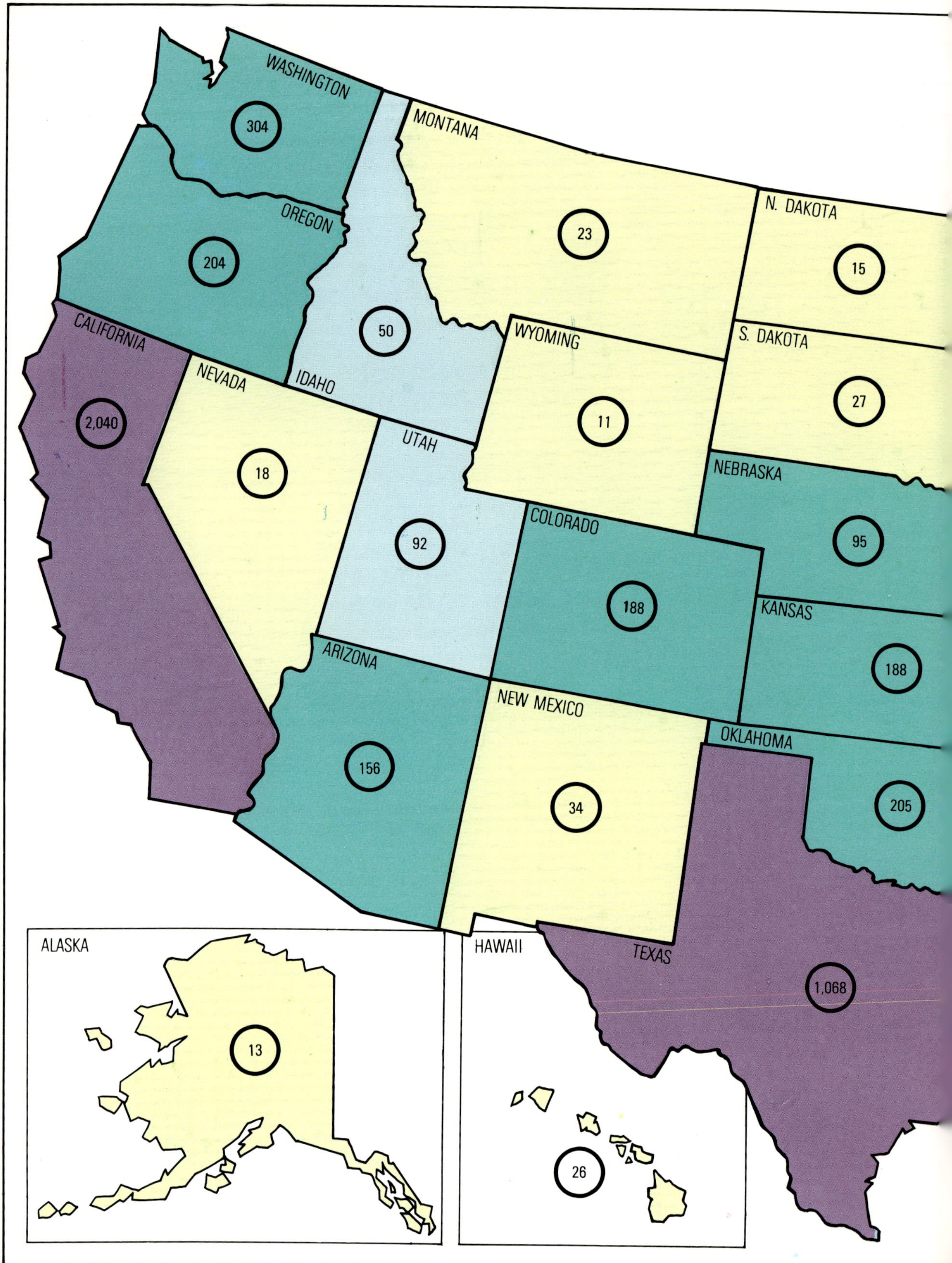

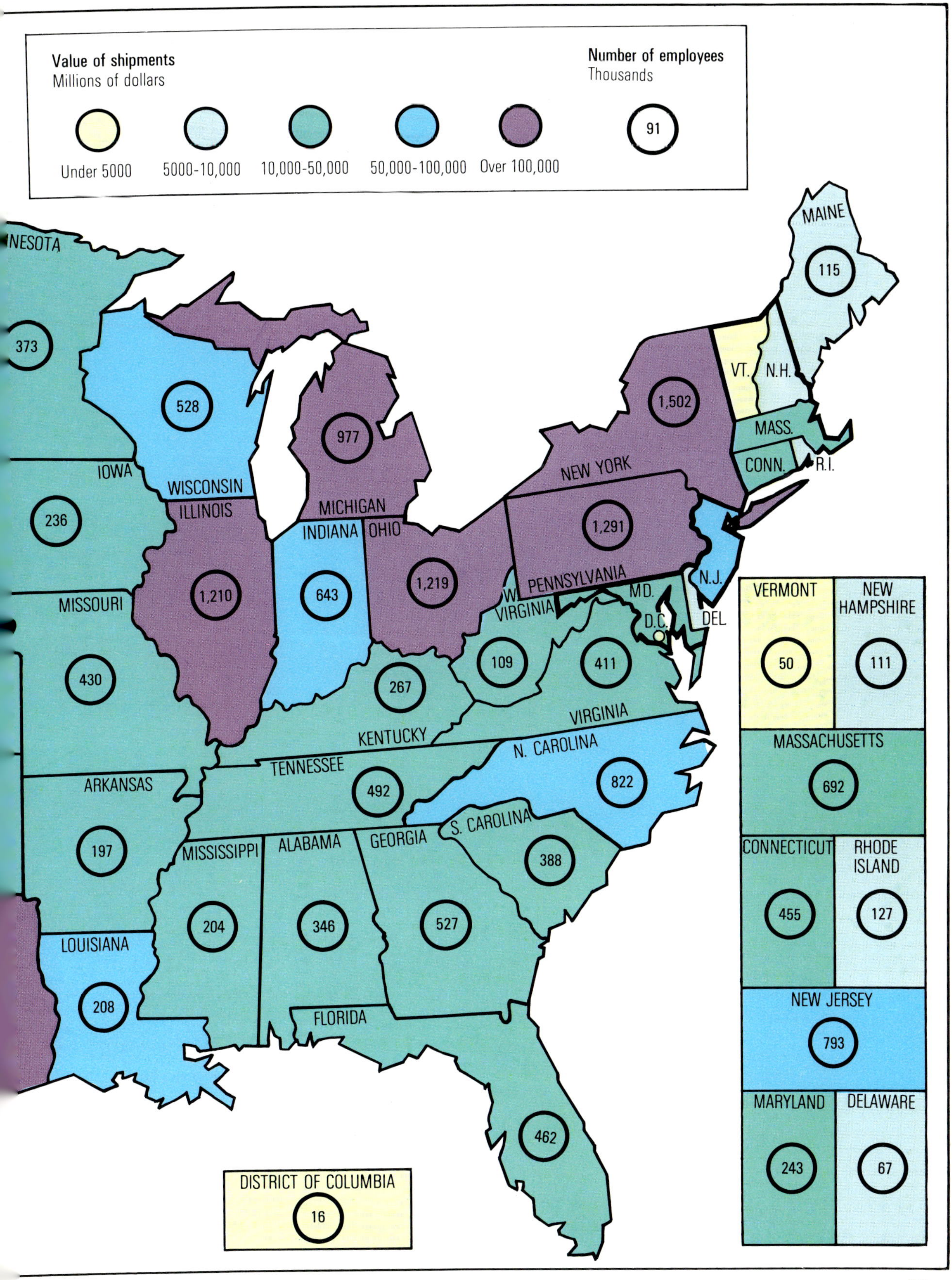
Value of shipments
Millions of dollars
Under 5000
5000-10,000
10,000-50,000
50,000-100,000
Over 100,000
Number of employees
Thousands
91
MAINE
115
VT.
N.H.
MASS.
CONN.
R.I.
NEW YORK
1,502
PENNSYLVANIA
1,291
N.J.
MD.
D.C.
DEL
NESOTA
373
WISCONSIN
528
MICHIGAN
977
IOWA
236
ILLINOIS
1,210
INDIANA
643
OHIO
1,219
MISSOURI
430
W. VIRGINIA
109
VIRGINIA
411
KENTUCKY
267
N. CAROLINA
822
TENNESSEE
492
ARKANSAS
197
MISSISSIPPI
204
ALABAMA
346
GEORGIA
527
S. CAROLINA
388
LOUISIANA
208
FLORIDA
462
DISTRICT OF COLUMBIA
16
VERMONT
50
NEW HAMPSHIRE
111
MASSACHUSETTS
692
CONNECTICUT
455
RHODE ISLAND
127
NEW JERSEY
793
MARYLAND
243
DELAWARE
67

MANUFACTURING

The United States ranks first in the world as a manufacturing nation in terms of both total value and output per capita. It achieved this enviable position through a combination of advantageous circumstances, chief of which was the rich abundance of raw materials. A large, flexible, and intelligent labour supply, the early development of mass-production methods and transportation networks, a substantial and prosperous domestic market — these have all contributed, along with such immeasurable factors as the individual pursuit of profit and traditional American enterprise.

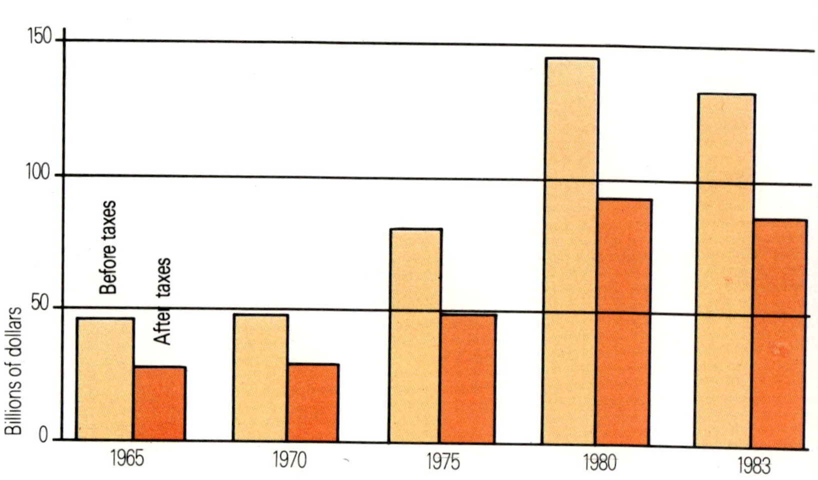

Diagram A: Net profits of U.S. manufacturing corporations, 1965-1983

TOP TEN: MANUFACTURING STATES IN TERMS OF VALUE, 1981
(Figures in parentheses show how they stood in 1967)

1	(2)	California
2	(8)	Texas
3	(4)	Illinois
4	(3)	Ohio
5	(1)	New York
6	(5)	Pennsylvania
7	(6)	Michigan
8	(7)	New Jersey
9	(9)	Indiana
10	(11)	North Carolina

Manufacturing has become the single largest sector of the economy, providing over one-third of all wages and salaries. The proportion of the national income derived from manufactures is 22 percent (about $580 billion), and although the percentage has declined during recent years (in 1963 it was 29 percent), manufacturing remains perhaps the single most vital indicator of the national economic performance.

The map illustrates the value of manufacturing output by state and the number of people employed in manufacturing industries in 1981. Measurement by shipment is the most reliable overall indicator of value, for although it includes some duplication as a result of shipments between two establishments within the same general industry, that has little effect on the relative performance of each state. The number of employees given includes administrative, clerical, and other staff, as well as production workers.

Recent trends in the manufacturing industry are obvious. The same map compiled thirty years ago would look rather different, with the Northeast more dominant by comparison with both West and South. Even now it may surprise some of us to find California so far ahead in terms of manufacturing employees. California is also the leader in total value of shipments.

Diagram A indicates the profitability of manufacturing business. This has shown an upward progression ever since the Depression of the 1930s with no serious interruption. Even the recession of the late 1970s made a comparatively minor impact (though its effect was greater than the figures suggest, taking inflation into account), and the upward trend was resumed by 1983.

The percentage of net profits paid in taxation registered a small but steady decline, from about 40 percent in 1965 to about 35 percent in 1983.

The varying contributions of the main sectors of the manufacturing industry are shown in Diagram B. The figures here are for "value added," which is, broadly, the value of the finished product less the value of raw materials. The largest item is "food," which includes everything from chocolate bars to diet cola. In general, this table should be interpreted flexibly, as it is difficult to group tens of thousands of different forms of manufacturers in ten categories. The extra category, "Others," includes tobacco products, rubber and many plastic products, leather goods, glass, pottery, and numerous miscellaneous items (the *Census of Manufactures* lists, for example, "guided missiles" and "costume jewellery and notions;" moreover, the latter category is considerably the larger of the two in terms of value added!).

Sources: U.S. Bureau of the Census;
U.S. Federal Trade Commission

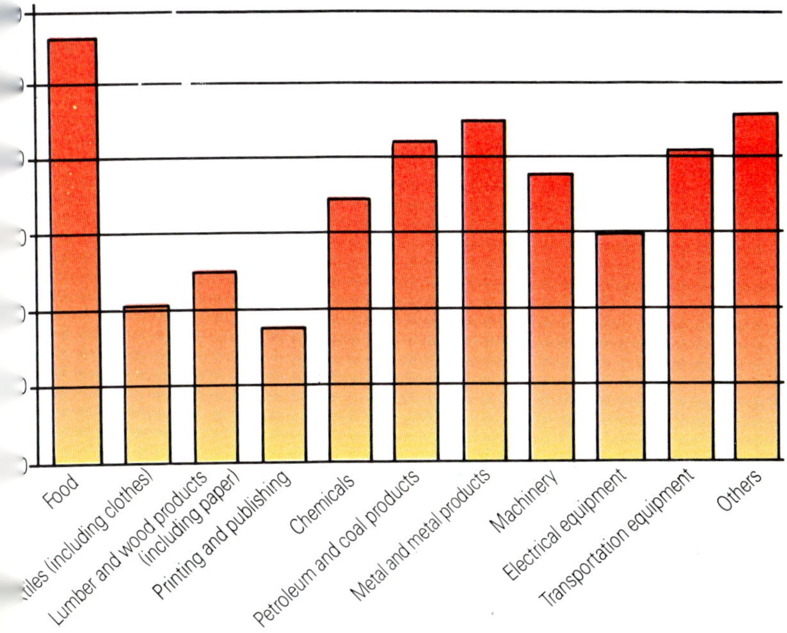

Diagram B: Value of major manufactures, 1982

EMPLOYMENT

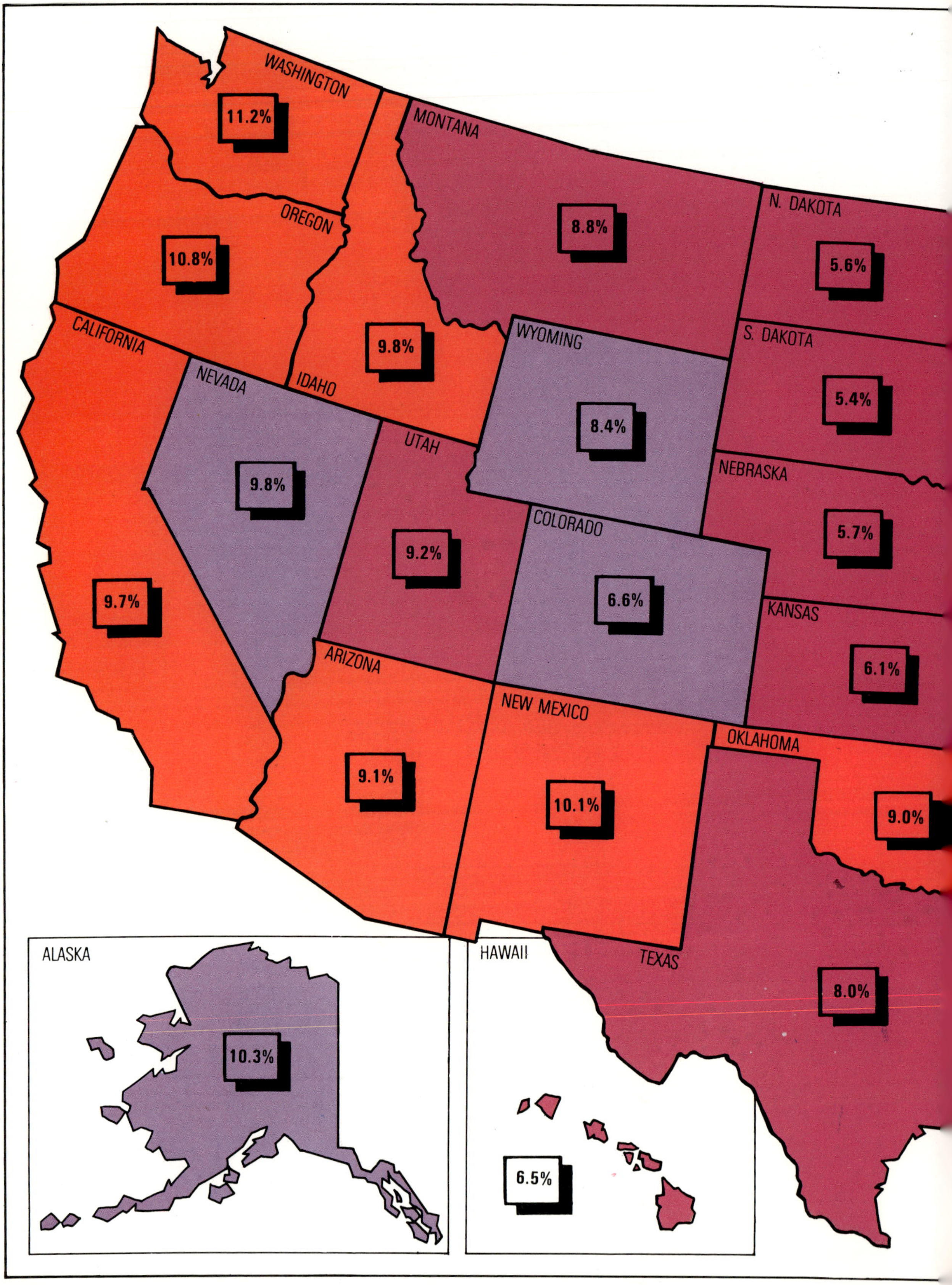

WASHINGTON
11.2%
OREGON
10.8%
CALIFORNIA
9.7%
IDAHO
9.8%
NEVADA
9.8%
MONTANA
8.8%
WYOMING
8.4%
UTAH
9.2%
COLORADO
6.6%
ARIZONA
9.1%
NEW MEXICO
10.1%
N. DAKOTA
5.6%
S. DAKOTA
5.4%
NEBRASKA
5.7%
KANSAS
6.1%
OKLAHOMA
9.0%
TEXAS
8.0%
ALASKA
10.3%
HAWAII
6.5%

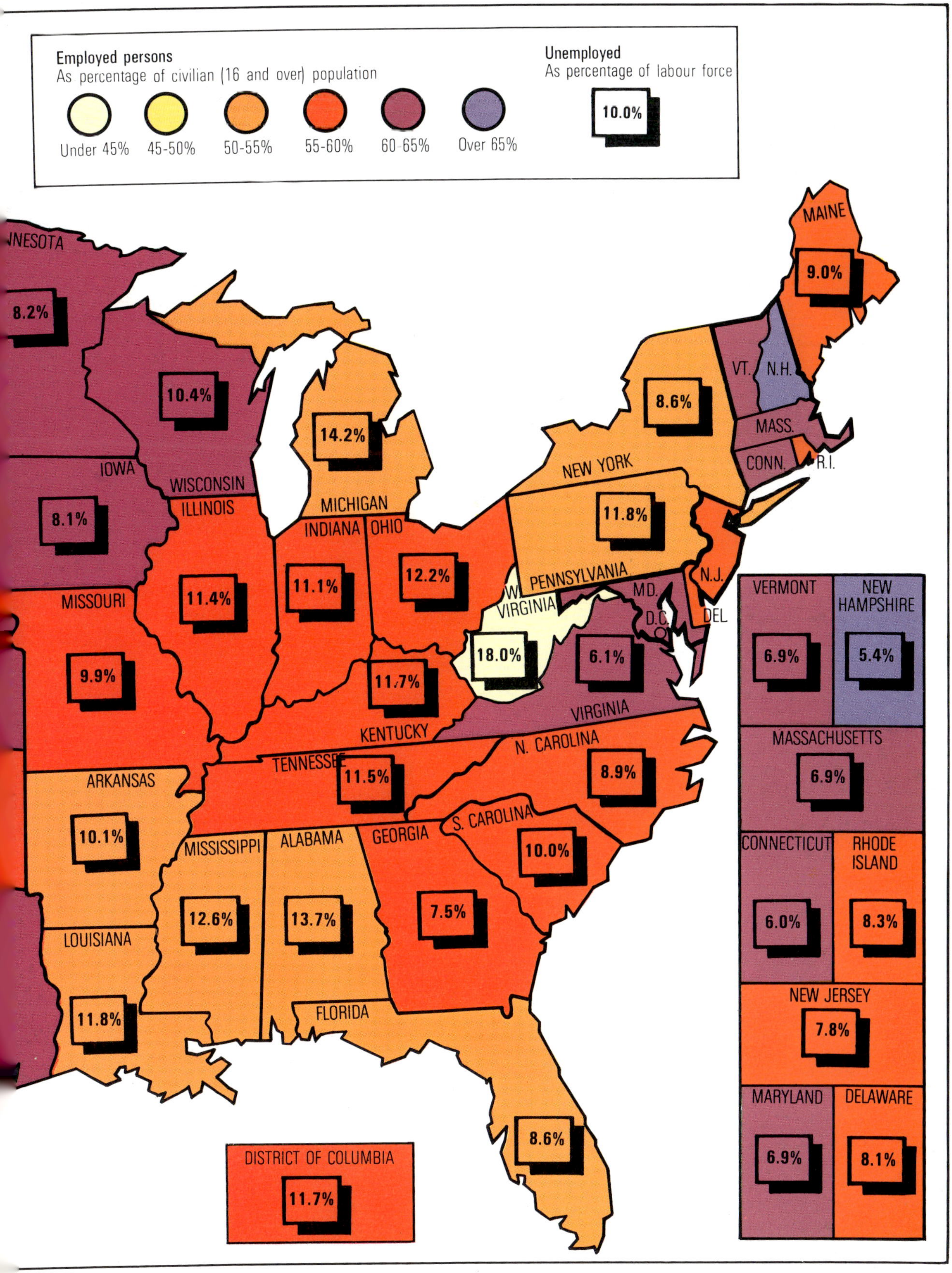

Employed persons
As percentage of civilian (16 and over) population
Under 45%
45-50%
50-55%
55-60%
60-65%
Over 65%
Unemployed
As percentage of labour force
10.0%
MINNESOTA 8.2%
WISCONSIN 10.4%
IOWA 8.1%
MICHIGAN 14.2%
ILLINOIS 11.4%
INDIANA 11.1%
OHIO 12.2%
MISSOURI 9.9%
KENTUCKY 11.7%
W. VIRGINIA 18.0%
VIRGINIA 6.1%
PENNSYLVANIA 11.8%
NEW YORK 8.6%
MAINE 9.0%
VT.
N.H.
MASS.
CONN.
R.I.
N.J.
MD.
D.C.
DEL
TENNESSEE 11.5%
N. CAROLINA 8.9%
S. CAROLINA 10.0%
ARKANSAS 10.1%
MISSISSIPPI 12.6%
ALABAMA 13.7%
GEORGIA 7.5%
LOUISIANA 11.8%
FLORIDA 8.6%
DISTRICT OF COLUMBIA 11.7%
VERMONT 6.9%
NEW HAMPSHIRE 5.4%
MASSACHUSETTS 6.9%
CONNECTICUT 6.0%
RHODE ISLAND 8.3%
NEW JERSEY 7.8%
MARYLAND 6.9%
DELAWARE 8.1%

EMPLOYMENT

The map illustrates two aspects of socioeconomic life: the percentage of civilian population aged 16 and over employed in 1983, and the average percentage of the labour force unemployed during the same year.

The Current Population Survey, from which these data are obtained, uses a monthly household survey to gather its information. People are classified as being employed, unemployed, or not in the labour force.

Several factors must be remembered in considering these data. Most important is sex, since women enter or leave the labour force with more frequency than do men, and this plays a major role in the calculation. The age structure of the population is also significant, and so are educational levels.

There is a great variation between different parts of the country. West Virginia has the lowest percentage of the population employed, 43 percent, and the lowest proportion of women who are classified as being in the labour force. It also has the highest rate of unemployment, 18 percent. As with some other southern states, this is associated with the decline in agricultural employment due to mechanization.

At the opposite end of the scale is New Hampshire, with 65 percent of the adult population employed, and only 5.4 percent of the labour force unemployed. However, the two percentages — employment and unemployment — are not always inversely related. Nevada and Alaska combine high percentages of the population employed with fairly high rates of unemployment. New York State and Florida, on the other hand, show fairly low percentages of employment and only moderate unemployment rates.

Diagram A: Proportions of the labour force in non-agricultural establishments, 1982

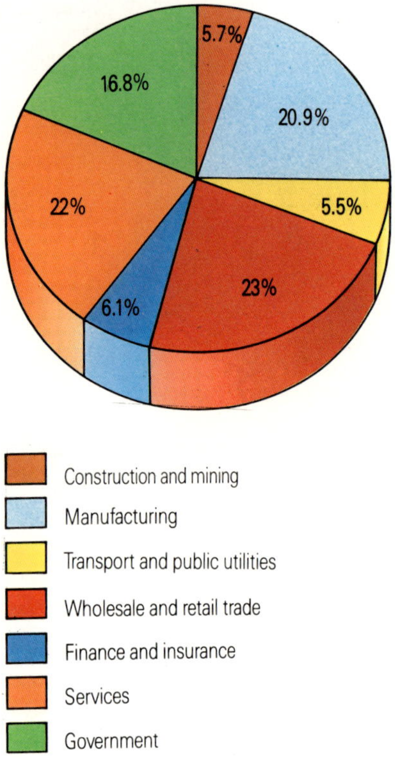

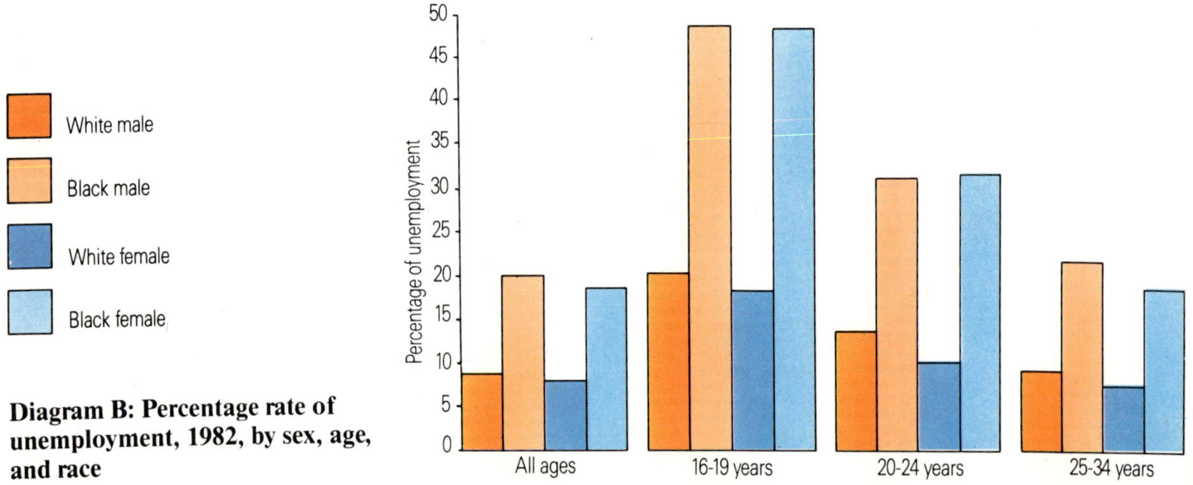

Diagram B: Percentage rate of unemployment, 1982, by sex, age, and race

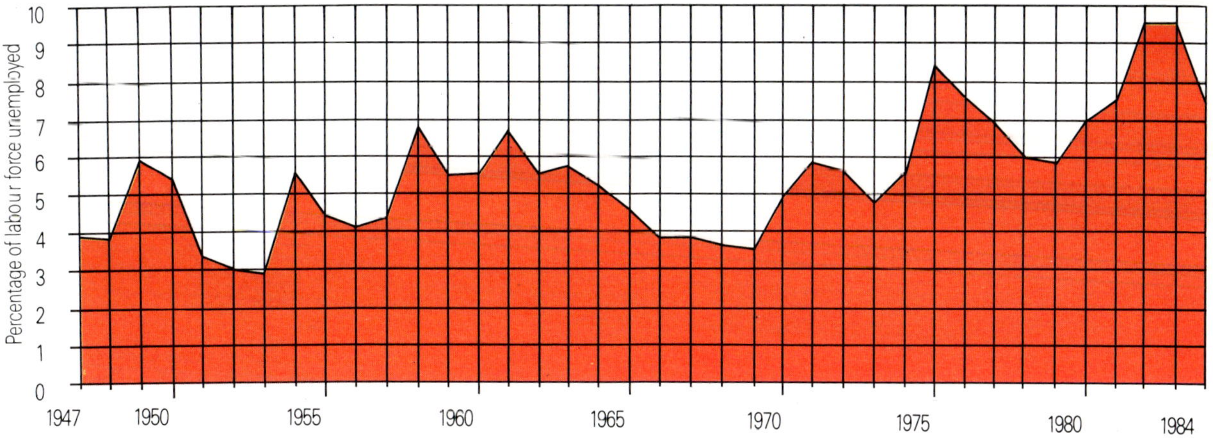

Diagram A shows the nonagricultural labour force divided into its main sectors. Wholesale and retail trade is the largest single category, just ahead of services and manufacturing. Government accounts for 17.6 percent of the total, although this proportion varies widely among the states.

Diagram B examines the rate of unemployment in relation to age, sex, and race. Its message is only too clear. The burden of unemployment falls most heavily on blacks, by a ratio of over 2 to 1. For both black and white groups, it is the youngest people who are affected most.

Diagram C traces the trend of unemployment since the end of World War II. The peak years — 1950, 1954, 1958, 1962, 1975 and 1982 — show a rising trend. It is more difficult to continue the picture back to earlier times, since methods of gathering and classifying data have changed too much to make direct comparison meaningful.

During the time period covered by Diagram C, another aspect of employment also changed considerably: the participation of women in the labour force. In 1950, only 34 percent of women aged 16 and over were included in the labour force. By 1960, this figure had risen to 38 percent, and this included over 30 percent of married women in the 20-34 age group. In 1984, these figures had risen to 53 percent of all women, and 64 percent of women aged 20-34.

Source: U.S. Bureau of labour Statistics

Diagram C: Percentage unemployment, 1947-1984

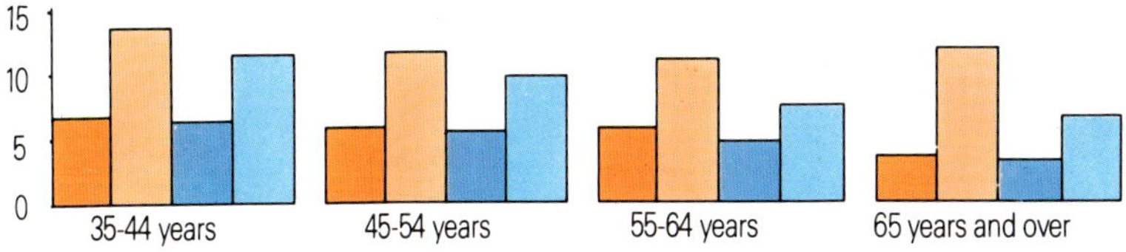

DIRECTION OF U.S. TRADE

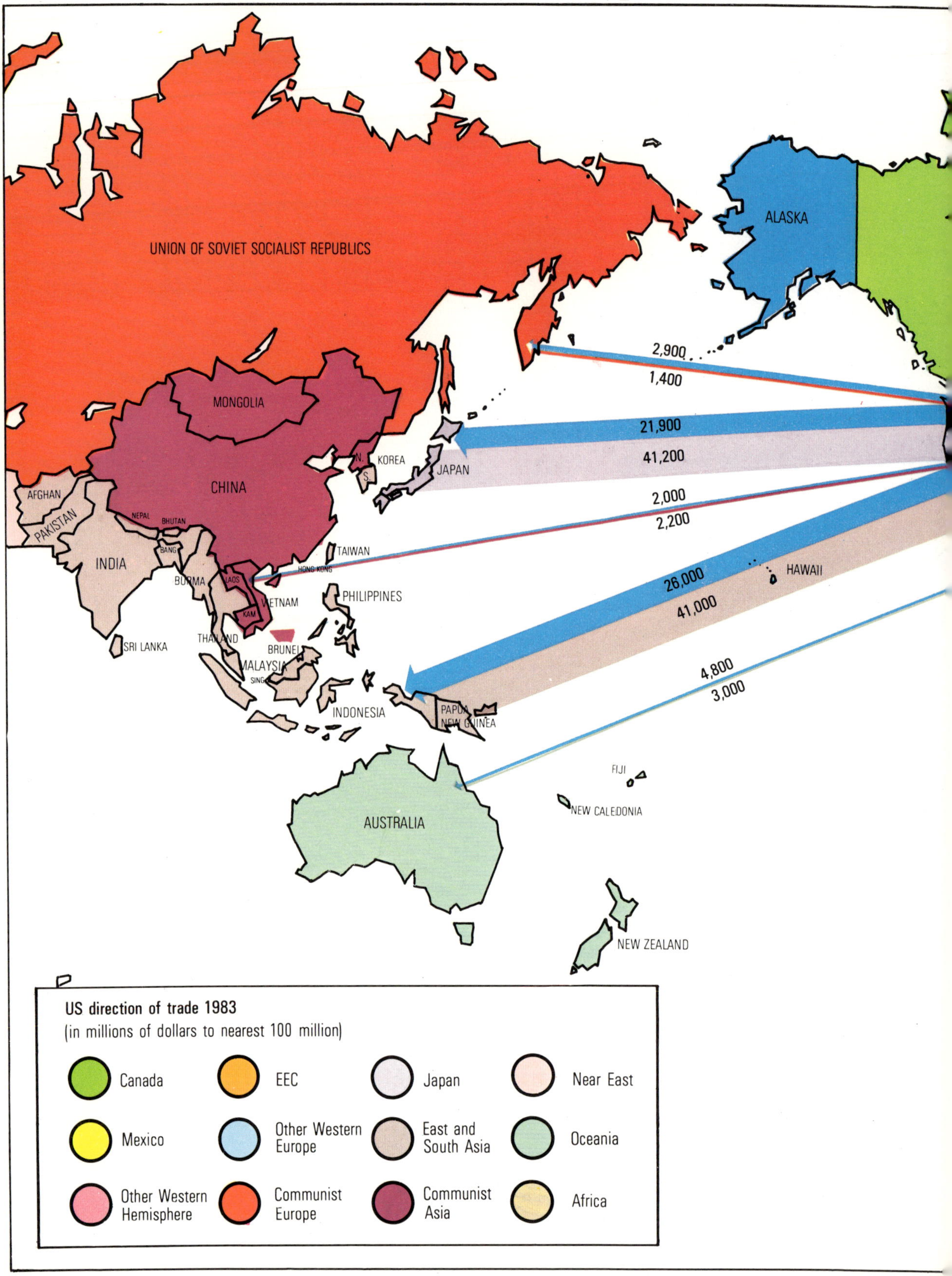

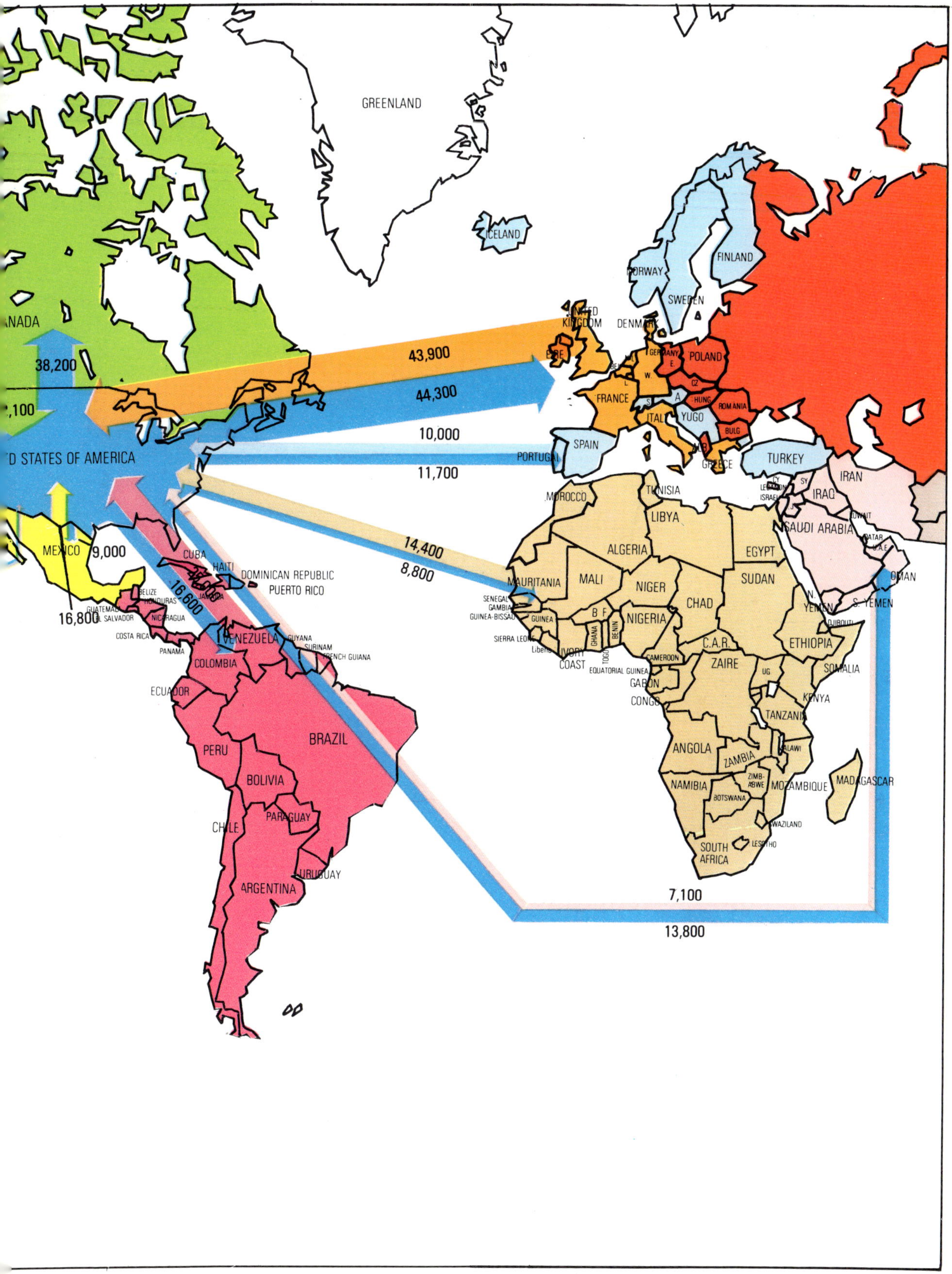
GREENLAND
ICELAND
NORWAY
FINLAND
SWEDEN
UNITED KINGDOM
DENMARK
EIRE
POLAND
FRANCE
ITALY
YUGO
HUNG
ROMANIA
BULG
SPAIN
PORTUGAL
GREECE
TURKEY
IRAN
IRAQ
SAUDI ARABIA
OMAN
S. YEMEN
N. YEMEN
MOROCCO
TUNISIA
LIBYA
ALGERIA
EGYPT
MAURITANIA
MALI
NIGER
CHAD
SUDAN
NIGERIA
ETHIOPIA
SOMALIA
KENYA
TANZANIA
ZAIRE
ANGOLA
ZAMBIA
NAMIBIA
BOTSWANA
MOZAMBIQUE
MADAGASCAR
SOUTH AFRICA
CAMEROON
GABON
CONGO
IVORY COAST
GHANA
BENIN
TOGO
GUINEA
SENEGAL
GAMBIA
GUINEA-BISSAU
SIERRA LEONE
EQUATORIAL GUINEA
C.A.R.
SWAZILAND
LESOTHO
CANADA
38,200
UNITED STATES OF AMERICA
MEXICO
9,000
16,800
CUBA
HAITI
DOMINICAN REPUBLIC
PUERTO RICO
JAMAICA
BELIZE
HONDURAS
GUATEMALA
EL SALVADOR
NICARAGUA
COSTA RICA
PANAMA
VENEZUELA
GUYANA
SURINAM
FRENCH GUIANA
COLOMBIA
ECUADOR
PERU
BRAZIL
BOLIVIA
PARAGUAY
CHILE
URUGUAY
ARGENTINA
43,900
44,300
10,000
11,700
14,400
8,800
16,600
7,100
13,800

DIRECTION OF U.S. TRADE

This map shows the destination of the exports of the United States, and the origin of its imports in 1983. The thickness of the arrows represents the relative value of the trade with different parts of the world.

The European Economic Community received 22 percent of U.S. exports, Canada 19 percent, East and South Asia 13 percent, and Japan 11 percent.

Turning to the pattern of U.S. imports, over 20 percent came from Canada and 15 percent from the EEC, but Japan accounted for a significant 16 percent.

In 1984 the picture remained about the same. Taking Europe as a whole, it received over 29 percent of the exports of the United States, and Asia nearly 30 percent. Japan alone accounted for 23.6 percent of the total, and the United Kingdom accounted for 12.2 percent. Asia supplied 37 percent of the imports of the United States, Japan's share amounting to 17.5 percent.

Diagram A looks at the tendencies in U.S. exports and imports in the period 1955-1983. Values of annual trade are here expressed in terms of constant (1967) dollars. The tremendous rise in the total real value of U.S. foreign trade is clear in both graphs, reaching a peak in 1980. Over this quarter of a century, there was a fivefold rise in U.S. exports, and nearly an eightfold rise in imports.

Diagram A: U.S. trade in billions of constant (1967) dollars, 1955-1983

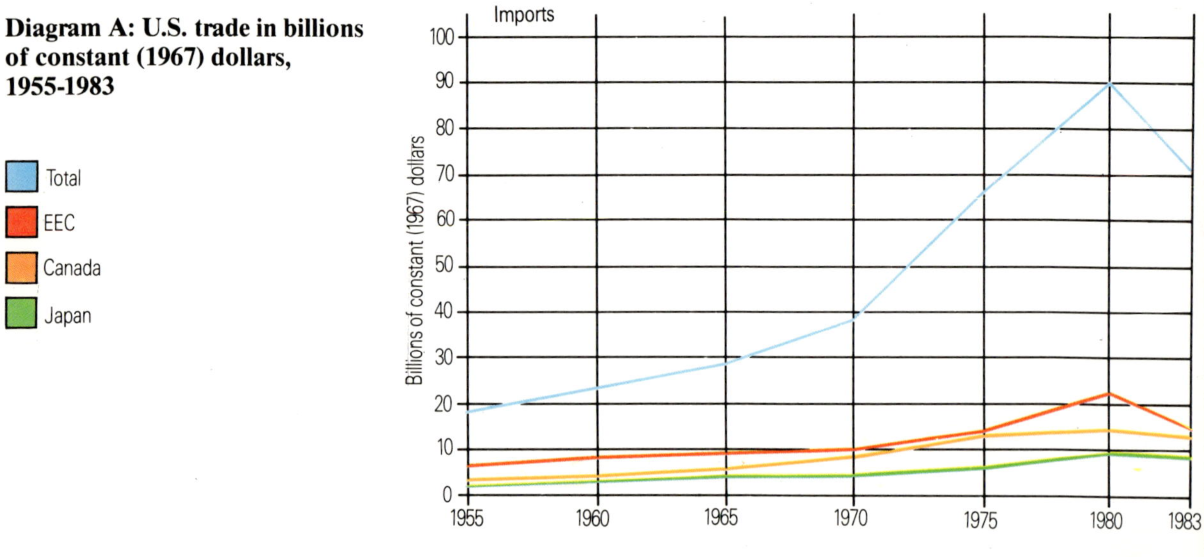

Within these totals, there have been some significant changes. Canada has come to account for a larger share of U.S. exports, and the EEC countries for a smaller one. Canadian exports to the United States, however, have tended to be less important, while Japan has obtained an increasingly larger share.

Diagram B looks at the types of commodity that made up U.S. exports and imports in 1983. The largest single group of goods by value in U.S. exports comprised machinery and transport equipment. Such items made up 45 percent of the total, while "other manufactured goods" amounted to another 15 percent.

The other pie chart in Diagram B shows that machinery and transport equipment also made up a large part of U.S. imports. Together with "other manufactured goods,'' these commodities accounted for 60 percent of U.S. imports in 1983.

It is interesting to contrast these features of U.S. trade in the 1980s with the pattern found in the past. In the last century, the United States received about 55 percent of its imports from Europe, and sent some 70 percent of its exports there. As noted above, finished manufactured goods account for a large part of both imports and exports these days. In former times, the picture was very different.

Thus, in 1930, such items made up 50 percent of U.S. exports; in 1900, 25 percent; in 1870, 15 percent. The trend in the importance of manufactured goods in imports is less simple. The percentages represented by them in U.S. imports was as follows: 1840, 45; 1870, 40; 1900, 21; 1930, 25; 1970, 55.

Sources: *Government Finance Statistics Yearbook, 1985; Survey of Current Business, 1985; Historical Statistics of the United States, Colonial Times to 1970, Volume II*

Diagram B: Distribution of foreign trade of the United States in 1983, by selected commodity groups, in millions of dollars

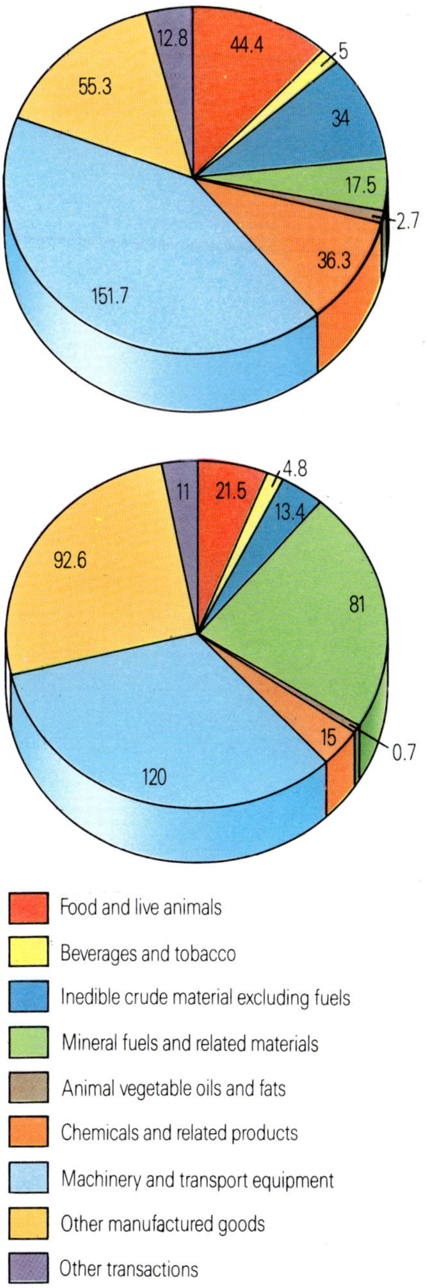

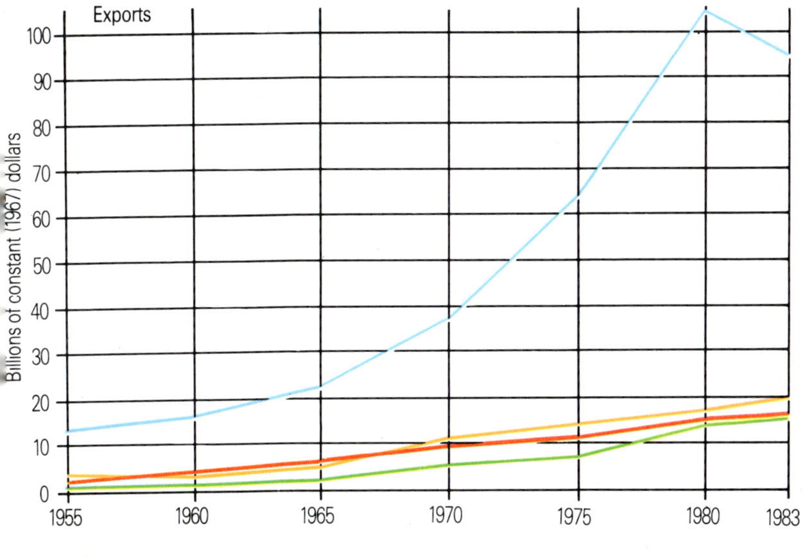

ROAD AND RAIL TRANSPORT

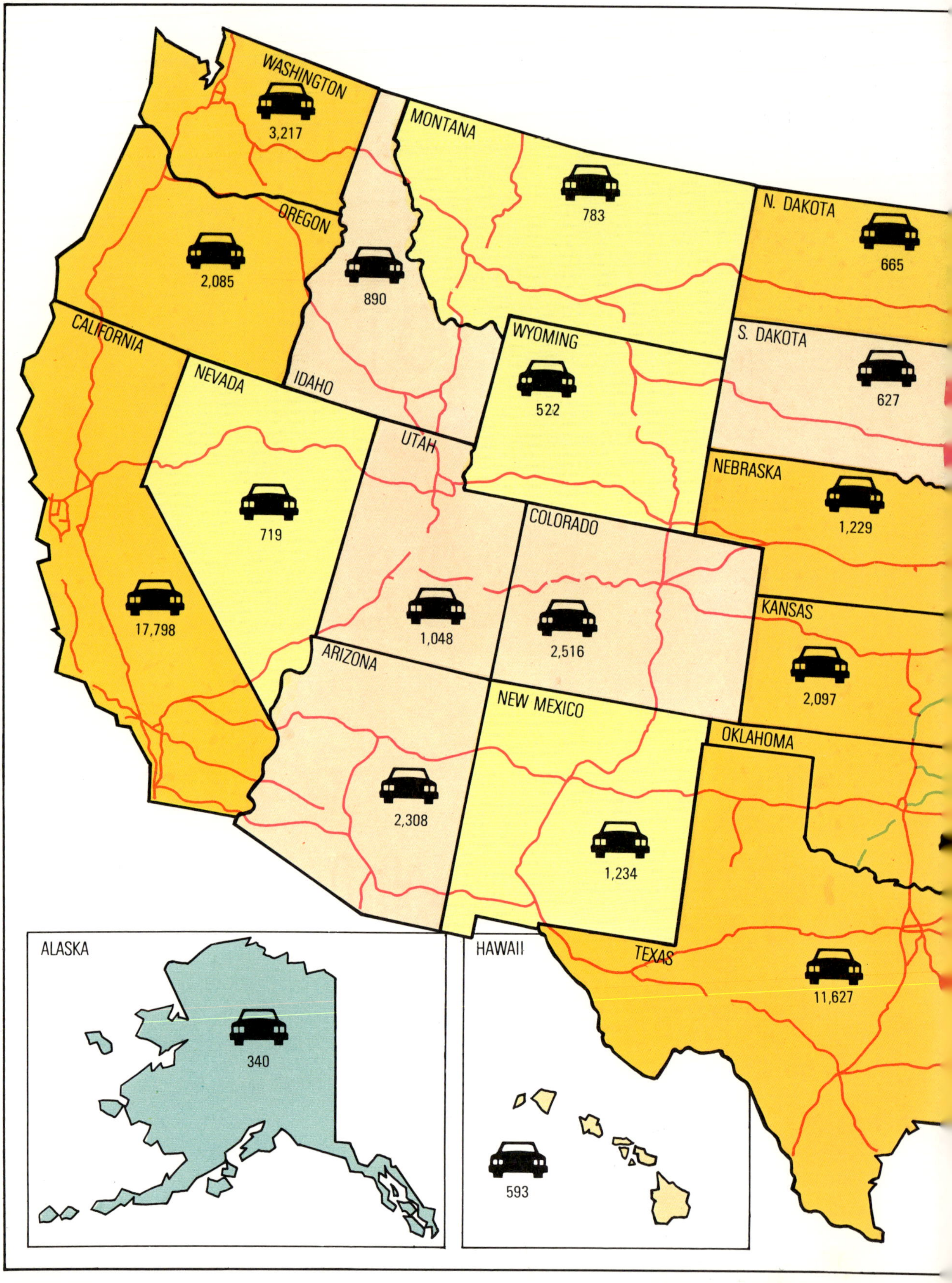

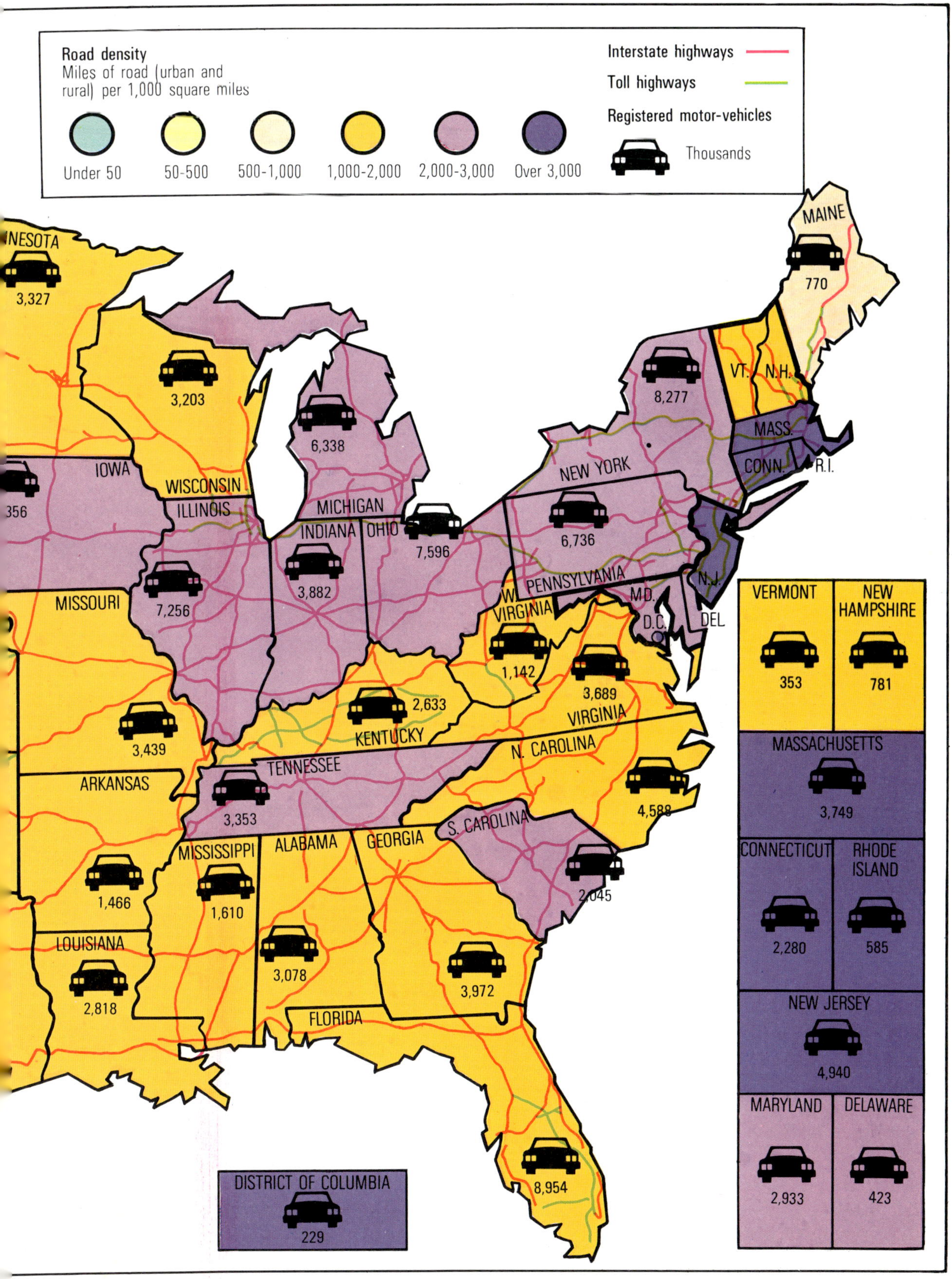
Road density
Miles of road (urban and rural) per 1,000 square miles
Under 50
50-500
500-1,000
1,000-2,000
2,000-3,000
Over 3,000
Interstate highways
Toll highways
Registered motor-vehicles
Thousands
NESOTA
3,327
IOWA
356
WISCONSIN
3,203
MICHIGAN
6,338
NEW YORK
8,277
MAINE
770
VT.
N.H.
MASS.
CONN.
R.I.
ILLINOIS
7,256
INDIANA
3,882
OHIO
7,596
PENNSYLVANIA
6,736
N.J.
MD.
D.C.
DEL
W. VIRGINIA
1,142
VIRGINIA
3,689
MISSOURI
3,439
KENTUCKY
2,633
TENNESSEE
3,353
N. CAROLINA
4,588
ARKANSAS
1,466
MISSISSIPPI
1,610
ALABAMA
3,078
GEORGIA
3,972
S. CAROLINA
2,045
LOUISIANA
2,818
FLORIDA
8,954
DISTRICT OF COLUMBIA
229
VERMONT
353
NEW HAMPSHIRE
781
MASSACHUSETTS
3,749
CONNECTICUT
2,280
RHODE ISLAND
585
NEW JERSEY
4,940
MARYLAND
2,933
DELAWARE
423

ROAD AND RAIL TRANSPORT

The map indicates the degree of utilization of road and rail transportation in the United States. States are coloured according to the density of roads, expressed in miles of urban and rural road per thousand square miles of territory. The map shows interstate and toll highways. The symbols give the number of motor vehicles (in thousands) registered in each state.

The densest road system is to be found in the District of Columbia, which packs 1,100 miles of road into its 64 square miles. At the other extreme, Alaska's 591,000 square miles contain only 10,000 miles of road. While there are 34 registered vehicles for every mile of road in Alaska, the equivalent number in D.C. is 200.

Part of the price paid for the ability to move large numbers of people along the roads at high speed includes the heavy toll in road

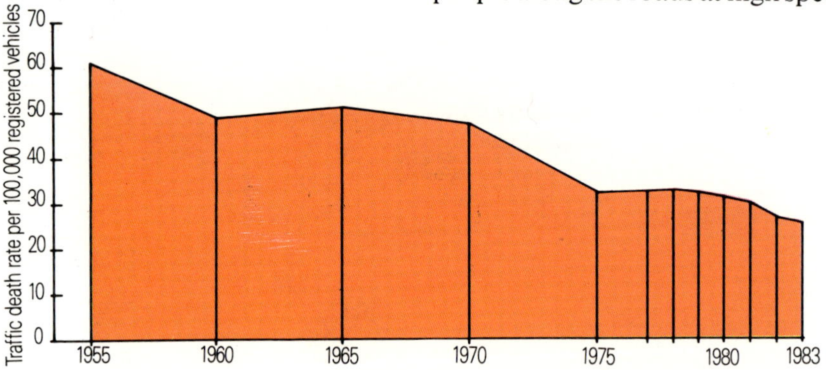

Diagram A: Traffic death rates per 100,000 registered vehicles, 1955-1983

Diagram B: Fuel consumption by cars and trucks, 1970-1982. "Cars" includes taxicabs and motorcycles

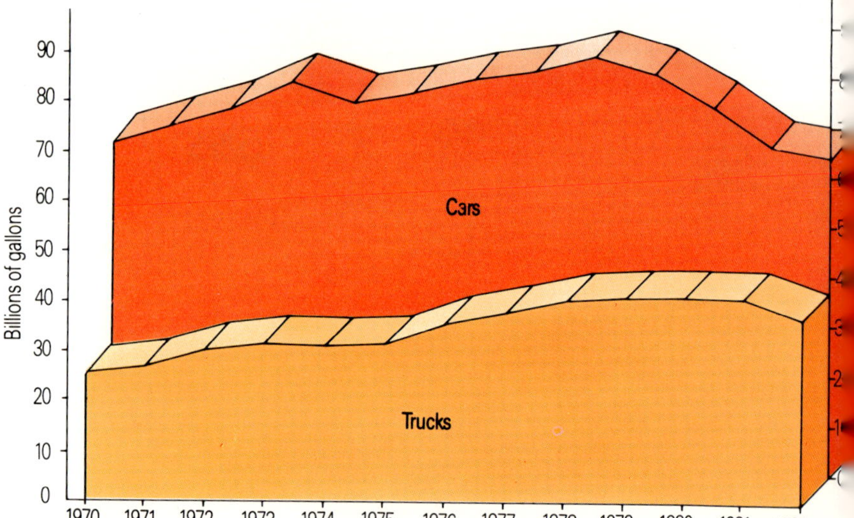

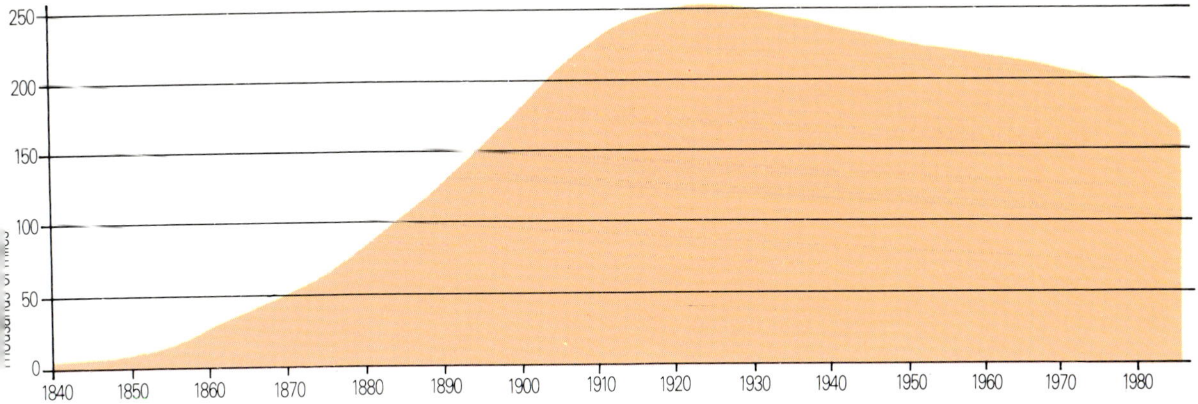

Diagram C: Mileage of railroad line, 1840-1980

accidents. It is interesting to see the effects of the attention paid to road safety in the numbers of traffic deaths recorded per 100,000 registered vehicles. Graphed in Diagram A, this shows a marked fall in fatalities since 1965.

The intense use of road transport — over 85 percent of eligible Americans hold driver licenses — is reflected in the figures for fuel consumption, graphed in Diagram B. Fuel consumption by cars, climbing steadily in the early 1970s, fell back in 1974 as the rise in fuel costs led to the use of vehicles with more efficient gas consumption. On the other hand, fuel consumption by trucks continued to rise almost without pause. The total amount of travel by trucks is now estimated to be well over 400 billion vehicle-miles per year, while passenger cars travel over 1,100 billion vehicle-miles.

Diagram C graphs the rise and decline of the railroads of the United States. The laying of thousands of miles of railroad track was a major feature of the transcontinental expansion in the period 1860-1920. As the diagram shows, this process of expansion reached its peak just before the Great Depression of the early 1930s. Although the U.S. railroad system played a vital part during World War II, it has shared the financial difficulties of railways in general since then.

In 1983, private automobiles accounted for by far the greatest proportion of intercity passenger traffic, 83 percent of the total in terms of passenger-miles. Bus and rail transportation accounted for only 1.6 and 0.7 percent respectively. In intercity freight transportation, however, railroads played a leading role, accounting for 36 percent of the total ton-mileage. Motor vehicles accounted for 24 percent.

Sources: U.S. Dept. of Transportation;
U.S. Federal Highway Administration

Note: A ton-mile is the movement of 1 ton (2,000 pounds) of freight for the distance of 1 mile. A passenger-mile is the movement of 1 passenger for the distance of 1 mile.

AIR AND WATER TRANSPORT

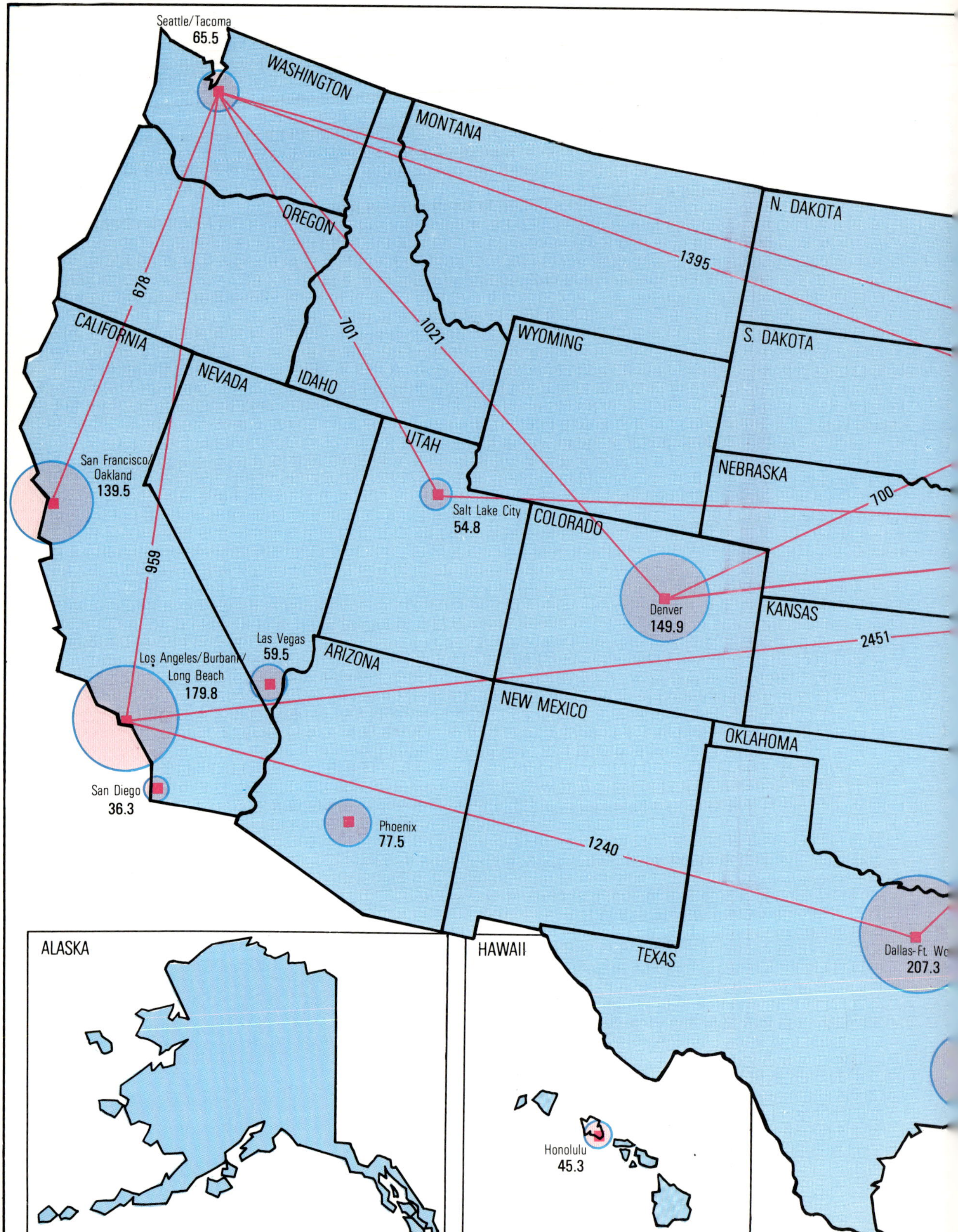

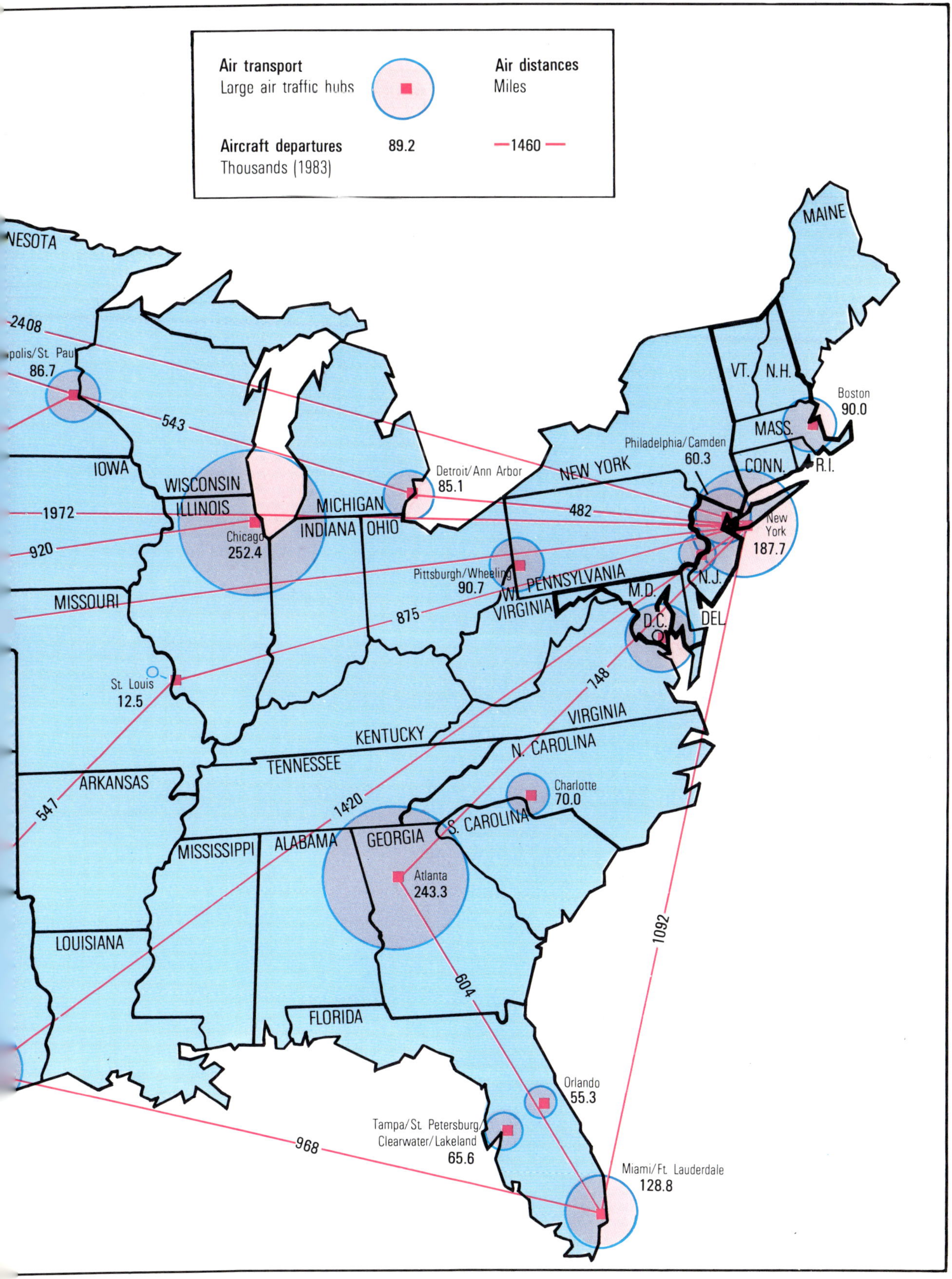
Air transport
Large air traffic hubs
Air distances
Miles
Aircraft departures
Thousands (1983)
89.2
1460
NESOTA
2408
polis/St. Paul
86.7
543
IOWA
WISCONSIN
ILLINOIS
1972
920
Chicago
252.4
MICHIGAN
INDIANA
OHIO
Detroit/Ann Arbor
85.1
MAINE
VT.
N.H.
Boston
90.0
MASS.
Philadelphia/Camden
60.3
CONN.
R.I.
NEW YORK
482
New York
187.7
Pittsburgh/Wheeling
90.7
PENNSYLVANIA
N.J.
M.D.
W. VIRGINIA
D.C.
DEL
MISSOURI
875
St. Louis
12.5
748
VIRGINIA
KENTUCKY
N. CAROLINA
TENNESSEE
Charlotte
70.0
ARKANSAS
547
1420
S. CAROLINA
MISSISSIPPI
ALABAMA
GEORGIA
Atlanta
243.3
LOUISIANA
1092
604
FLORIDA
Orlando
55.3
Tampa/St. Petersburg/
Clearwater/Lakeland
65.6
968
Miami/Ft. Lauderdale
128.8

AIR AND WATER TRANSPORT

There were 16,029 civil airports in the United States in 1983, including heliports, seaplane bases, and military airports with joint civil and military use. The majority of flights, however, were from airports making up the large air-traffic hubs. An "air-traffic hub" is a city or metropolitan area requiring aviation services. A large air-traffic hub is defined as one responsible for at least 1 percent of the total number of revenue passengers using U.S. certificated route air carriers (often referred to as "scheduled airlines"). In 1983 these large air-traffic hubs numbered 26. They included 40 airports and accounted for 220 billion passengers. The 26 large air-traffic hubs are shown on the map, together with the number of aircraft departures from each in 1983.

The expansion of domestic air travel has been a major feature of U.S. transportation since World War II. One of the graphs on Diagram A shows the number of passenger-miles flown on domestic routes between 1970 and 1983. During that period, this number more than doubled, although there was a significant dip between 1979 and 1982.

The other graph on this diagram shows the average rate charged for these flights, expressed in constant (1983) dollars per passenger-mile. In general, the rate has fallen as the number of passenger-miles has increased.

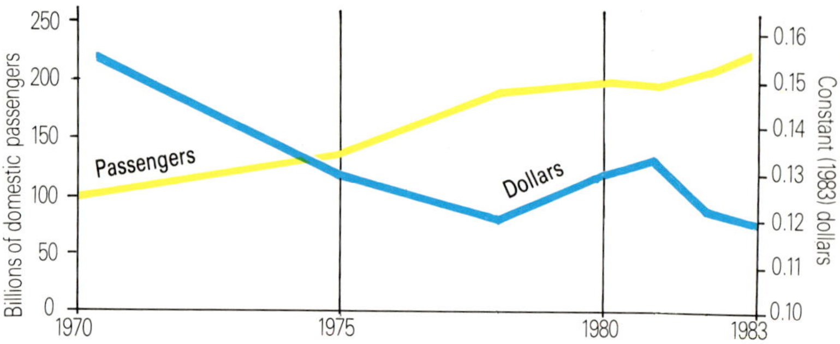

Diagram A: Domestic passenger traffic, 1970-1983, showing passenger-miles flown, and rates in constant (1983) dollars per passenger-mile

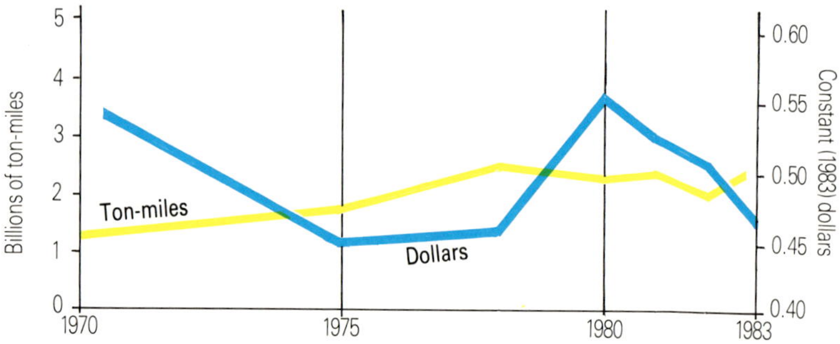

Diagram B: Domestic air freight, 1970-1983, showing ton-miles flown, and rates in constant (1983) dollars per ton-mile

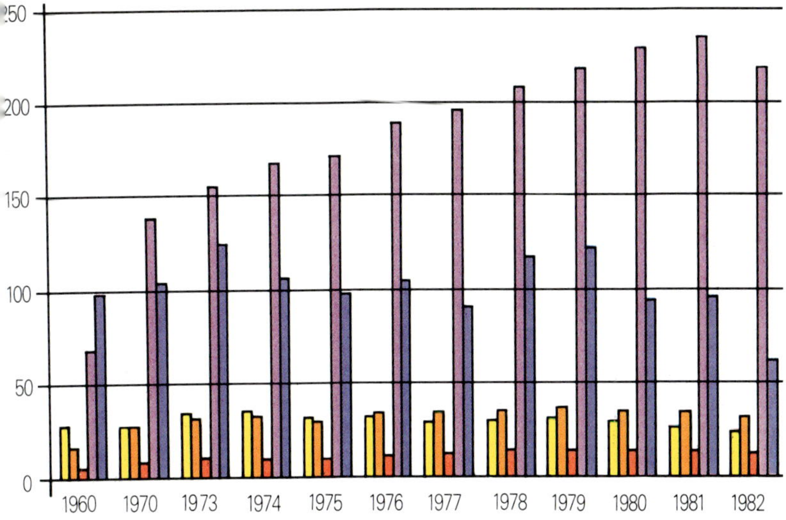

Diagram C: Freight carried on inland waterways, by system, 1960-1982

Domestic air flights have also carried an increasing amount of freight and mail over the same period. Diagram B graphs the domestic freight carried between 1970 and 1983, in ton-miles. This rose sharply until 1979, remaining relatively constant thereafter. The diagram also shows the average rate charged for this freight, in constant (1983) dollars per ton-mile. The rate fell strikingly from 1970 to 1979.

The volume of freight carried on U.S. domestic flights is considerable, but it is insignificant compared with the volume carried on the inland waterways. In 1982, this totalled 351 billion ton-miles.

Diagram C graphs the freight traffic on inland waterways, by system, between 1970 and 1982. The expansion of the Mississippi River system is particularly notable.

Inland waterborne traffic played a major part in the opening up of the interior of the continent in the nineteenth century. In the 1830s and 1840s, a considerable amount of capital was invested in canals. One major undertaking was the construction of the Illinois-Michigan Canal connecting the Mississippi and its tributaries with the Great Lakes, and, incidentally, leading to the expansion of Chicago from a small village to a major industrial centre.

Over a century later, the history of the U.S. inland waterways took another leap forward, when agreement between the U.S. and Canadian governments made possible the opening of the St. Lawrence Seaway in 1959. This opened the Great Lakes to ocean-going vessels.

Note: A ton-mile is the movement of 1 ton (2,000 pounds) of freight for the distance of 1 mile. A passenger-mile is the movement of 1 passenger for the distance of 1 mile.

Sources: United States Federal Aviation Administration; U.S. Corps of Engineers

COMMUNICATIONS

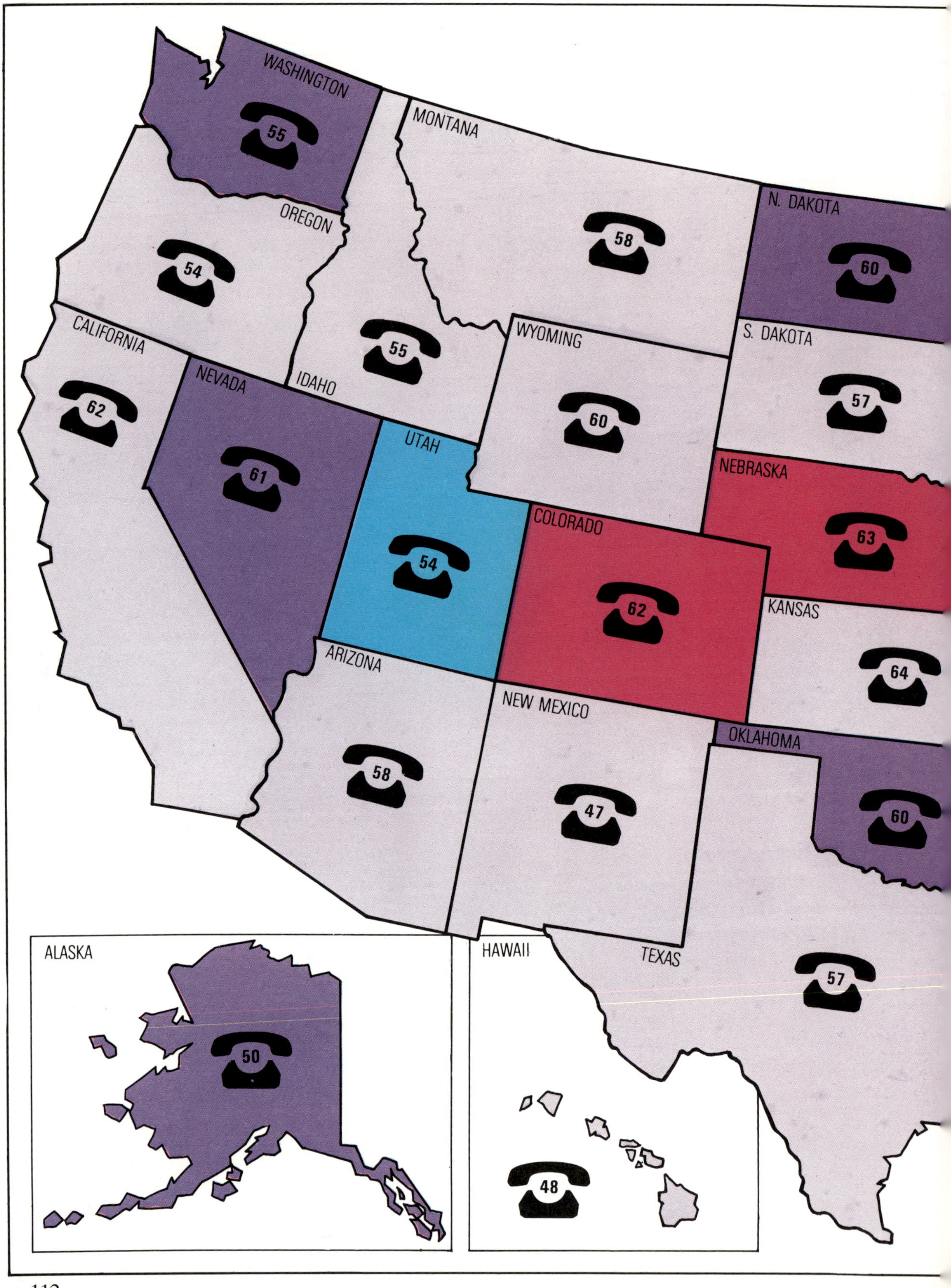

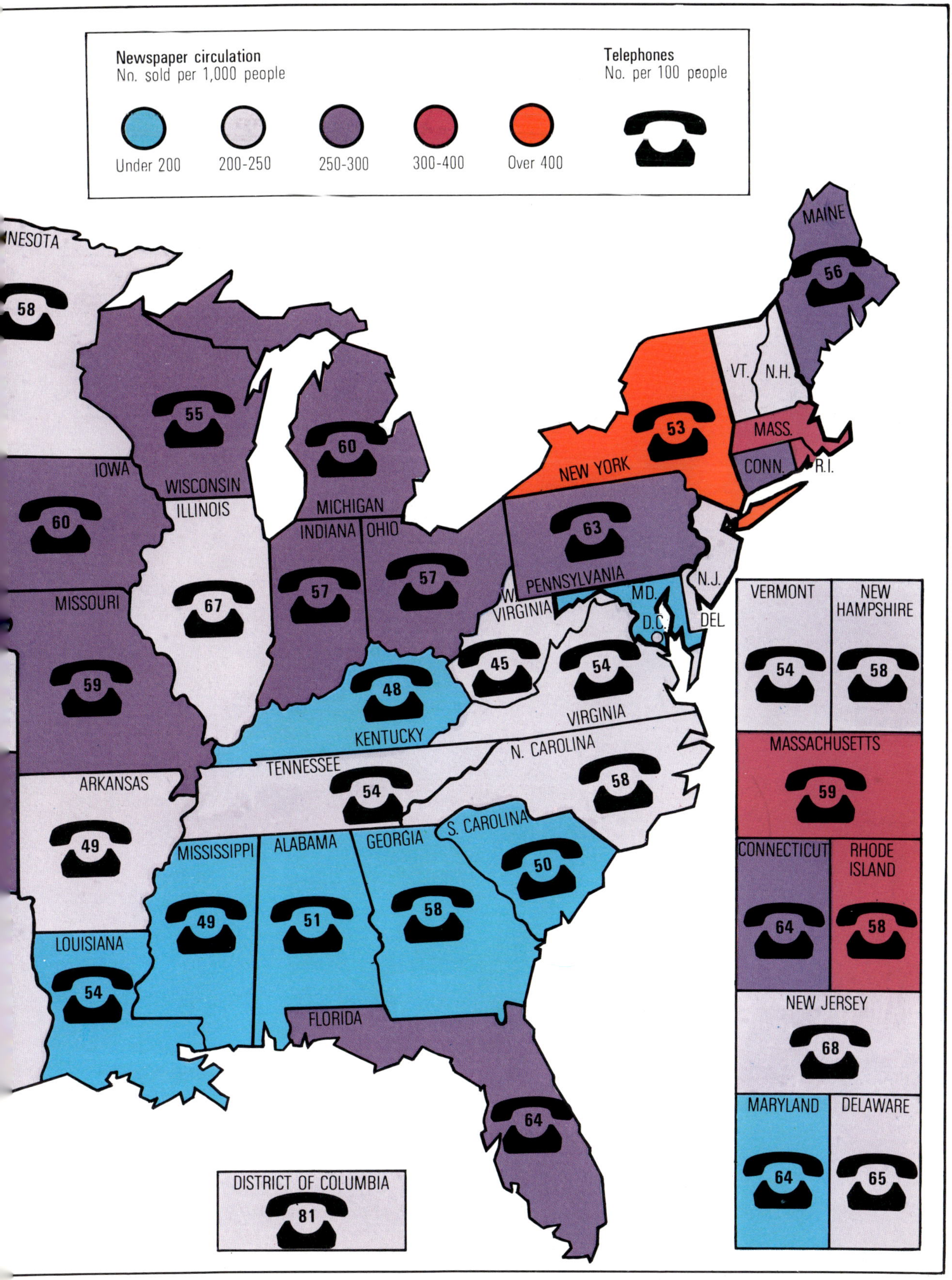

Newspaper circulation
No. sold per 1,000 people
Under 200
200-250
250-300
300-400
Over 400
Telephones
No. per 100 people
NESOTA
58
WISCONSIN
55
MICHIGAN
60
IOWA
60
ILLINOIS
67
INDIANA
57
OHIO
57
MISSOURI
59
KENTUCKY
48
W. VIRGINIA
45
VIRGINIA
54
PENNSYLVANIA
63
NEW YORK
53
MAINE
56
VT.
N.H.
MASS.
CONN.
R.I.
N.J.
MD.
D.C.
DEL
TENNESSEE
54
N. CAROLINA
58
ARKANSAS
49
S. CAROLINA
50
MISSISSIPPI
49
ALABAMA
51
GEORGIA
58
LOUISIANA
54
FLORIDA
64
DISTRICT OF COLUMBIA
81
VERMONT
54
NEW HAMPSHIRE
58
MASSACHUSETTS
59
CONNECTICUT
64
RHODE ISLAND
58
NEW JERSEY
68
MARYLAND
64
DELAWARE
65

COMMUNICATIONS

One of the most striking features of social development in the twentieth century has been the expansion of the communications media, and in this change the United States has led the world. Nearly every U.S. home today has at least one TV set and radio. Over 1,700 daily newspapers circulate over 62.5 million copies in total. Billions of pieces of mail are delivered each year.

The map shows how the states compare in two respects. The colour of each state indicates the circulation of daily newspapers per 1,000 people, and the symbols show the number of telephones per 100 people. The District of Columbia is once again far ahead of others: 2.44 daily papers are bought there per capita, and there are more telephones than households. Mississippi is at the other end of the scale, with 161 daily newspapers for every 1,000 people, and 49 telephones for every 100 inhabitants.

In 1960 there were 74 million telephones in use in the United States, making 182 million calls each day. In 1981 this had risen to 158 million telephones, and 800 million calls per day. In 1960 312 morning daily newspapers circulated over 24 million copies. In 1982 the number of morning daily newspapers had increased to

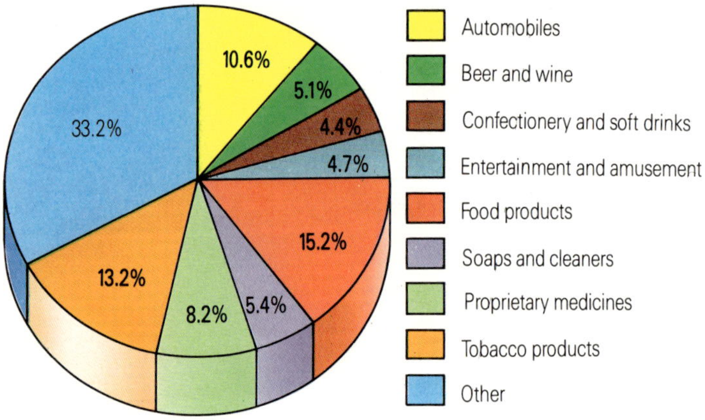

Diagram B: Percentages of total expenditure for network advertising spent on main types of product, 1982

Diagram A: Gross broadcast revenue, 1960-1980, for TV and radio

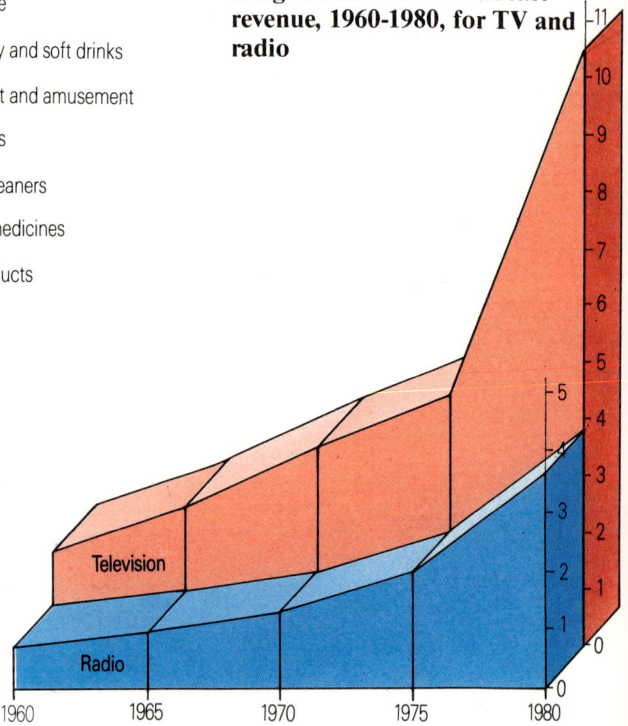

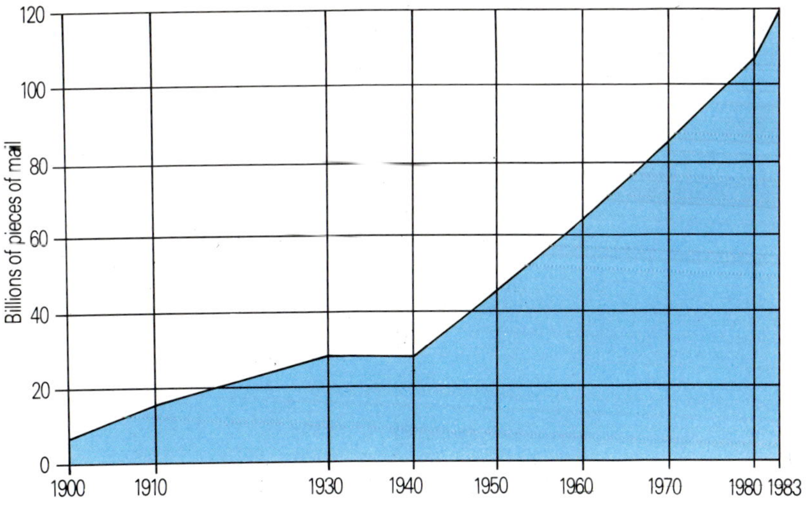

Diagram C: Number of pieces of mail, in billions, handled each year by the U.S. Postal Service, 1900-1983

434 and circulation to over 33 million copies. The number of evening papers, however, decreased over the same period from 1,459 to 1,284 and circulation from 34.9 million to 28.8 million.

Television is now the most influential form of mass communication. The average American watches about 7 hours of TV each day. Whereas in 1961 56 TV stations broadcast a total of 2,186 hours each week, in 1982 there were 291 stations broadcasting 30,337 hours weekly.

Diagram A shows how commercial TV has grown since 1960 in terms of gross broadcast revenues. While the figure for radio expanded from $665 million to $3.58 billion in the period 1960-1980, the equivalent amounts for television are $1.5 billion and $10.5 billion.

Diagram B shows the main source of these massive funds — TV network advertising expenditures. Food, tobacco, and automotive products account for a large part of the total. TV advertising expenditures are now on the way to overtaking the total amount spent on local and national newspaper advertising.

Diagram C graphs the expansion of the U.S. Postal Service. At the turn of the century it handled 7.1 billion pieces of mail in a year. By 1983 this figure had risen to 120 billion. Over the same period, Postal Service revenues increased from $108 million to over $25 billion. This amounts to a rise from $1.34 per capita in 1900, to over $24 per capita in 1983.

Source: U.S. Federal Communications Commission

REVENUE AND EXPENDITURE

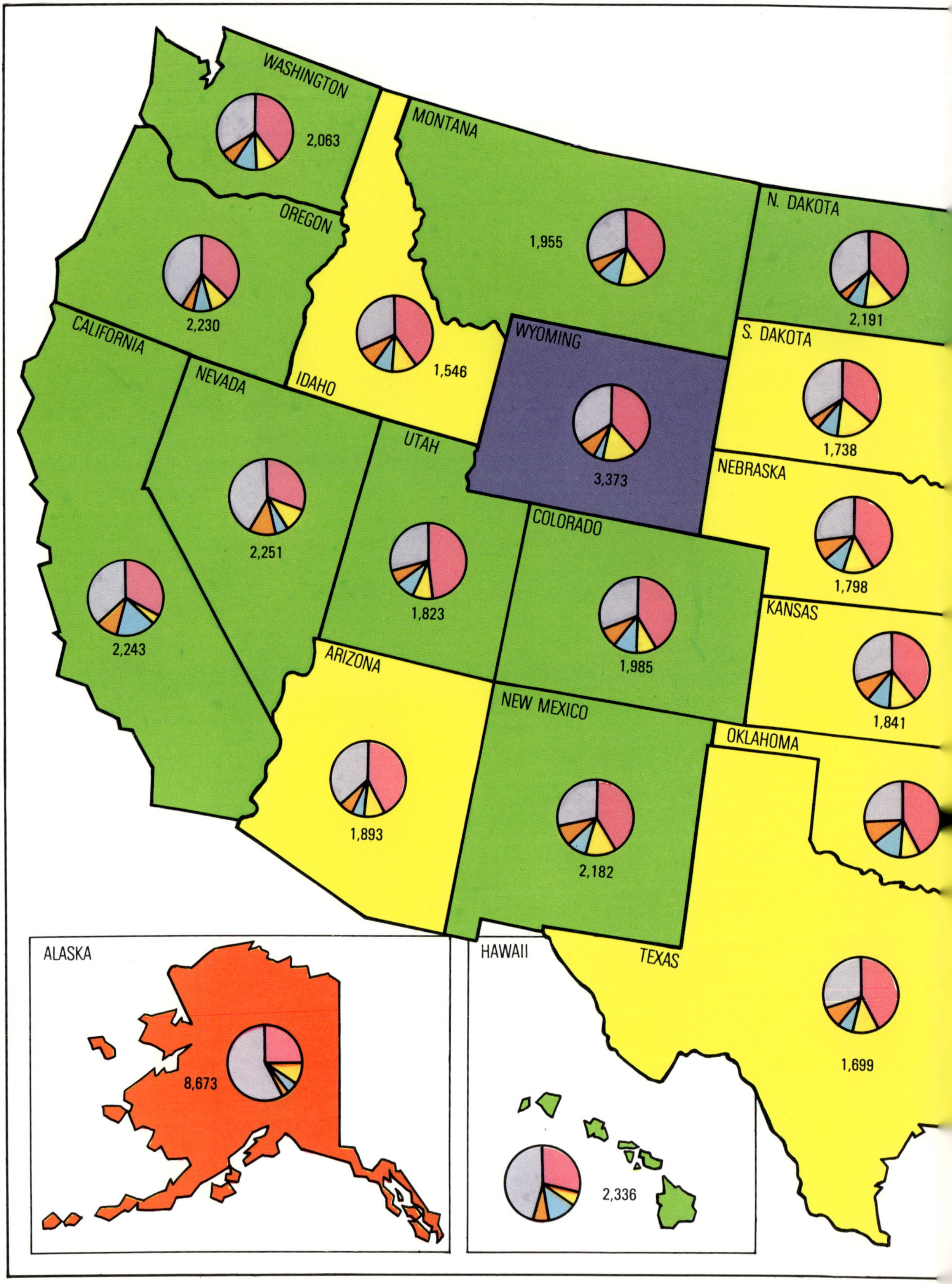

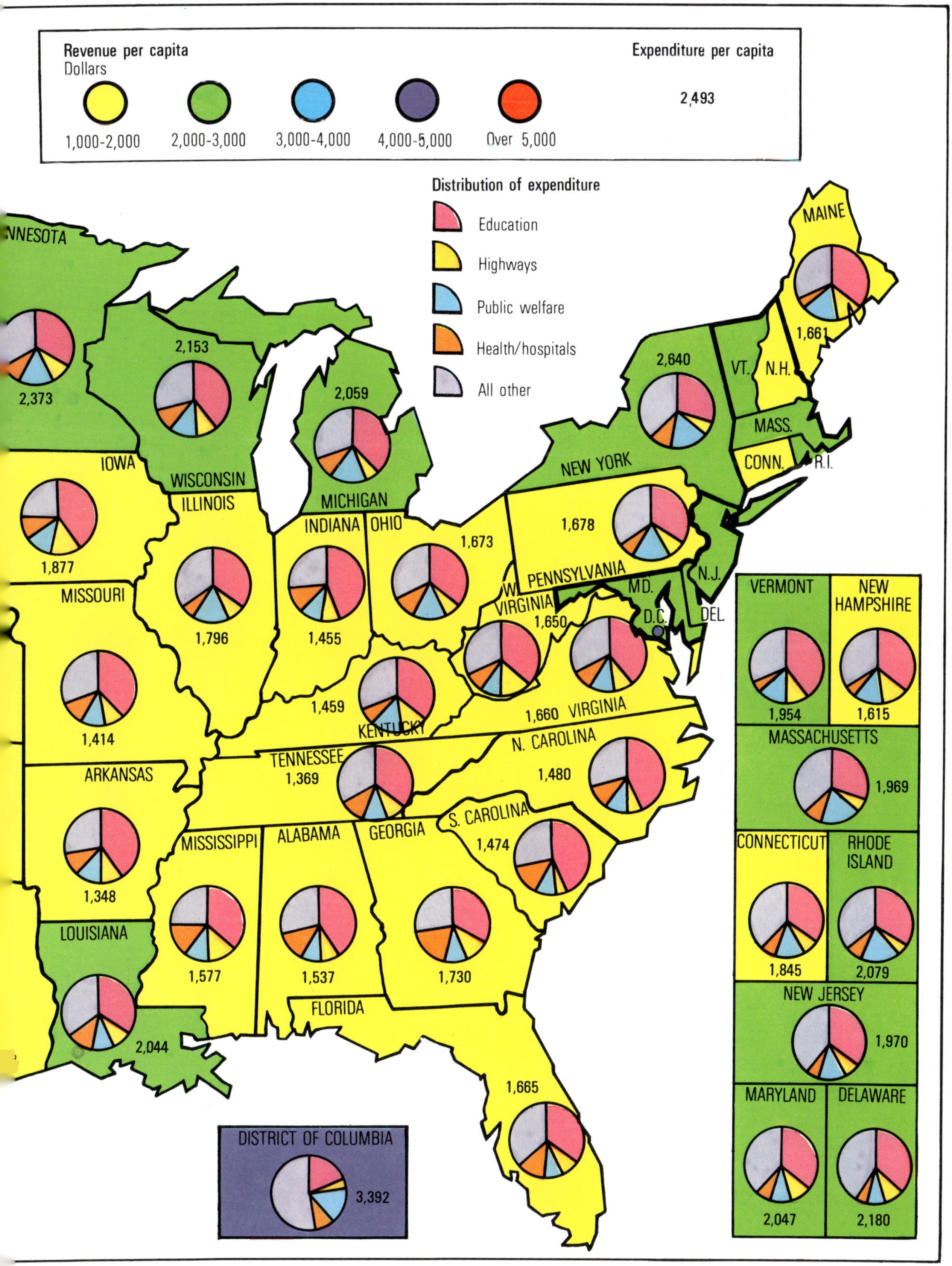
Revenue per capita
Dollars
1,000-2,000
2,000-3,000
3,000-4,000
4,000-5,000
Over 5,000
Expenditure per capita
2,493
Distribution of expenditure
Education
Highways
Public welfare
Health/hospitals
All other
MINNESOTA
2,373
WISCONSIN
2,153
MICHIGAN
2,059
NEW YORK
2,640
MAINE
1,661
VT.
N.H.
MASS.
CONN.
R.I.
IOWA
1,877
ILLINOIS
1,796
INDIANA
1,455
OHIO
1,673
PENNSYLVANIA
1,678
N.J.
MD.
D.C.
DEL
W. VIRGINIA
1,650
VIRGINIA
1,660
MISSOURI
1,414
KENTUCKY
1,459
TENNESSEE
1,369
N. CAROLINA
1,480
ARKANSAS
1,348
MISSISSIPPI
1,577
ALABAMA
1,537
GEORGIA
1,730
S. CAROLINA
1,474
LOUISIANA
2,044
FLORIDA
1,665
DISTRICT OF COLUMBIA
3,392
VERMONT
1,954
NEW HAMPSHIRE
1,615
MASSACHUSETTS
1,969
CONNECTICUT
1,845
RHODE ISLAND
2,079
NEW JERSEY
1,970
MARYLAND
2,047
DELAWARE
2,180

REVENUE AND EXPENDITURE

The map deals with state and local revenuc and expenditure. The states are coloured according to the per capita revenue raised, while the numbers in the symbols give the corresponding per capita expenditure. Alaska and the District of Columbia are by far the highest, because of their unique nature. Of the other states, Wyoming is the highest, both for revenue and expenditure, while Arkansas is the lowest.

The pie chart on each state is divided according to the distribution of expenditure by function. On average, about 36 percent of state and local expenditure is spent on education. Utah, spending 48 percent on education, comes first in this respect, followed by Indiana and South Carolina with 44 percent each.

Diagram A: Distribution of federal and state and local government expenditure, by main functions, 1970 and 1982

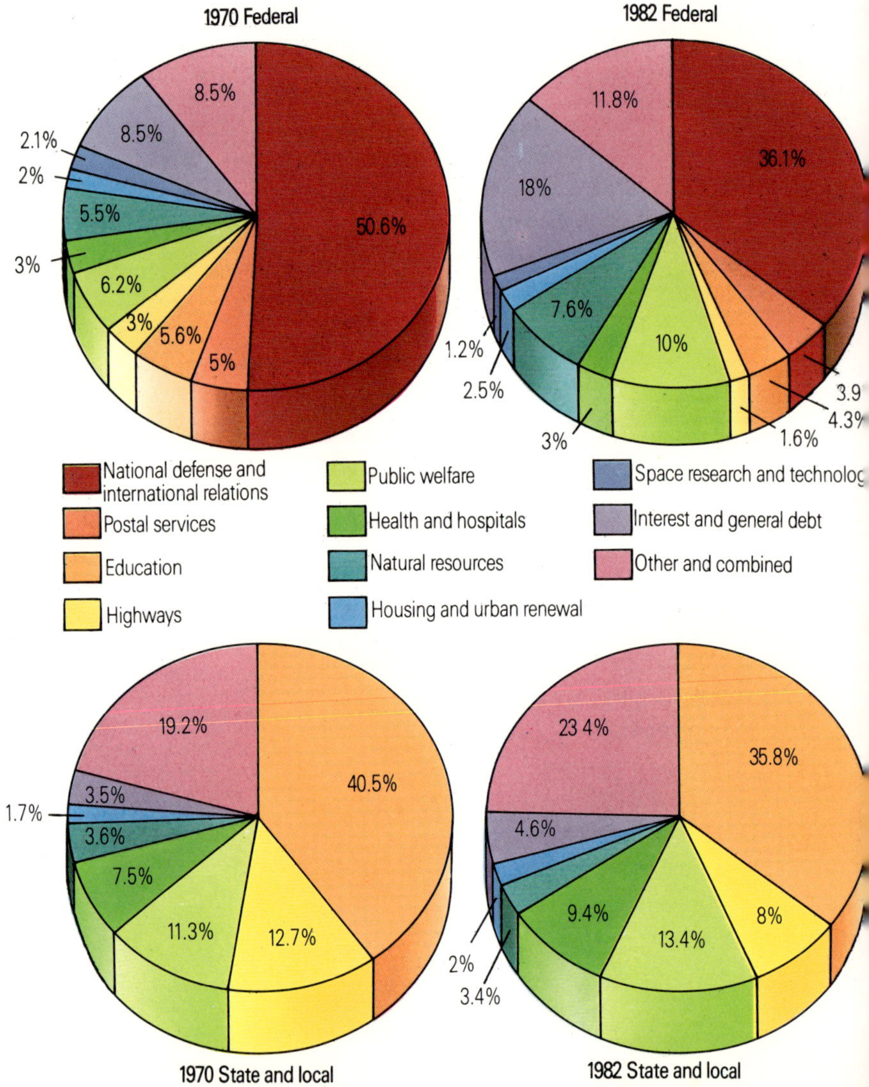

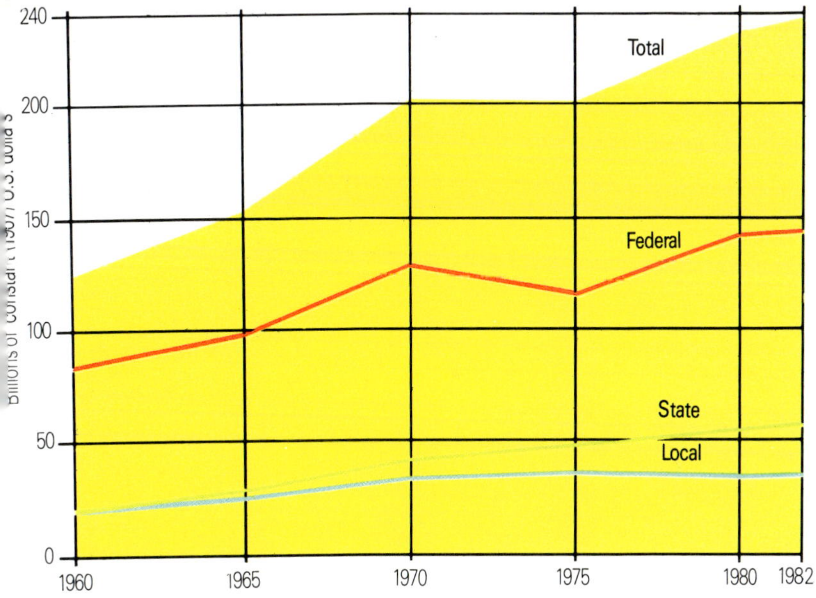

Diagram B: Tax revenue, 1960-1982, for all governments and for federal, state, and local governments

The four pie charts of Diagram A show the proportions of total national expenditure devoted to various purposes, both by federal, and state and local authorities, in 1970 and in 1982.

Diagram B depicts the steady rise in tax revenue since 1960, graphing federal, state and local, and total taxes, allowing for inflation. State and local taxes represent a rising proportion of the total.

In 1960, total tax revenue of all governments amounted to $113 billion. Of this, 68 percent went to the federal government, 16 percent to state governments, and 16 percent to local governments. In 1982, when the total tax revenue amounted to $671 billion, 60 percent went to federal government, 24 percent to state government and 16 percent to local governments.

A major factor in economic life is the indebtedness of the government. In 1983 the total public debt amounted to $1,377.2 billion, or $5,870 per capita. In 1970, the total was $370.1 billion, or $1,814 per capita. Interest payments on this debt made up 9.9 percent of total federal outlays in 1970. In 1983, it was 16.2 percent.

The debts of some of the large cities are now also substantial. In 1982 New York City owed $1,472 per capita. But this was far behind some others, notably Atlanta, Georgia ($2,354), Washington, D.C. ($2,783), Wichita, Kansas ($2,860), and Austin, Texas ($2,899). In the years since then, the debt of some cities has increased while the debt of others has decreased.

Source: U.S. Bureau of the Census

PERSONAL WEALTH

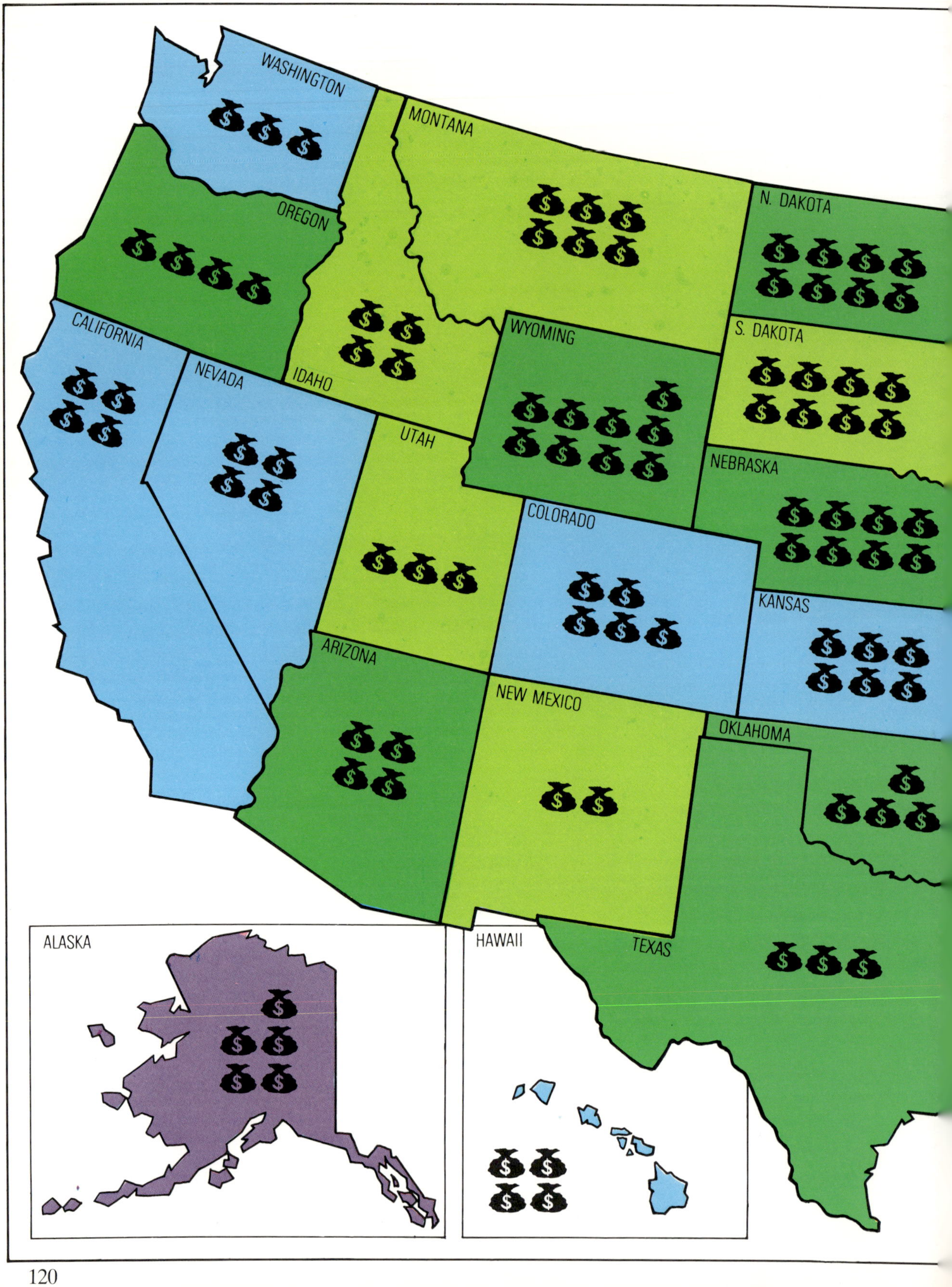

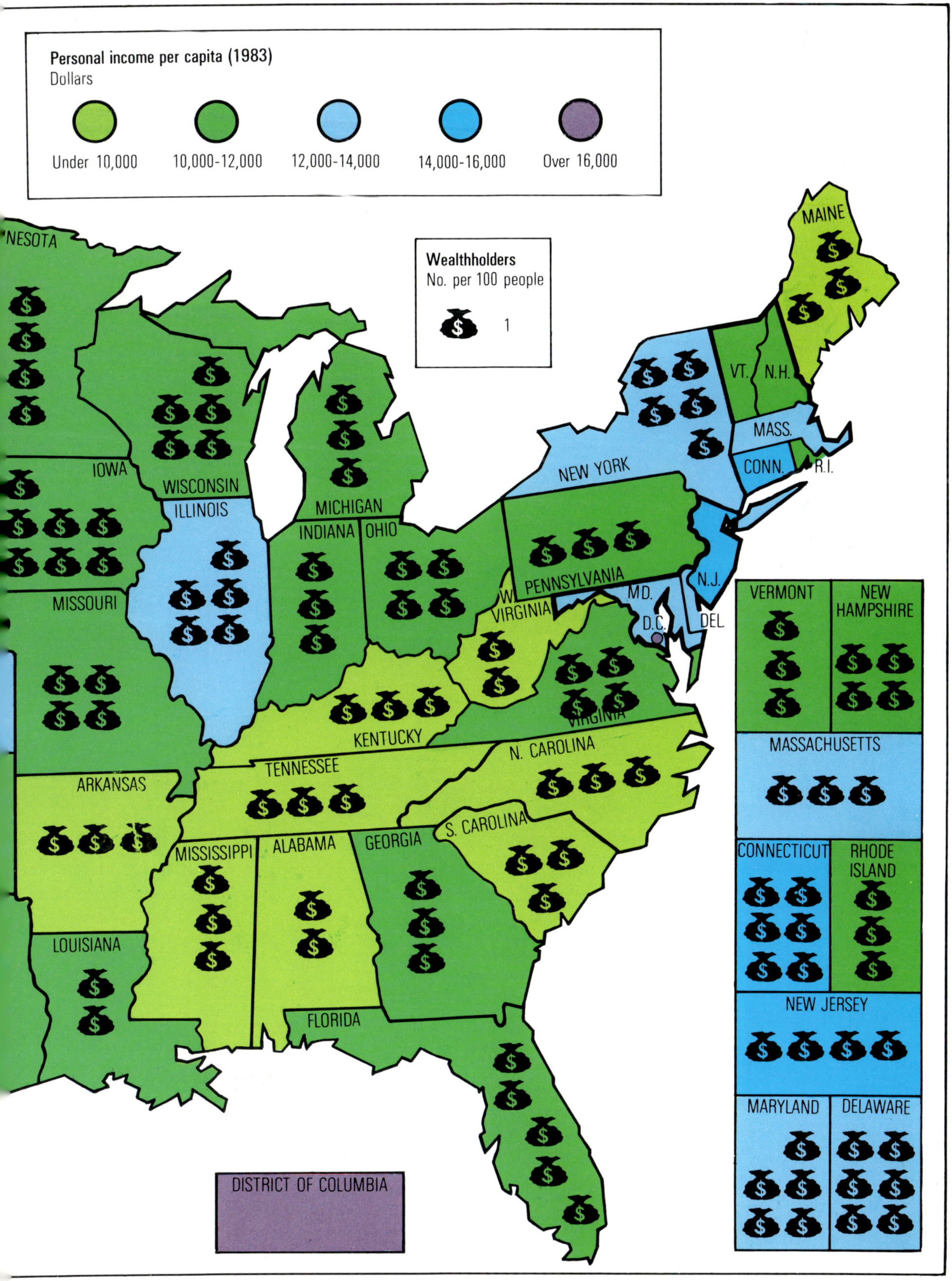
Personal income per capita (1983)
Dollars
Under 10,000
10,000-12,000
12,000-14,000
14,000-16,000
Over 16,000
Wealthholders
No. per 100 people
1
NESOTA
MAINE
IOWA
WISCONSIN
MICHIGAN
NEW YORK
VT.
N.H.
MASS.
CONN.
R.I.
ILLINOIS
INDIANA
OHIO
PENNSYLVANIA
N.J.
MD.
D.C.
DEL
MISSOURI
W. VIRGINIA
VIRGINIA
KENTUCKY
TENNESSEE
N. CAROLINA
ARKANSAS
S. CAROLINA
MISSISSIPPI
ALABAMA
GEORGIA
LOUISIANA
FLORIDA
DISTRICT OF COLUMBIA
VERMONT
NEW HAMPSHIRE
MASSACHUSETTS
CONNECTICUT
RHODE ISLAND
NEW JERSEY
MARYLAND
DELAWARE

PERSONAL WEALTH

This map deals with the distribution of personal wealth. States are coloured according to the average personal income per capita of residents in 1983. Also shown are the number of wealthholders, those whose gross estate is $60,000 or more. "Gross estate" is the total value of all assets, including life insurance. Numbers of wealthholders are estimates derived by the Internal Revenue Service from a sample of federal estate tax returns for deceased people.

On average, the residents of the United States had an income of $11,675 per capita in 1983. (This rose to $12,707 in 1984.) The average for individual states in 1983 varied from $8,072 in Mississippi and $8,937 in Arkansas, to $14,826 in Connecticut and $16,820 in Alaska. The District of Columbia's average was $16,409. The table shows the per capita income for each of the states and its relation to other states.

Overall, the people with $60,000 or more gross estate make up 3.7 percent of the population. In Alaska this percentage is 6, in Connecticut 5.7, in Mississippi 2.8, and in Arkansas 1.8, correlating with the per capita income levels. (These figures relate to 1976.)

In 1965, per capita personal income in the United States was $2,782, and in 1975 $5,857. In terms of constant (1972) dollars, the per capita incomes were:

1965	$3,171
1975	$4,051
1983	$4,670

In 1983, the median family income — the level at which 50 percent of all U.S. families received this amount or less — was estimated at $24,580. Diagram A shows the distribution of the aggregate income received by families in 1983. The percentage of the total aggregate income for the entire country is plotted against the percentage of families receiving the corresponding income or less.

At the bottom end of the scale, 20 percent of all families received 4.7 percent of the total income, and 40 percent received 15.8 percent of the total. At the other end of the scale, the top 5 percent of families received 15.8 percent of the total income.

Diagram B graphs the growth in the median family income since 1950 in constant (1983) dollars. It also shows black and white families separately. The rise in income levels in all cases is striking, until 1973, when the steady increase came to an end. Although the percentage difference between white and black families is plain, it has slowly been decreasing.

Diagram A: Percentage of aggregate personal income received by various percentages of all families, 1983

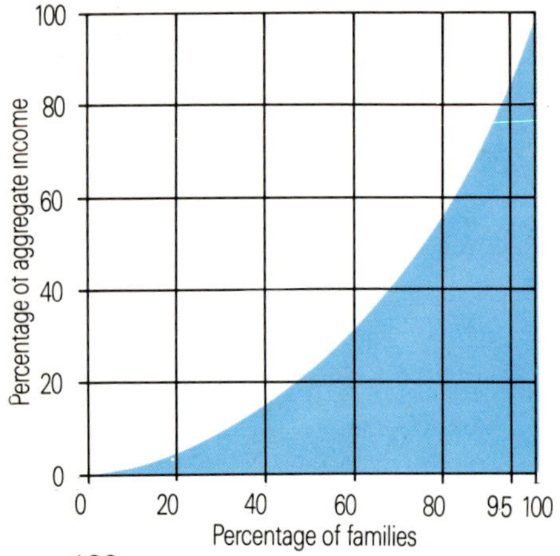

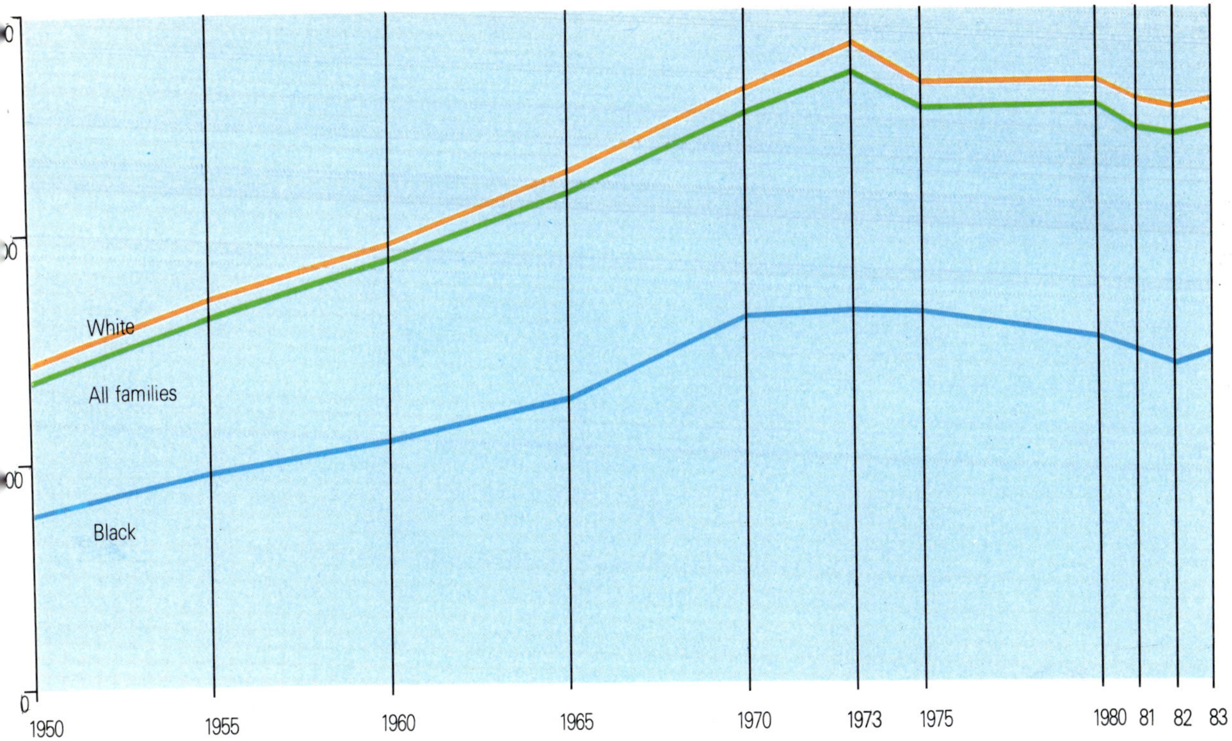

Diagram B: Median income of families, in constant (1983) dollars, all families, black and white

In 1983, 10.3 percent of households had an income of $50,000 or more. The percentage for white households was 11.1, for black households 3.1, and for households of Spanish origin 4.5. At the other end of the scale, 9.2 percent of households received a money income of $5,000 or less, 7.7 percent for whites, 21.1 percent for blacks, and 12.5 percent for households of Spanish origin.

Families are classified as being above or below the poverty level using the poverty index originated in 1964. This is based on income and reflects the different food consumption requirements of families according to their size. The poverty thresholds are updated every year to reflect changes in the Consumer Price Index. In 1983 the threshold for a family of four stood at $10,178, and 35.5 million people were classified as being below the poverty level. They accounted for 12.1 percent of the white population, 35.7 percent of the black population, and 28.4 percent of people of Spanish origin.

Turning to the distribution of personal wealth, data are less plentiful and less up-to-date. (Most of the data come from the U.S. Internal Revenue Service.) In 1976, it is estimated, 1 percent of the population held 19.2 percent of the nation's total personal wealth, and just 0.5 percent owned 14.3 percent.

Sources: U.S. Bureau of Economic Analysis, *Survey of Current Business;*
U.S. Bureau of the Census, *Current Population Reports;*
U.S. Internal Inland Revenue Service, *Statistics of Income*

THE FAMILY

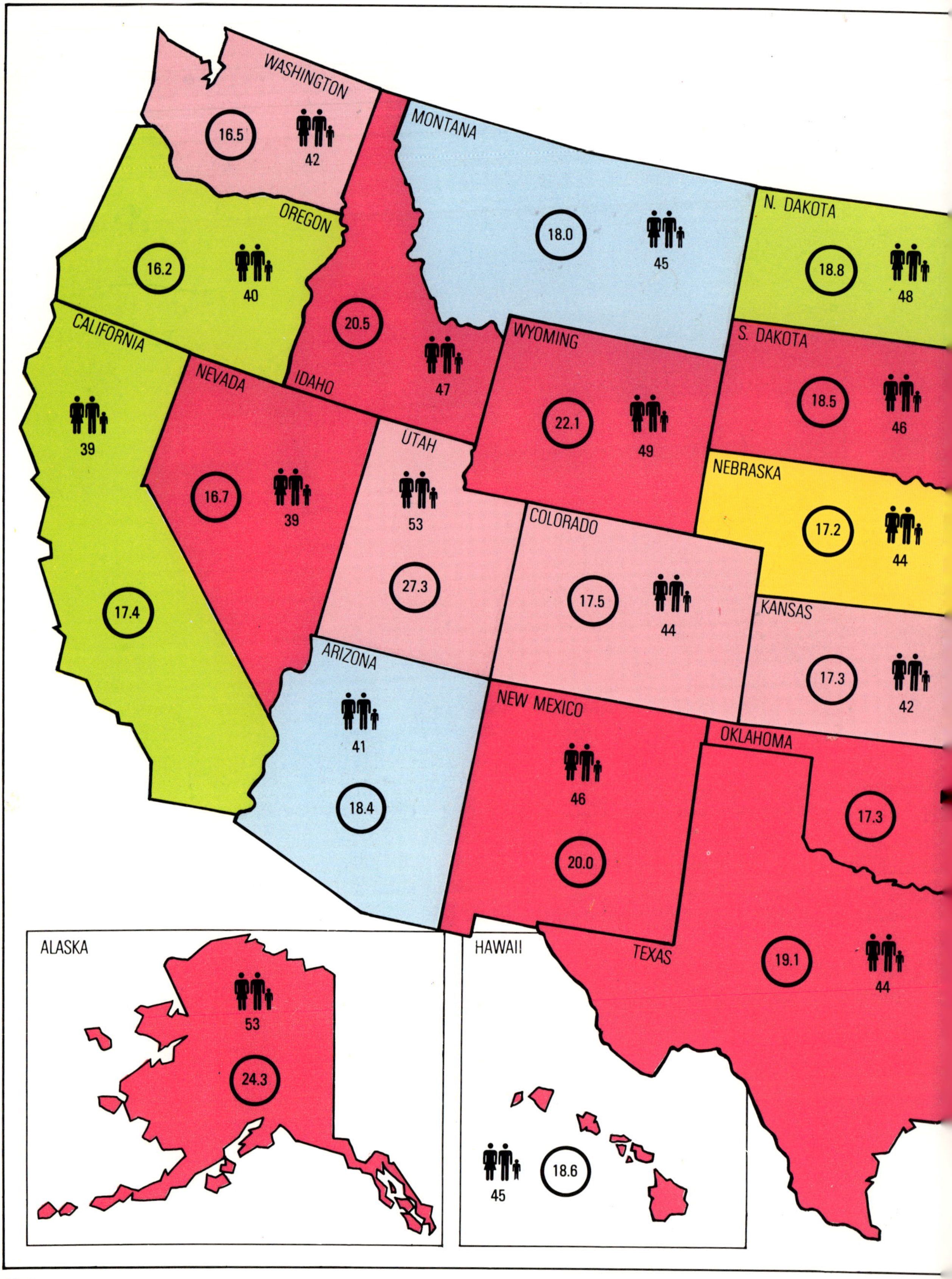

WASHINGTON
16.5
42
MONTANA
18.0
45
N. DAKOTA
18.8
48
OREGON
16.2
40
IDAHO
20.5
47
WYOMING
22.1
49
S. DAKOTA
18.5
46
CALIFORNIA
39
17.4
NEVADA
16.7
39
UTAH
53
27.3
NEBRASKA
17.2
44
COLORADO
17.5
44
KANSAS
17.3
42
ARIZONA
41
18.4
NEW MEXICO
46
20.0
OKLAHOMA
17.3
TEXAS
19.1
44
ALASKA
53
24.3
HAWAII
45
18.6

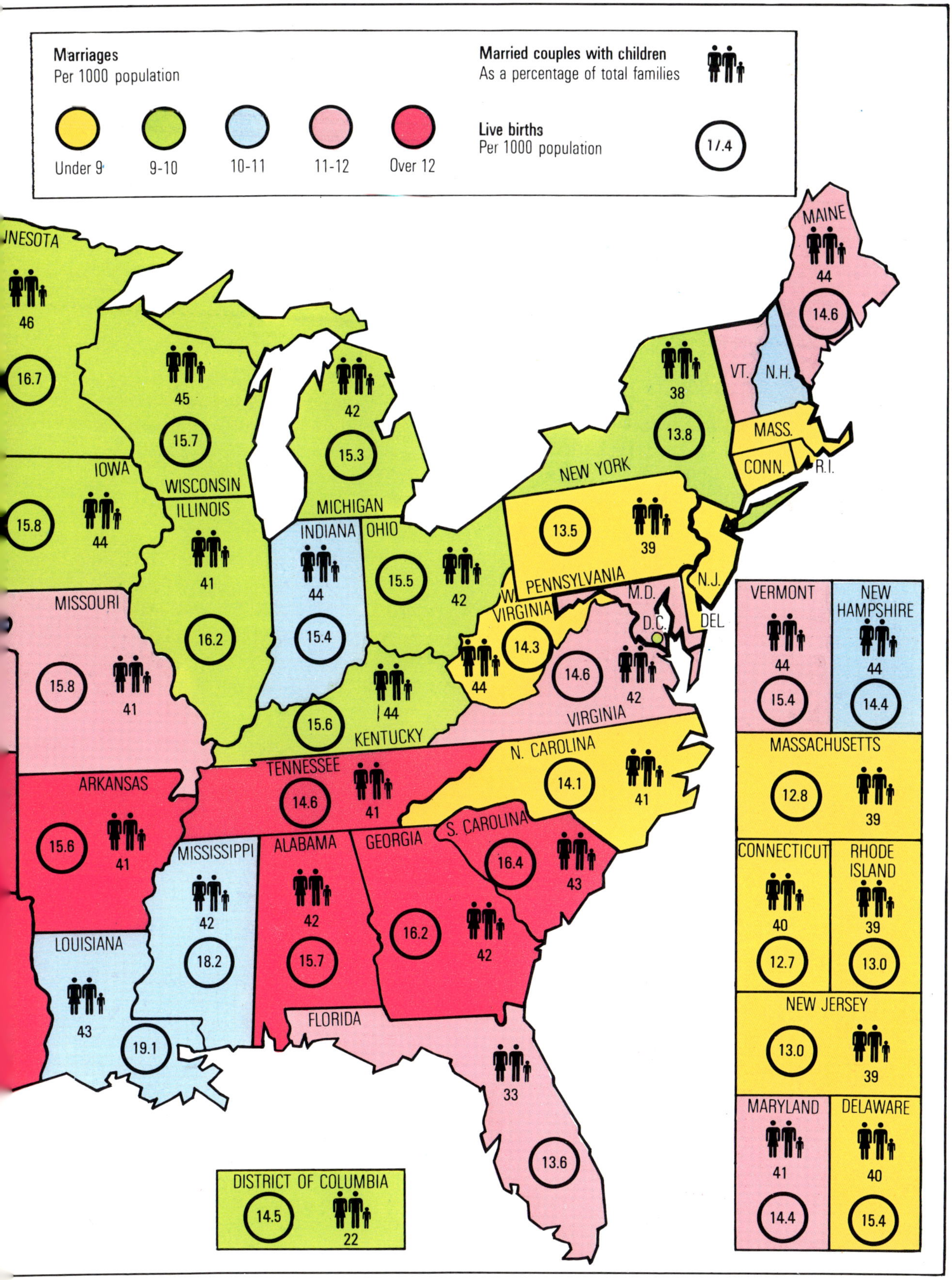
Marriages
Per 1000 population
Under 9
9-10
10-11
11-12
Over 12
Married couples with children
As a percentage of total families
Live births
Per 1000 population
17.4
INESOTA
46
16.7
WISCONSIN
45
15.7
MICHIGAN
42
15.3
IOWA
44
15.8
ILLINOIS
41
16.2
INDIANA
44
15.4
OHIO
42
15.5
MISSOURI
41
15.8
KENTUCKY
44
15.6
NEW YORK
38
13.8
PENNSYLVANIA
39
13.5
W. VIRGINIA
44
14.3
VIRGINIA
42
14.6
MAINE
44
14.6
VT.
N.H.
MASS.
CONN.
R.I.
N.J.
M.D.
D.C.
DEL
TENNESSEE
41
14.6
N. CAROLINA
41
14.1
ARKANSAS
41
15.6
MISSISSIPPI
42
18.2
ALABAMA
42
15.7
GEORGIA
42
16.2
S. CAROLINA
43
16.4
LOUISIANA
43
19.1
FLORIDA
33
13.6
DISTRICT OF COLUMBIA
14.5
22
VERMONT
44
15.4
NEW HAMPSHIRE
44
14.4
MASSACHUSETTS
12.8
39
CONNECTICUT
40
12.7
RHODE ISLAND
39
13.0
NEW JERSEY
13.0
39
MARYLAND
41
14.4
DELAWARE
40
15.4

THE FAMILY

This map deals with statistics about the family. States are coloured according to the number of marriages per 1,000 people in 1982. The average marriage rate for the whole country was 10.8.

It must be pointed out, that the rate for a state refers to the number of marriages *performed* there, related to the population *residing* in that state. This explains the anomalous figure for Nevada in particular, which recorded 123.9 marriages for every thousand residents in 1982. Apart from this state, marriage rates per thousand in 1982 ranged from 8.1 in New Jersey to 16.7 in South Carolina.

It should also be borne in mind that the marriage rate measured in this way is strongly affected by the age structure, that is, by the proportion of the population in the age groups most likely to be marrying. This is important when considering trends in the marriage rate, since the percentage of the population in the 25 to 44 year age group declined up to 1970, and then rose again.

The map also contains two symbols for each state. One indicates the number of married couples with children, as a percentage of all families. (The Bureau of the Census defines a family to be "a group of two or more persons related by birth, marriage, or adoption and residing together in a household.") The other symbol shows the birth rate per 1,000 people for 1981.

The variations between states are in all cases affected by their age distribution. So it is not surprising that the lowest figure for married couples with children per 100 families is 22 for the District of Columbia, followed by 33 for Florida.

Similarly, the fact that Alaska shows the second highest birth rate — 24.3 per 1,000 — is clearly related to the age distribution. Utah comes first with 27.3, while Connecticut has the lowest figure, 12.7 per 1,000 people.

Diagram A shows that, in 1983, 63.9 percent of the population aged 18 and over were married, a decline from the 1970 figure of 71.7 percent. Conversely 6.9 percent of people aged 18 and over in 1983 were divorced, compared with the 1970 figure of 3.2 percent. In 1970, there were 47 divorced people for every 1,000 married people, while in 1983 the figure had risen to 114.

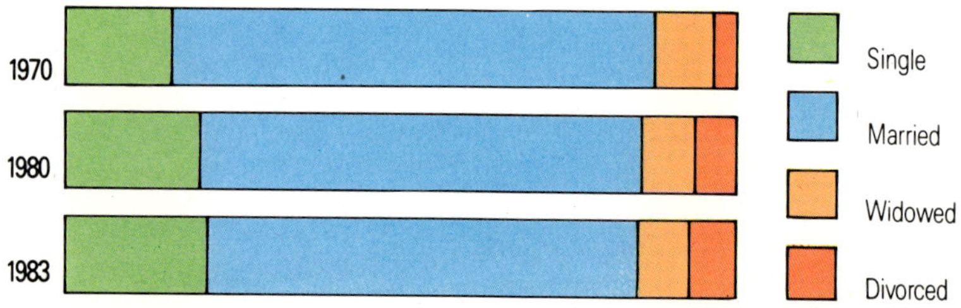

Diagram A: Marital status, 1970, 1980, and 1983

The rate of divorce per 1,000 of total population rose rapidly during the 1960s and early 1970s, from 2.2 in 1960, to 3.5 in 1970, reaching 4.8 in 1975. However, the rate of increase then slowed down. In 1981 the figure had reached 5.3; it then began to fall again, in 1982 to 5.1 and in 1983 to 5.0.

Diagram B graphs the marriage rate, per 1,000 unmarried women aged 15 and over, and the divorce rate, also expressed per 1,000 married women, aged 15 and over, from 1960 to 1981. The marriage rate reached its peak in 1969, and declined quite rapidly from 1973 to 1978. It then showed signs of rising again. The divorce rate expressed per 1,000 married women reached a peak of 22.8 in 1979.

Many states now report a "median duration of marriage" figure, and an estimate can be made for the country as a whole. In 1981 it was 7.0 years.

The median age at first marriage is also estimated by the Bureau of the Census. In 1981 it was 23.9 years for men and 22.0 for women. Both figures had shown a tendency to rise over the past two decades. In 1960, the median age for men was 22.8, that for women, 20.3.

The median age at remarriage, on the other hand, also estimated by the Bureau, has fallen. In 1965 it was 39.6 years for men, and 35.5 for women. In 1981 it was 35.3 for men, and 32.1 for women.

Diagram C shows the characteristics of family households in 1983, separating black and white. Almost 85 percent of white households included a married couple, compared to 53.4 percent of black households. In 12.2 percent of white households, the householder was a woman, with no spouse present. For black households, the percentage was 41.9. In the remaining 3.1 percent of white and 4.7 percent of black households, the householder was male, with no spouse present.

Sources: U.S. National Center for Health Statistics; U.S. Bureau of the Census

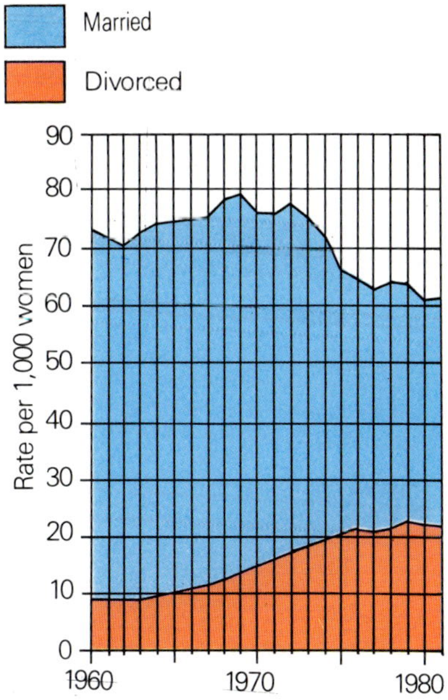

Diagram B: Marriage rate, per 1,000 unmarried women, and divorce rate, per 1,000 married women, 1960-1981

Diagram C: Distribution of family households by characteristics 1983

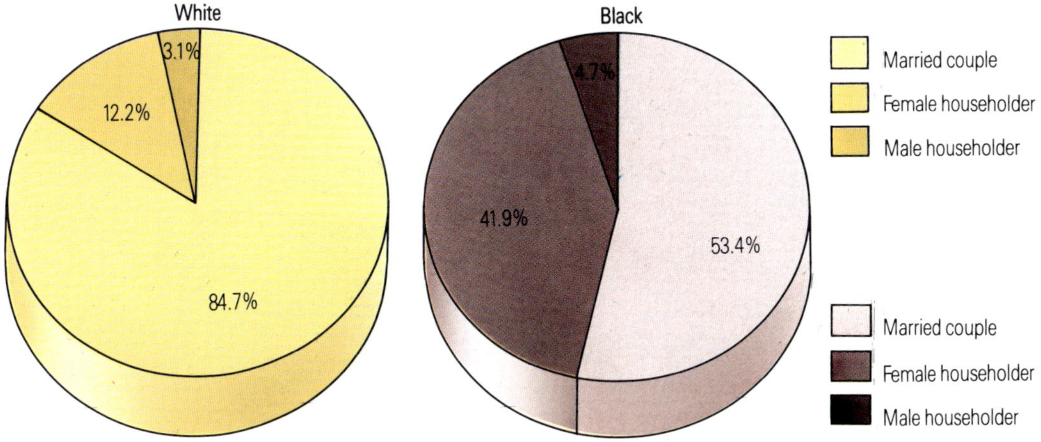

EDUCATIONAL ENROLLMENT

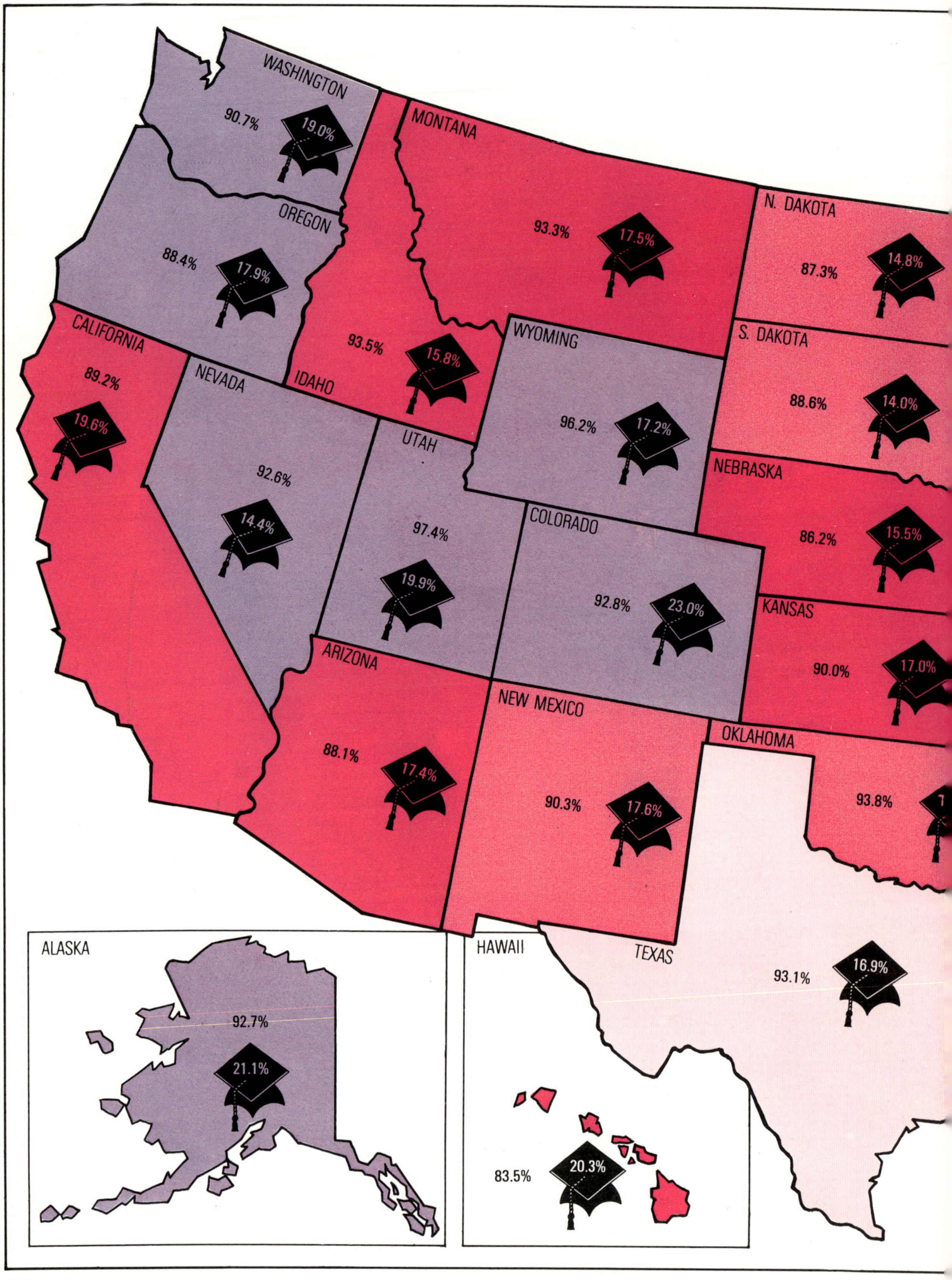

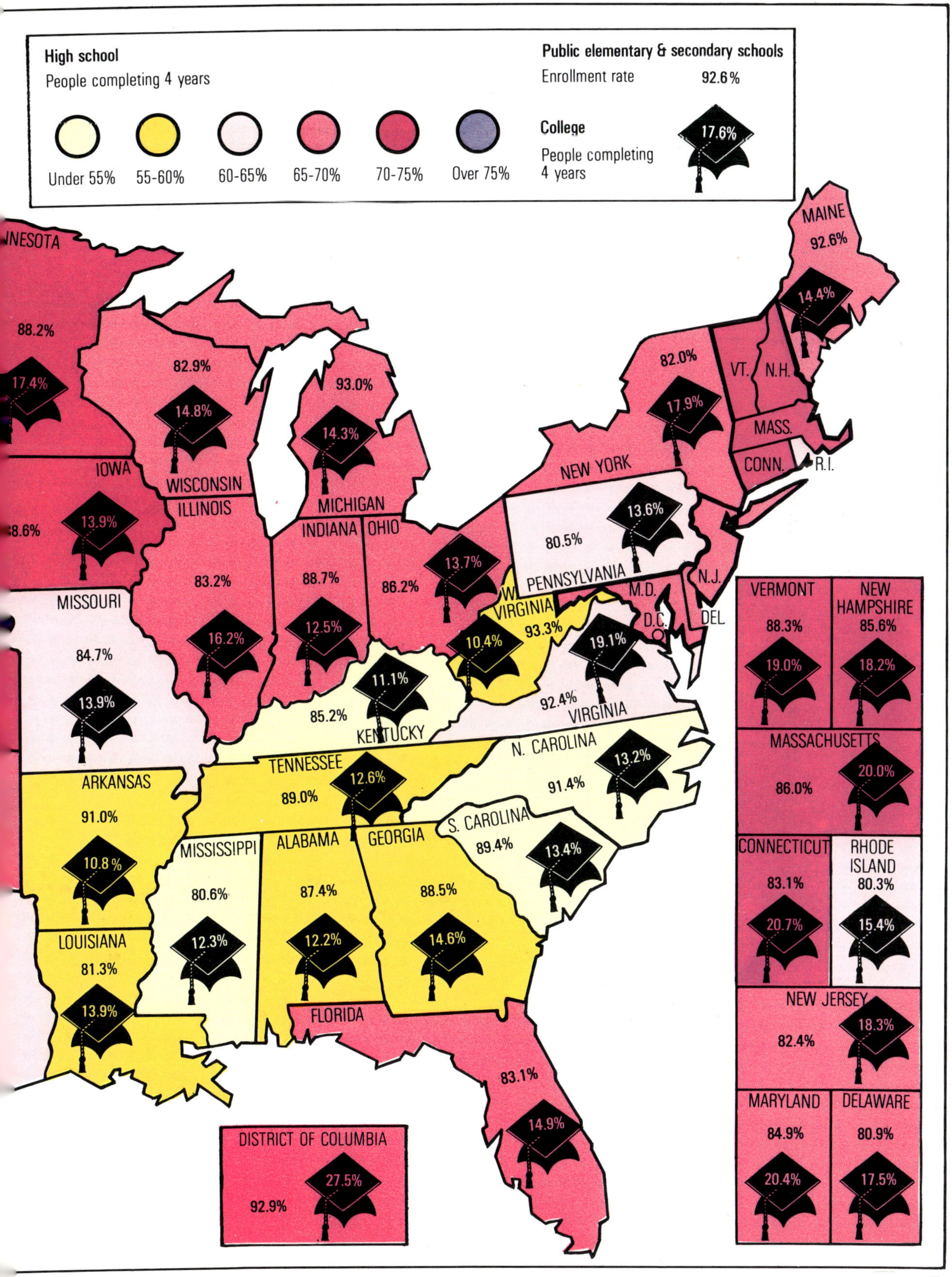

High school
People completing 4 years
Under 55%
55-60%
60-65%
65-70%
70-75%
Over 75%
Public elementary & secondary schools
Enrollment rate
92.6%
College
People completing 4 years
17.6%
MINNESOTA
88.2%
17.4%
IOWA
88.6%
13.9%
WISCONSIN
82.9%
14.8%
MICHIGAN
93.0%
14.3%
ILLINOIS
83.2%
16.2%
INDIANA
88.7%
12.5%
OHIO
86.2%
13.7%
MISSOURI
84.7%
13.9%
NEW YORK
82.0%
17.9%
PENNSYLVANIA
80.5%
13.6%
MAINE
92.6%
14.4%
VT.
N.H.
MASS.
CONN.
R.I.
N.J.
M.D.
D.C.
DEL
W. VIRGINIA
93.3%
10.4%
VIRGINIA
92.4%
19.1%
KENTUCKY
85.2%
11.1%
TENNESSEE
89.0%
12.6%
N. CAROLINA
91.4%
13.2%
S. CAROLINA
89.4%
13.4%
ARKANSAS
91.0%
10.8%
LOUISIANA
81.3%
13.9%
MISSISSIPPI
80.6%
12.3%
ALABAMA
87.4%
12.2%
GEORGIA
88.5%
14.6%
FLORIDA
83.1%
14.9%
DISTRICT OF COLUMBIA
92.9%
27.5%
VERMONT
88.3%
19.0%
NEW HAMPSHIRE
85.6%
18.2%
MASSACHUSETTS
86.0%
20.0%
CONNECTICUT
83.1%
20.7%
RHODE ISLAND
80.3%
15.4%
NEW JERSEY
82.4%
18.3%
MARYLAND
84.9%
20.4%
DELAWARE
80.9%
17.5%

EDUCATIONAL ENROLLMENT

On this map, the states are coloured according to the percentage of adults – 25 years and over – in 1980, who had completed at least 4 years of high school education. Nationwide, this percentage was 66.5, but there is a considerable variation between the states.

In Kentucky 53.1 percent of adults had completed 4 years of high school, and in Mississippi 54.8 percent, while 80 percent of Utah adults had reached this level of education, exceeded only by Alaska's 82.5 percent.

The map also shows two other percentages for each state: the enrollment rate in public elementary and secondary schools, and the percentage of adults who had completed 4 years or more of college. The enrollment rate expresses the number of schoolchildren in autumn 1982 as a percentage of the number of children aged between 5 and 17 years. Rhode Island shows the lowest enrollment rate, at 80.3 percent, followed by Pennsylvania, with 80.5 percent. At the other end of the scale, Utah again stands out with 97.4, followed by Wyoming, with 96.2. The average for the whole country was 87.3.

The percentage of people with 4 years' college education, which was 16.2 percent nationwide in 1980, was highest in the District of Columbia, where 27.5 percent of adults had attained this educational level. Next came Colorado, with 23 percent. Lowest were Arkansas, with 10.8, and Kentucky, with 11.1 percent.

Diagram A traces the history of school enrollment for the years 1960 to 1983, showing the total numbers of pupils, and the numbers in elementary and high schools, and in colleges. The numbers reflect changes in the age structure over the post-war period, as well as changes in educational standards.

Diagram A: School enrollment, by level of instruction, 1960-1983

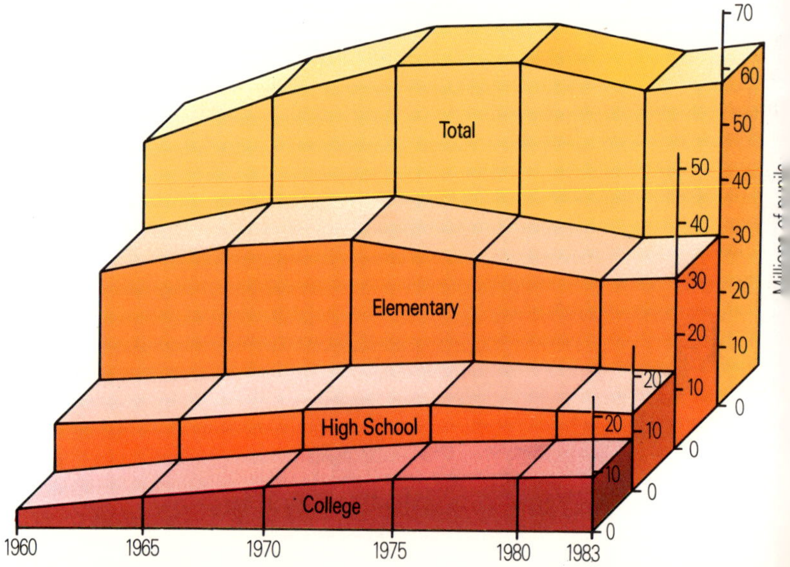

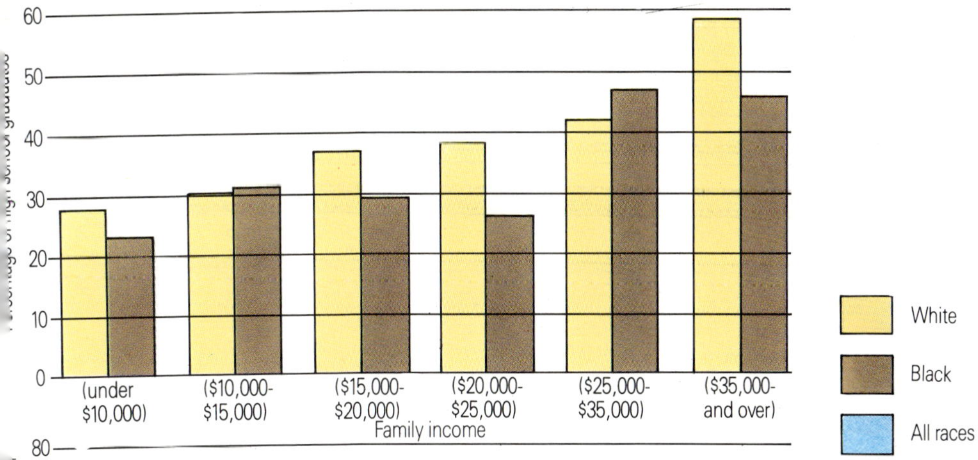

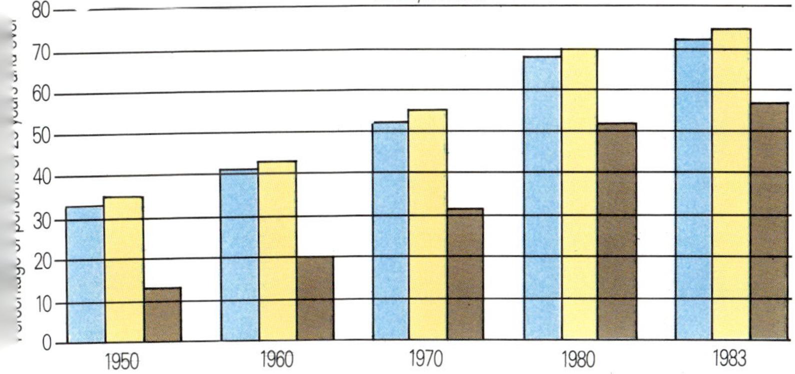

Diagram B: Percentage of high school graduates enrolling in college, by family income, 1983. Figures are for dependent family members, 18-24 years old

Diagram C: Percentage of adults — 25 years or over — who have completed 4 years or more of high school education, 1950-1983

In 1980, 42 percent of the population aged between 16 and 24 were enrolled in school. In 1950, this percentage was only 27. Most striking was the rise in the number of girls who continued their education. In 1950, 103,000 women were awarded bachelor's degrees, and 329,000 men, but in 1982 the women obtaining bachelor's degrees outnumbered men, by 480,000 to 473,000.

Enrollment rates are strongly affected by family income and by race. Diagram B shows the percentage of high school graduates aged 18 to 24, broken down into black people and white people, and into family income groups. While 27.9 percent of high school graduates from families with an annual income of under $10,000 were in college, the percentage rose to 58.2 percent for the "$35,000 and over" group.

The overall percentage for black people is lower than that for white people, but this difference is not found in every income group. Diagram C also bears on the difference in educational levels achieved by black people and white people in the period 1950-1983. While, at the start of this period, the percentage of black people aged 25 or over who had completed 4 years or more of high school was far smaller than the percentage of white people, the gap has decreased steadily as the overall percentage has increased.

Sources: U.S. Bureau of the Census;
U.S. National Center for Education Statistics

EDUCATION RESOURCES

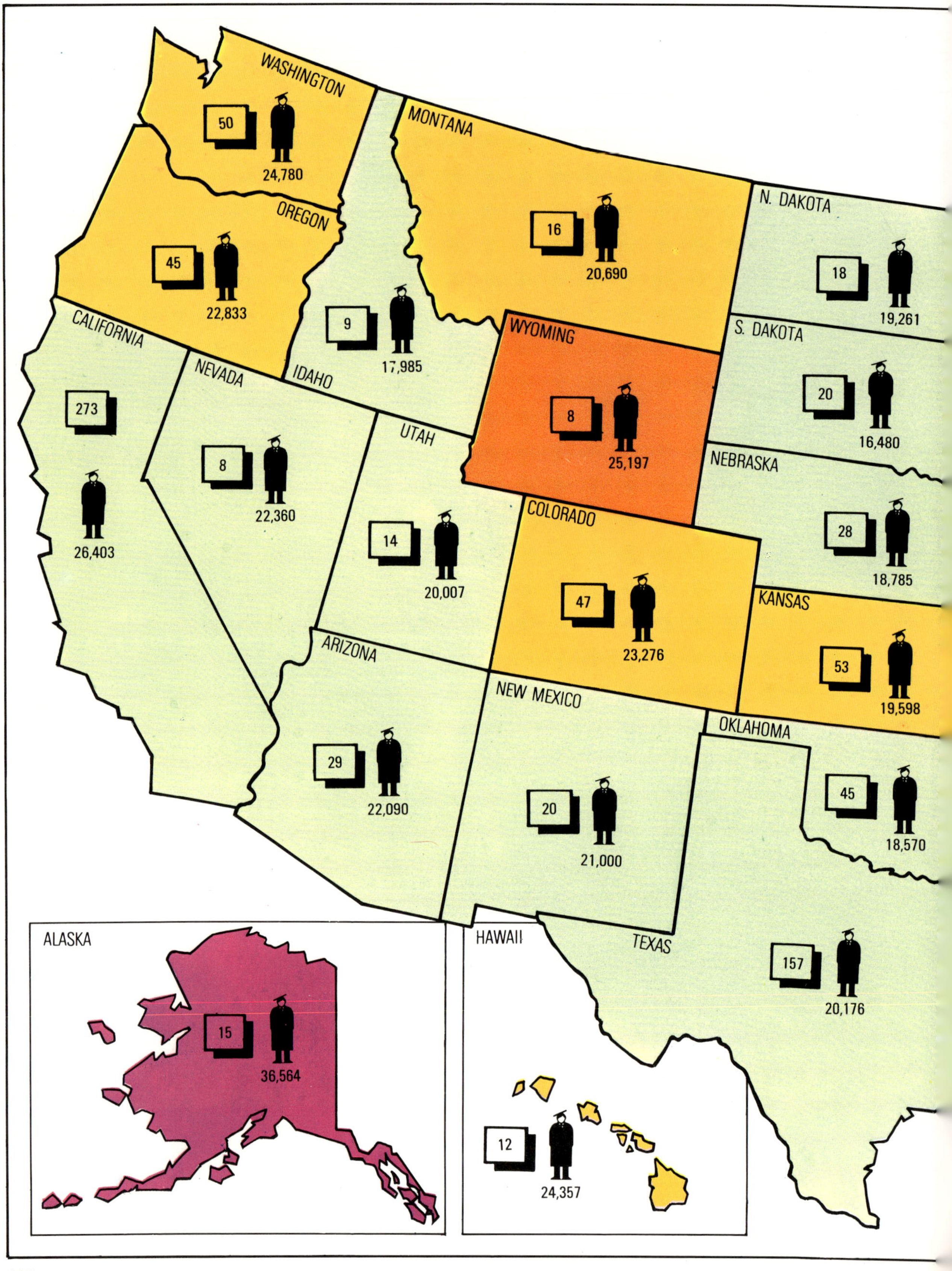

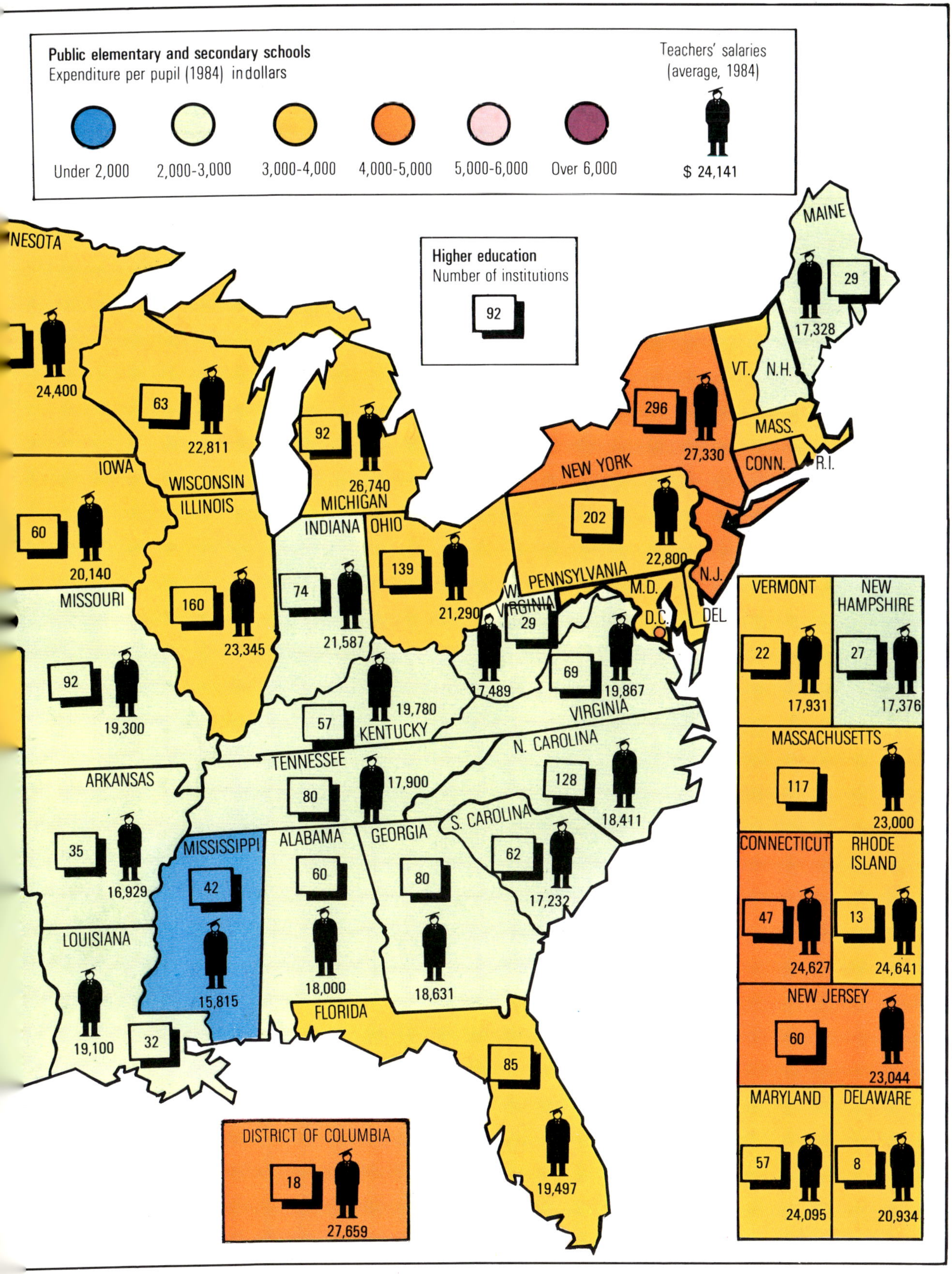

Public elementary and secondary schools
Expenditure per pupil (1984) in dollars
Under 2,000
2,000-3,000
3,000-4,000
4,000-5,000
5,000-6,000
Over 6,000
Teachers' salaries (average, 1984)
$ 24,141
Higher education
Number of institutions
92
MAINE
29
17,328
VT.
N.H.
MASS.
CONN.
R.I.
NEW YORK
296
27,330
PENNSYLVANIA
202
22,800
N.J.
M.D.
D.C.
DEL
NESOTA
24,400
WISCONSIN
63
22,811
MICHIGAN
92
26,740
IOWA
60
20,140
ILLINOIS
160
23,345
INDIANA
74
21,587
OHIO
139
21,290
W. VIRGINIA
29
17,489
VIRGINIA
69
19,867
MISSOURI
92
19,300
KENTUCKY
57
19,780
TENNESSEE
80
17,900
N. CAROLINA
128
18,411
ARKANSAS
35
16,929
MISSISSIPPI
42
15,815
ALABAMA
60
18,000
GEORGIA
80
18,631
S. CAROLINA
62
17,232
LOUISIANA
19,100
32
FLORIDA
85
19,497
DISTRICT OF COLUMBIA
18
27,659
VERMONT
22
17,931
NEW HAMPSHIRE
27
17,376
MASSACHUSETTS
117
23,000
CONNECTICUT
47
24,627
RHODE ISLAND
13
24,641
NEW JERSEY
60
23,044
MARYLAND
57
24,095
DELAWARE
8
20,934

EDUCATION RESOURCES

This map shows information about the resources devoted to education. States are coloured to represent the 1984 expenditure per pupil, according to the average daily attendance at public elementary and secondary schools.

Alaska had the highest expenditure per pupil, $7,026. This is far above the second highest, New Jersey, which spent $4,943 per pupil. At the other end of the scale, Mississippi spent $1,962 per pupil in 1984. The average for the entire country was $3,173.

Diagram A presents expenditure per capita in 1982 for each state, in descending order. Wyoming comes first on this list, spending $724 per pupil. Some way behind is New York State, with $564. At the bottom are Kentucky, with $328 per pupil, and Mississippi with $317.

Also shown on the map for each state are average teachers' salaries for the year ending in June 1984. This figure covers all teachers in public elementary and secondary schools. The national average was $22,000, but there is a remarkable variation in teachers' salaries between different parts of the country. In

Diagram A: Per capita expenditure on education, 1982, by state

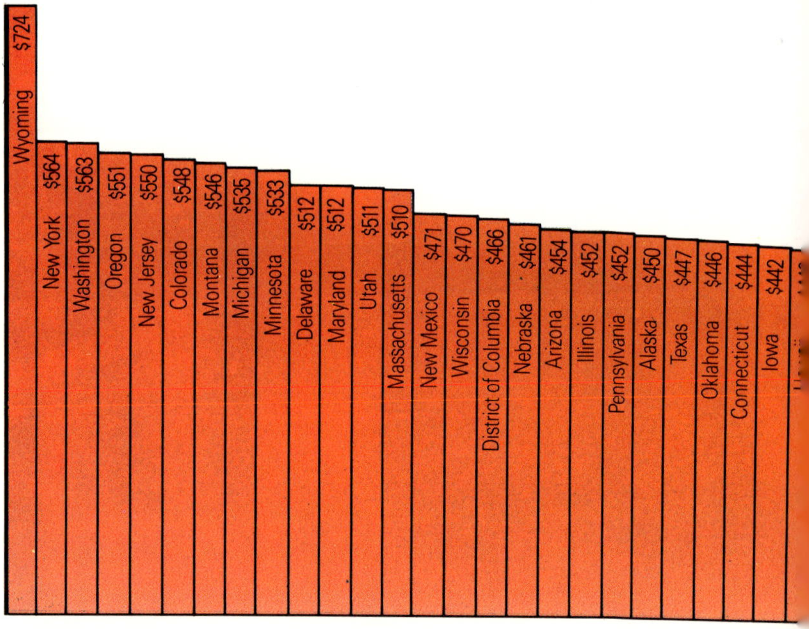

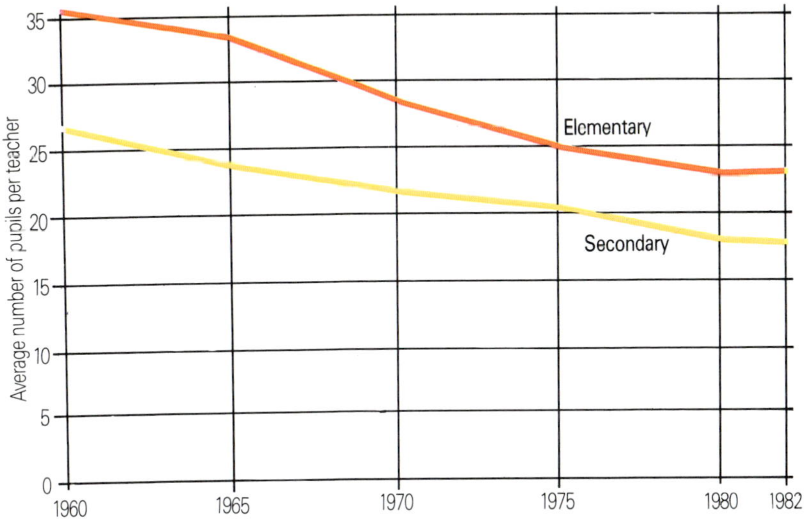

Diagram B: Average number of pupils per teacher in public elementary and secondary schools, 1960-1982

Alaska, the average salary was $36,564. The District of Columbia came next with $27,659, followed by New York State at $27,330. In South Dakota, on the other hand, teachers averaged $16,480 per year, and in Arkansas, $16,929.

Diagram B graphs the number of children per teacher. This "pupil-teacher ratio" has fallen fairly steadily over the period, and further falls are projected in the next decade.

The map also gives the number of institutions of higher education in 1982 for each state. This covers universities, colleges, professional schools, and junior and teachers' colleges. There was a total of 3,280 such institutions in the United States in 1982, with a total enrollment of 8.58 million. Of these, 296 were in New York State, and 273 in California.

Source: U.S. National Center for Education Statistics

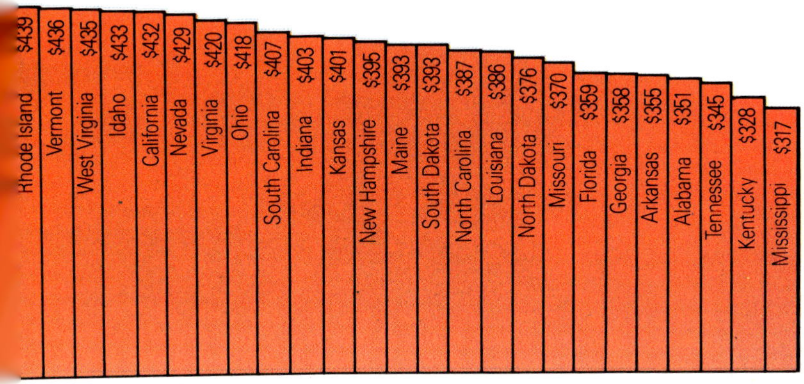

PUBLIC HEALTH

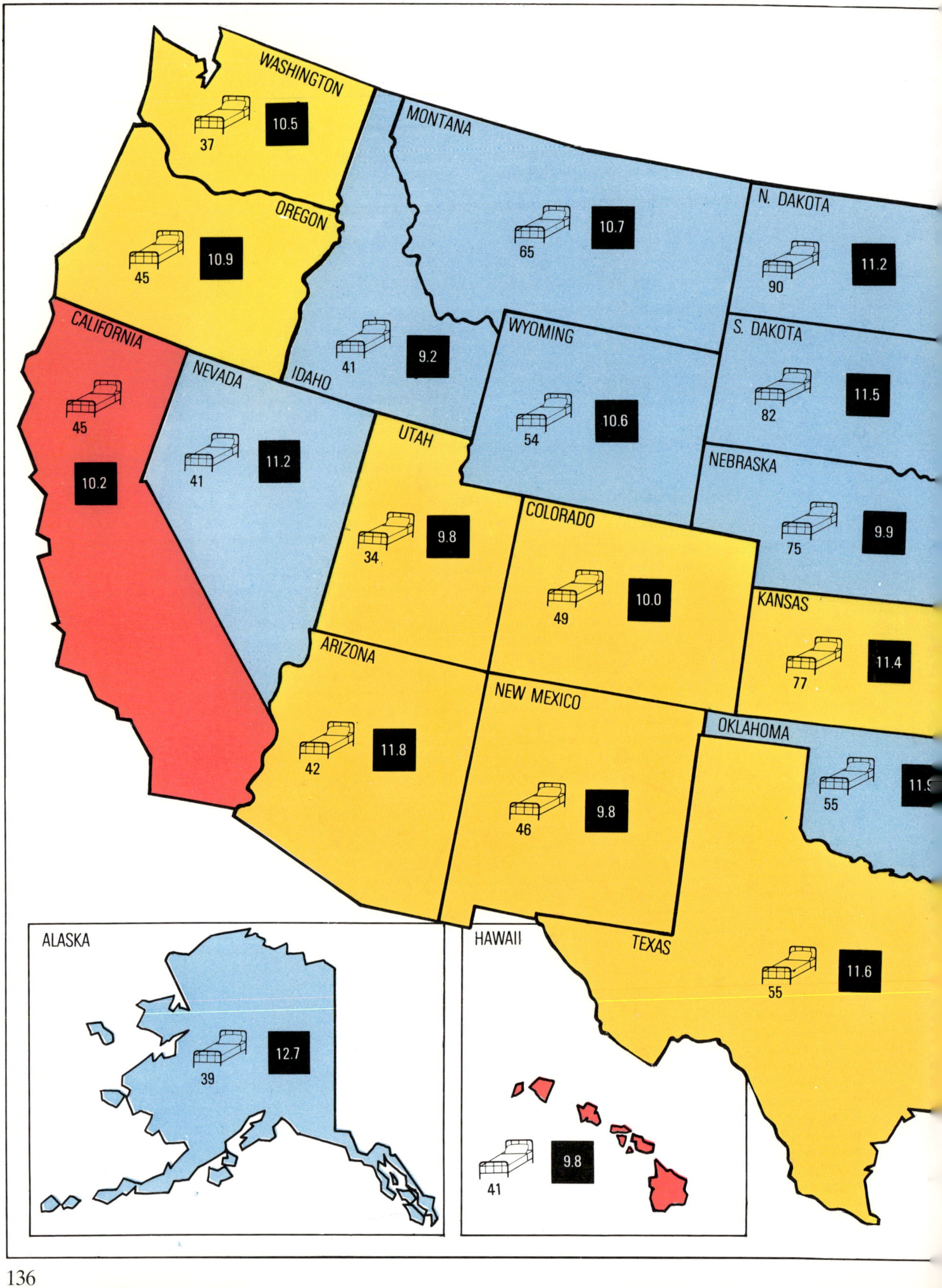

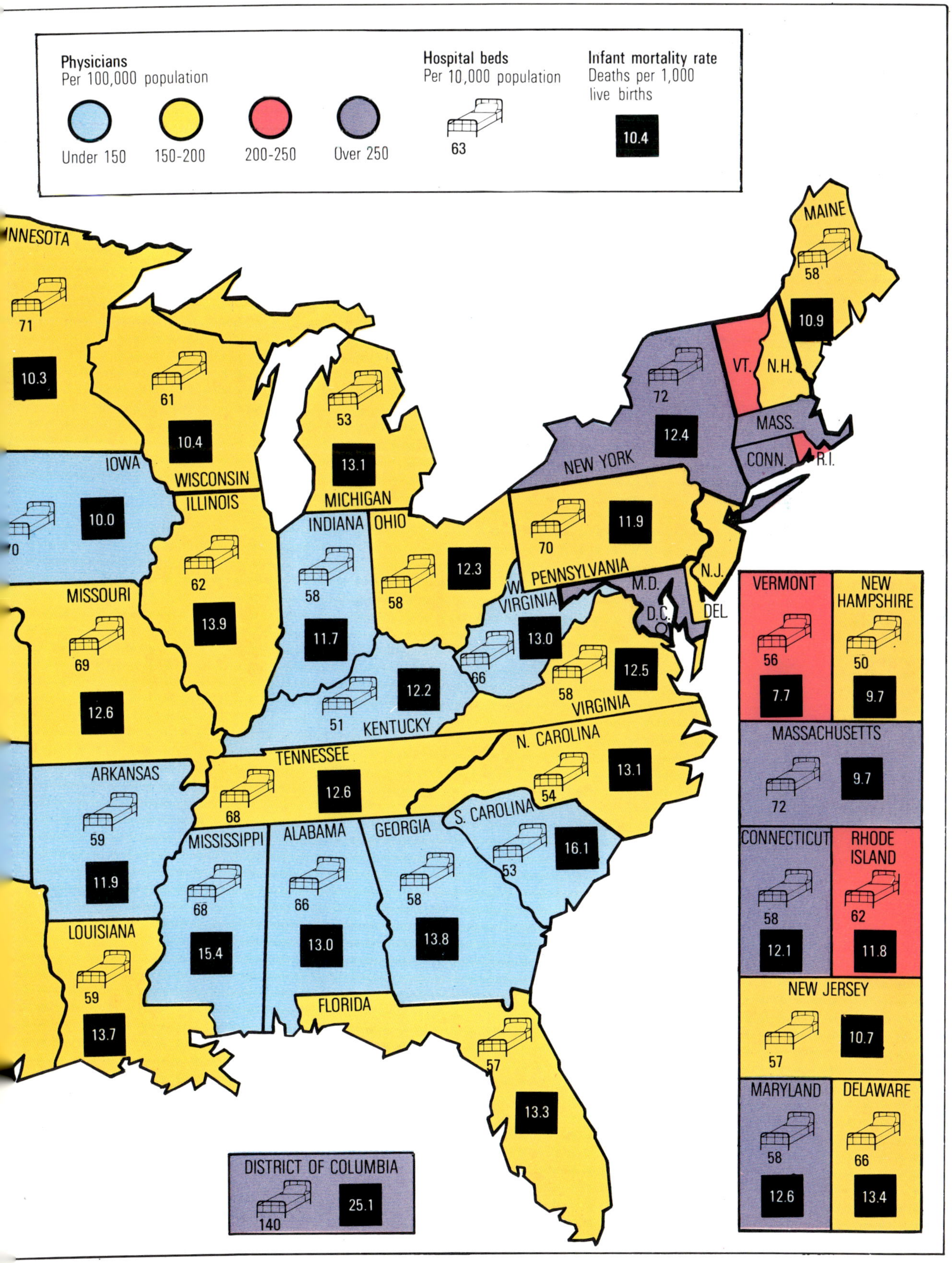
Physicians
Per 100,000 population
Under 150
150-200
200-250
Over 250
Hospital beds
Per 10,000 population
63
Infant mortality rate
Deaths per 1,000
live births
10.4
INNESOTA
71
10.3
WISCONSIN
61
10.4
MICHIGAN
53
13.1
IOWA
10.0
ILLINOIS
62
13.9
INDIANA
58
11.7
OHIO
58
12.3
MISSOURI
69
12.6
KENTUCKY
51
12.2
W. VIRGINIA
66
13.0
VIRGINIA
58
12.5
PENNSYLVANIA
70
11.9
NEW YORK
72
12.4
MAINE
58
10.9
VT.
N.H.
MASS.
CONN.
R.I.
N.J.
M.D.
D.C.
DEL
TENNESSEE
68
12.6
N. CAROLINA
54
13.1
ARKANSAS
59
11.9
S. CAROLINA
53
16.1
MISSISSIPPI
68
15.4
ALABAMA
66
13.0
GEORGIA
58
13.8
LOUISIANA
59
13.7
FLORIDA
57
13.3
DISTRICT OF COLUMBIA
140
25.1
VERMONT
56
7.7
NEW HAMPSHIRE
50
9.7
MASSACHUSETTS
72
9.7
CONNECTICUT
58
12.1
RHODE ISLAND
62
11.8
NEW JERSEY
57
10.7
MARYLAND
58
12.6
DELAWARE
66
13.4

PUBLIC HEALTH

In 1983 the total expenditure on the nation's health amounted to over $355 billion, or $1,459 per capita (and 11 percent of the GNP). In 1960 the expenditure per capita was exactly one-tenth of that (and 5 percent of the GNP). Allowing for inflation, the cost of health services and supplies rose during the 1960s and 1970s and, according to informed forecasts, is likely to go on rising.

The map provides three general indicators of health and health services: the ratio of physicians to total population, the availability of hospital beds, and infant mortality rates.

The ratio of physicians to total population is generally high, and highest of all in the Northeast and California, traditionally prosperous regions with high urban population. The true figures are probably slightly higher than the map suggests since certain small categories, such as physicians in federal employment or doctors of osteopathy, are excluded.

In general, there are fewer differences between the states in health care now than there were one or two generations ago. Thus, the availability of hospital beds is reasonably consistent nationwide (the national average is 6 beds per 1,000 people), and the comparatively low figure in Alaska, for example, may be largely explained by the low proportion of elderly Alaskans. The term "hospital" here encompasses all institutions registered by the American Hospital Association (approximately 7,000 in all), including psychiatric and other specialized hospitals.

Infant mortality rates are used all over the world as an indication of health care. They represent babies that were born alive but died before their first birthday. These figures are encouraging inasmuch as they show an improvement of 40 percent in the decade ending in 1981. Moreover, the gap between white and black

Diagram A: Life expectancy at birth, 1920-1980

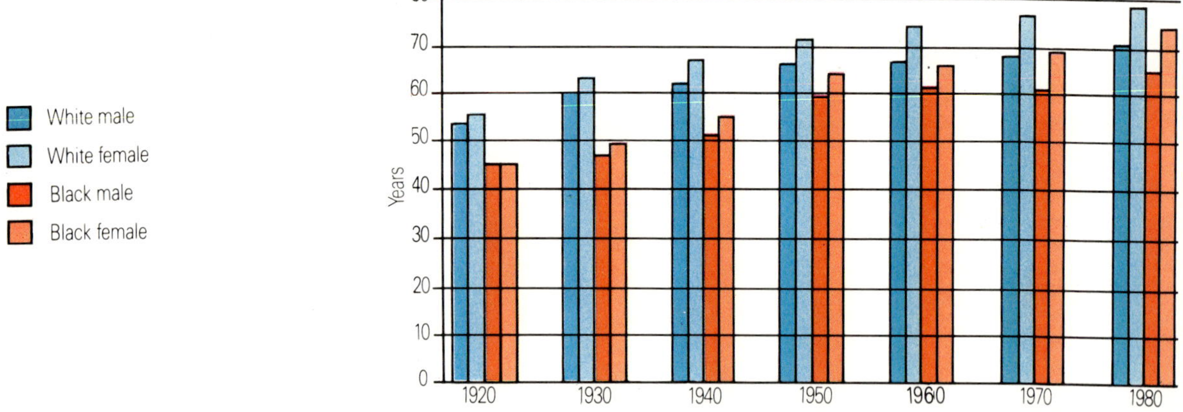

people has tended to close, although the mortality rate is still markedly higher among black babies.

It is largely this fact that explains the very high figure for infant mortality in the District of Columbia (notwithstanding its high proportion of hospital beds) and contributes to the relatively high figures in the South. Every southern state has a rate higher than the national average, with Mississippi the highest at 15 per thousand live births.

Diagram A shows the life expectancy at birth for white and black people. Although the life expectancy at birth of a black male is still six years less than that of a white male, it has improved. The figures overall are inspiring: general life expectancy has increased from 54 to 74 years in half a century.

Diagram B lays out, in broad categories, expenditure on health services and supplies in 1983. This category includes personal expenses, hospital care, physicians', dentists', and other professional services, drugs, eyeglasses, home nursing and other services, but not medical research or building works, etc. The gap between private and public (federal, state, local) expenditure has narrowed considerably in recent years. In 1960, before the introduction of Medicare, public expenditure amounted to less than 21 percent of the total; by 1980 this percentage had almost doubled.

A notable feature of private expenditure is the rising cost of medical insurance. In 1960 insurance premiums accounted for less than 45 percent of total expenditure in the private sector. In 1983 they accounted for over 55 percent.

Source: U.S. National Center for Health Statistics

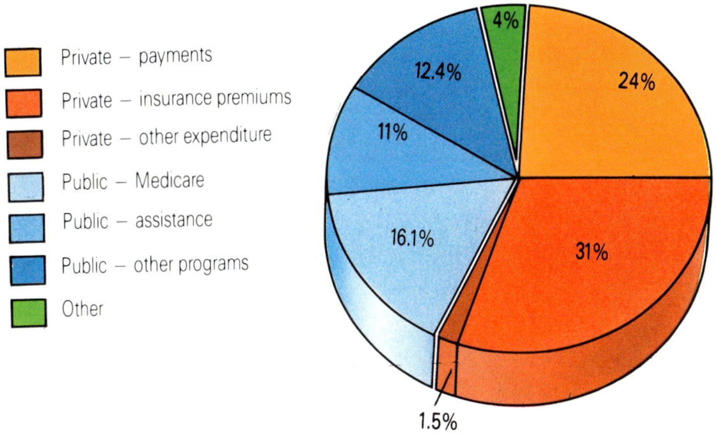

Diagram B: National health expenditure, 1983

CRIME

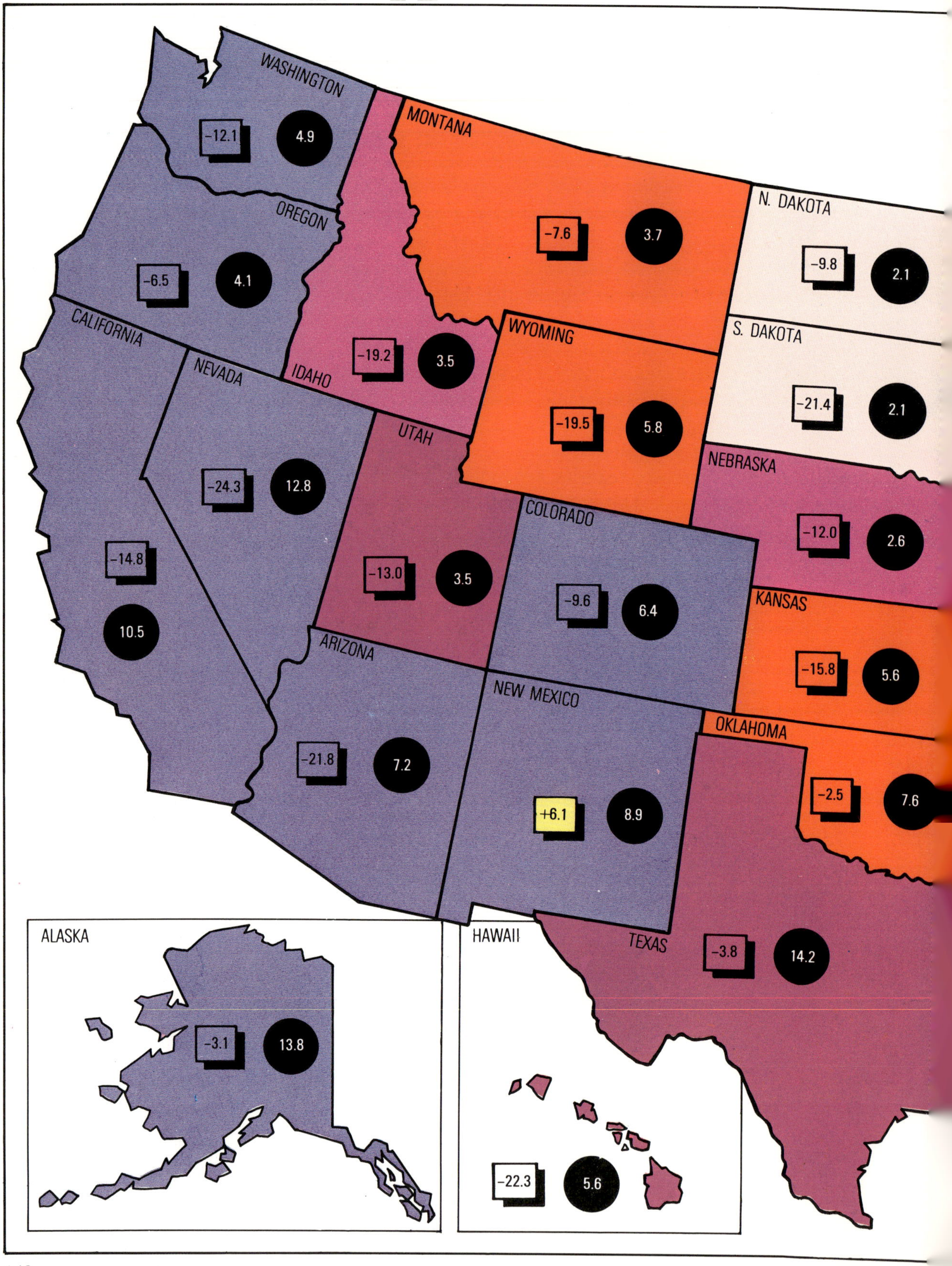

WASHINGTON
-12.1
4.9
MONTANA
-7.6
3.7
N. DAKOTA
-9.8
2.1
OREGON
-6.5
4.1
IDAHO
-19.2
3.5
WYOMING
-19.5
5.8
S. DAKOTA
-21.4
2.1
CALIFORNIA
-14.8
10.5
NEVADA
-24.3
12.8
UTAH
-13.0
3.5
COLORADO
-9.6
6.4
NEBRASKA
-12.0
2.6
KANSAS
-15.8
5.6
ARIZONA
-21.8
7.2
NEW MEXICO
+6.1
8.9
OKLAHOMA
-2.5
7.6
TEXAS
-3.8
14.2
ALASKA
-3.1
13.8
HAWAII
-22.3
5.6

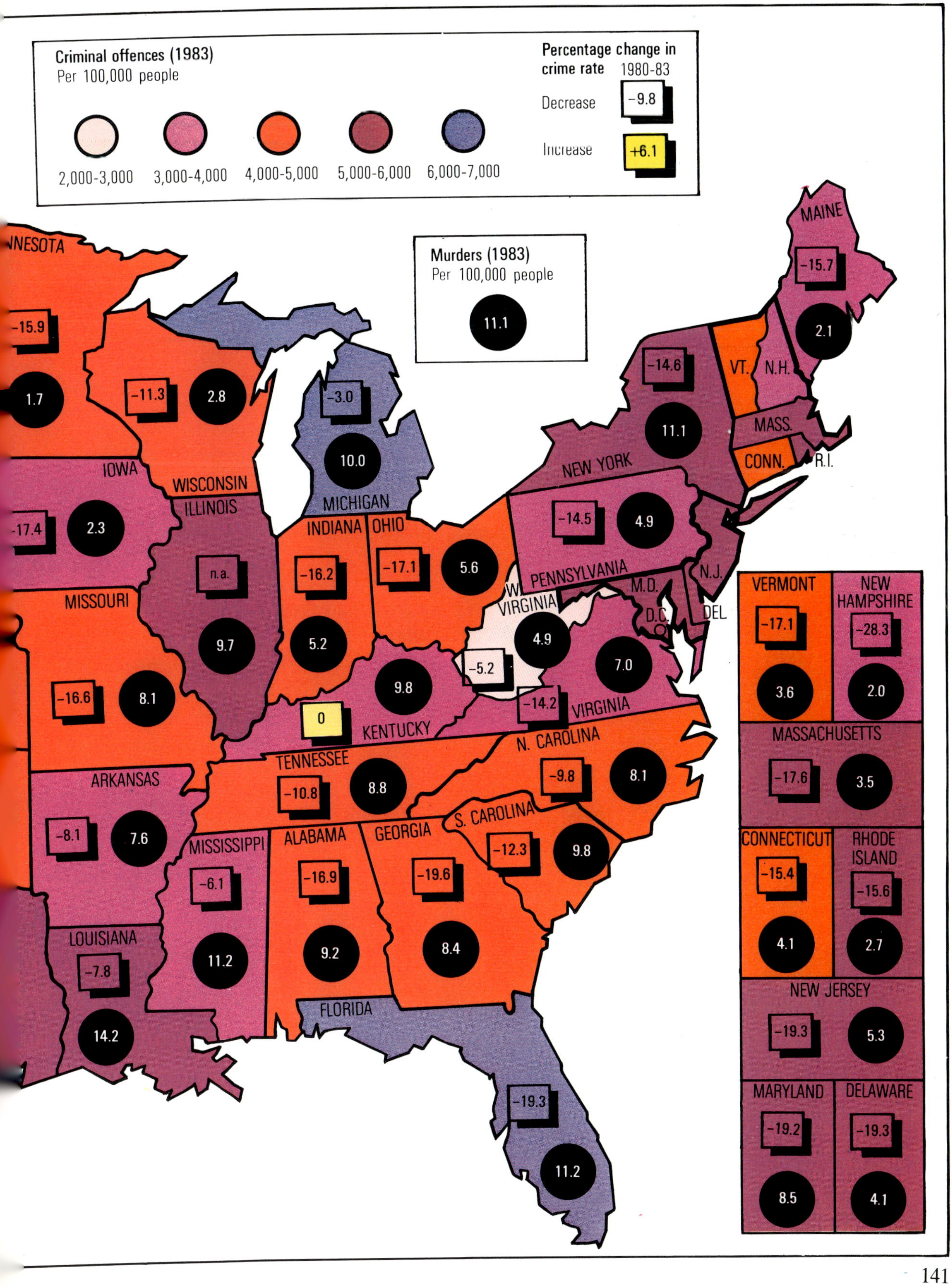
Criminal offences (1983)
Per 100,000 people
2,000-3,000
3,000-4,000
4,000-5,000
5,000-6,000
6,000-7,000
Percentage change in crime rate 1980-83
Decrease
-9.8
Increase
+6.1
Murders (1983)
Per 100,000 people
11.1
NNESOTA
-15.9
1.7
-11.3
2.8
WISCONSIN
-3.0
10.0
MICHIGAN
IOWA
-17.4
2.3
ILLINOIS
n.a.
9.7
INDIANA
-16.2
5.2
OHIO
-17.1
5.6
MISSOURI
-16.6
8.1
KENTUCKY
0
9.8
W. VIRGINIA
-5.2
4.9
VIRGINIA
-14.2
7.0
PENNSYLVANIA
-14.5
4.9
NEW YORK
-14.6
11.1
MAINE
-15.7
2.1
VT.
N.H.
MASS.
CONN.
R.I.
N.J.
M.D.
D.C.
DEL
TENNESSEE
-10.8
8.8
N. CAROLINA
-9.8
8.1
S. CAROLINA
-12.3
9.8
ARKANSAS
-8.1
7.6
MISSISSIPPI
-6.1
11.2
ALABAMA
-16.9
9.2
GEORGIA
-19.6
8.4
LOUISIANA
-7.8
14.2
FLORIDA
-19.3
11.2
VERMONT
-17.1
3.6
NEW HAMPSHIRE
-28.3
2.0
MASSACHUSETTS
-17.6
3.5
CONNECTICUT
-15.4
4.1
RHODE ISLAND
-15.6
2.7
NEW JERSEY
-19.3
5.3
MARYLAND
-19.2
8.5
DELAWARE
-19.3
4.1

CRIME

This map deals with crime and law enforcement. States are coloured according to the number of criminal offences known to the police, per 100,000 population in 1983. The average for the entire country was 5,159.

The crime rate for individual states varies from 2,419 for West Virginia, to 6,251 for California. Variations in the crime rate closely match the varying degrees of urbanization. The rate of crime in metropolitan areas in 1983 averaged 5,852, while the rate in rural areas was 1,881 offences per 100,000 population.

Diagram A graphs the rate of all criminal offences, including non-violent crimes in the period 1974-1983. The rate has decreased since 1980 for every category of crime. On the map, the percentage fall in the crime rate is shown for each state.

Diagram B is a pie chart showing the distribution of serious criminal offences between various categories of crime according to arrests. Larceny (theft of property without use of force or fraud) forms the largest category, making up 56 percent of the total. Burglary comes next, at 19 percent. Violent crimes (comprising murder, forcible rape, robbery and aggravated assault) make up 21 percent of all serious criminal offences.

The contrast between metropolitan and rural areas is more striking in the incidence of violent crime than for crime in general. In metropolitan areas in 1983, there were 627 violent crimes per 100,000 population, compared with 161 in rural areas. In cities with populations of 250,000 or more, the rate for violent crime was 1,294, and for "property crime" 7,345 offences per 100,000 people.

Detroit, Michigan, had the highest rate of violent crime in 1983: 2,169 per 100,000 residents. It was followed by Baltimore, Maryland, at 2,003, and Washington, D.C. at 1,915.

There were a total of 10.3 million arrests for serious crimes in 1983: 74 percent of these were of people in the 18-44 year age

Diagram A: Crime rate showing violent and property crimes, 1974-1983. The area marked in red represents violent crime

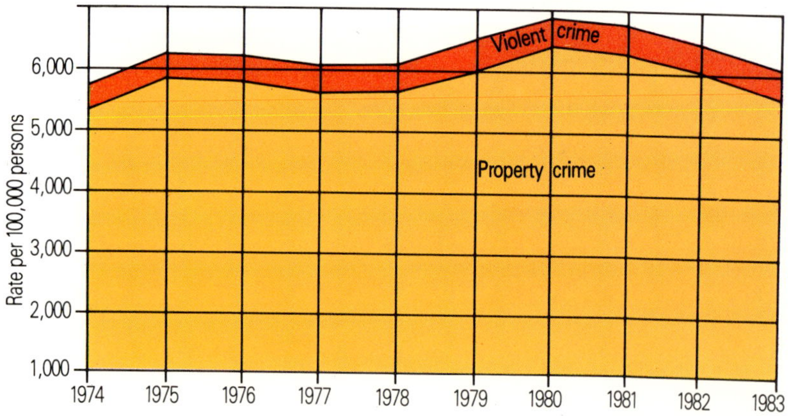

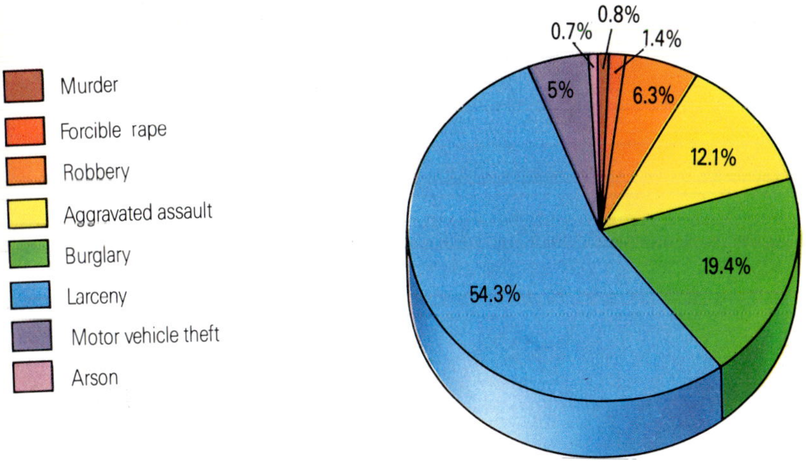

Diagram B: Distribution of criminal offences by type of crime, 1983

group, and 83 percent were males. The proportion of persons arrested who were under 18 has been declining steadily since the mid-1970s, while the proportion in the 18-44 year age group has been rising.

In 1982, 608,000 persons were in locally operated jails or in state or federal prisons — 38 for every 10,000 adult residents. There were 1,287,300 people under the supervisory authority of a probation agency. In 1983, 11,896 persons were released from their first term of imprisonment in a federal institution. On average they had served 15.9 months of an average sentence of 35.4 months.

Diagram C graphs the number of prisoners in federal and state prisons, per 100,000 population, from 1950 to 1983. This rate fell during the 1960s, but thereafter rose rapidly. In 1983, there were well over twice as many prisoners as in 1970.

In 1981, Juvenile Courts disposed of 1.35 million delinquency cases, 44 for every 1,000 people in the 10-17 years age group. This was an improvement on the 1980 figure, when the rate was 46.4. However, in 1960, the rate was 20.1. At that time 19.3 percent of these cases concerned girls, but in 1981 the percentage had risen to 24.0.

Sources: U.S. Federal Bureau of Investigation;
U.S. Bureau of Justice Statistics

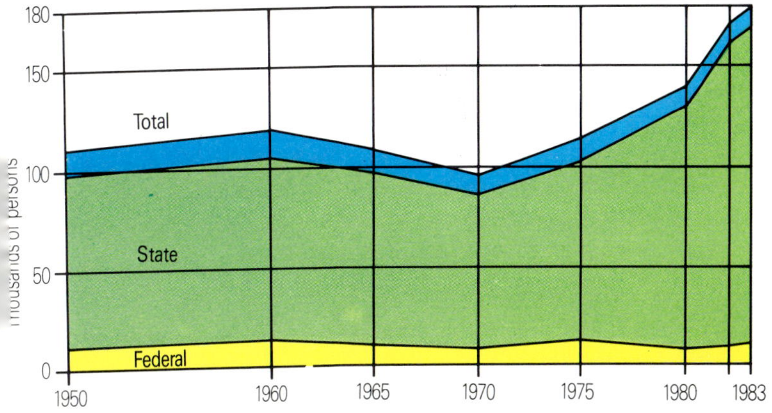

Diagram C: Federal and state prisoners, 1950-1983

ELECTIONS

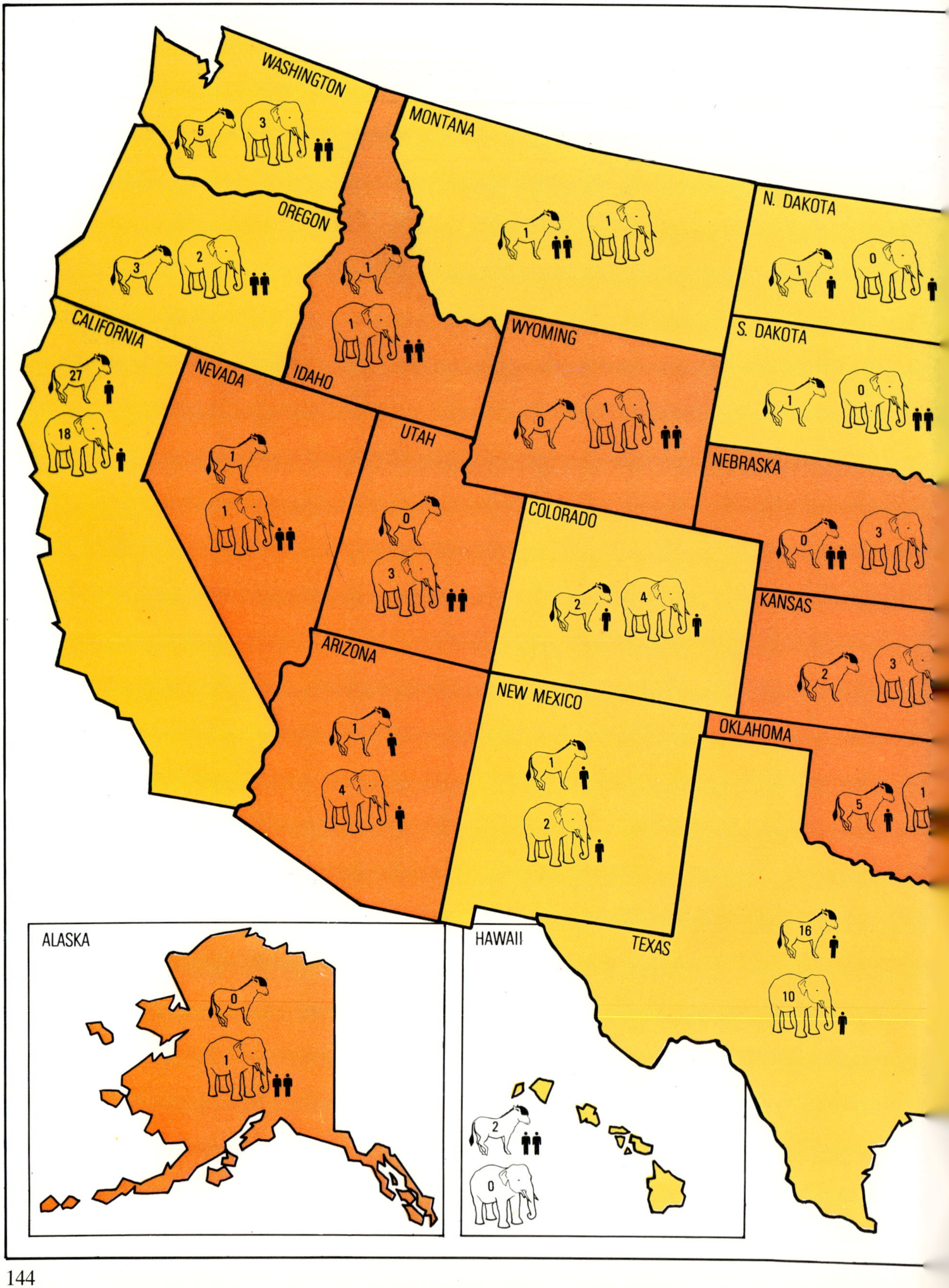
WASHINGTON
5
3
OREGON
3
2
CALIFORNIA
27
18
IDAHO
1
1
MONTANA
1
1
N. DAKOTA
1
0
S. DAKOTA
1
0
WYOMING
0
1
NEVADA
1
1
UTAH
0
3
NEBRASKA
0
3
COLORADO
2
4
KANSAS
2
3
ARIZONA
1
4
NEW MEXICO
1
2
OKLAHOMA
5
TEXAS
16
10
ALASKA
0
1
HAWAII
2
0

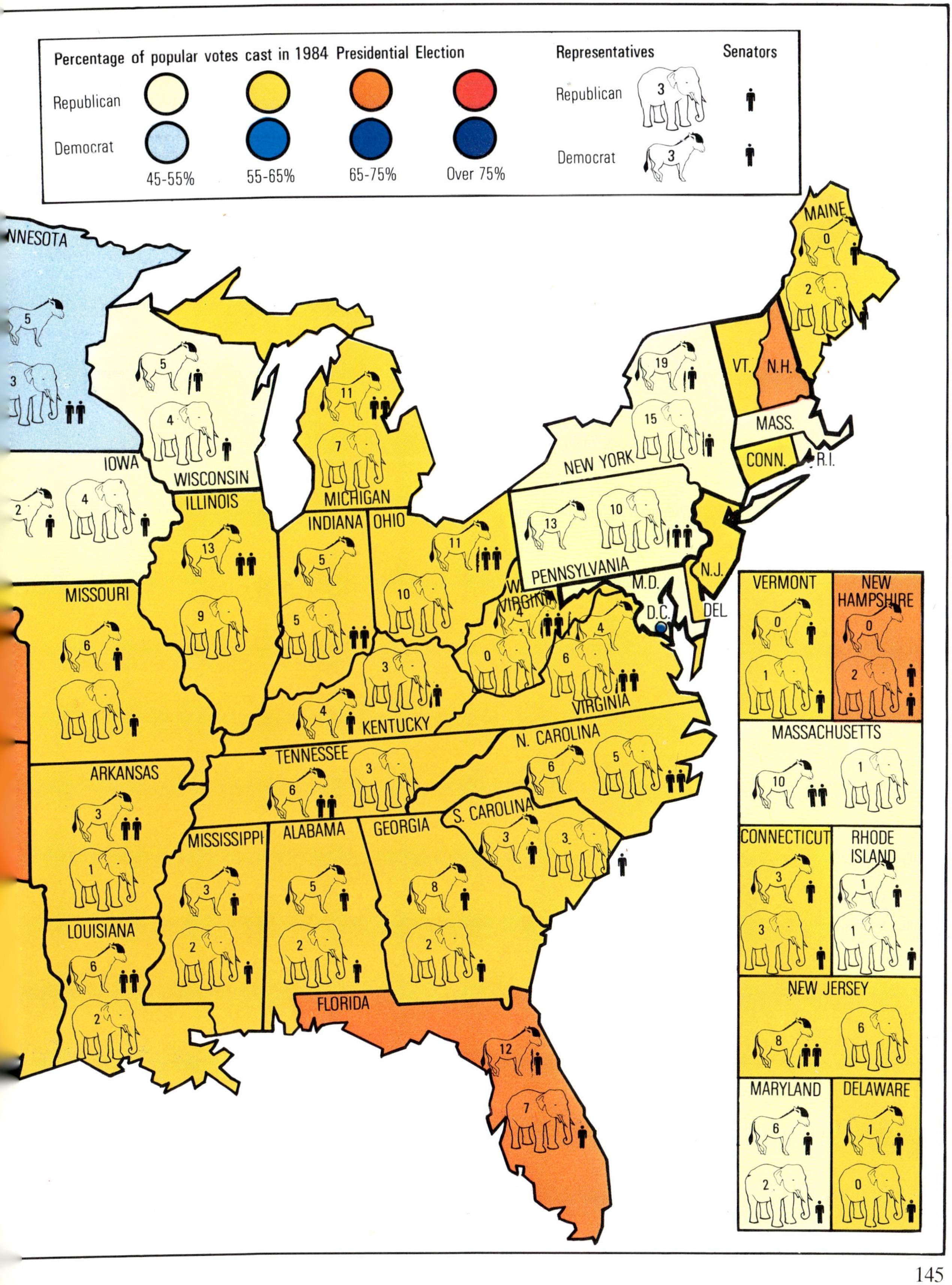
Percentage of popular votes cast in 1984 Presidential Election
Republican
Democrat
45-55%
55-65%
65-75%
Over 75%
Representatives
Senators
Republican
Democrat
3
3
MINNESOTA
IOWA
WISCONSIN
ILLINOIS
MICHIGAN
INDIANA
OHIO
MISSOURI
KENTUCKY
TENNESSEE
ARKANSAS
MISSISSIPPI
ALABAMA
GEORGIA
LOUISIANA
FLORIDA
S. CAROLINA
N. CAROLINA
VIRGINIA
W. VIRGINIA
PENNSYLVANIA
NEW YORK
MAINE
VT.
N.H.
MASS.
CONN.
R.I.
N.J.
M.D.
D.C.
DEL
VERMONT
NEW HAMPSHIRE
MASSACHUSETTS
CONNECTICUT
RHODE ISLAND
NEW JERSEY
MARYLAND
DELAWARE

ELECTIONS

The presidential elections of 1984 were won by the Republican candidate, the incumbent President Reagan. As the map shows, he won every state except Minnesota, the home state of his Democratic opponent, and the District of Columbia.

In terms of the total popular vote, however, President Reagan's victory was less overwhelming. He obtained 58.8 percent of the votes cast, against 40.5 percent for the Democratic candidate (Mondale). That is certainly a substantial majority, but it was exceeded by Johnson's victory over Goldwater in 1964 and by Nixon's over McGovern in 1972.

When people vote in a presidential election, they are voting for a group of electors who make up the electoral college (equal in number to the members of Congress for each state), which decides by a simple majority the winning candidate in each state. It was only in 1961, after the adoption of the Twenty-Third Amendment to the Constitution, that the people living in the District of Columbia were able to vote for president. They still do not have a representative or senator in Congress.

The map also shows the state of the two parties in Congress after the 1984 elections. In spite of the "coattail" effect (the tendency for the head of the ticket to pull along the other candidates with him), the Democrats held a comfortable majority in the House of Representatives, which is elected as a whole every two years. In the Senate, where one-third of the members are elected every two years (two senators for each state regardless of population), the Republicans held a small majority.

Citizens of other democratic countries are often surprised by the low proportion of persons voting in federal elections. Less than three-quarters of eligible citizens are registered to vote, and of

TABLE A
PARTY AFFILIATION OF STATE GOVERNORS, 1960-1984

	Dem.	Rep.
1960	34	16
1964	34	16
1968	24	26
1972	30	20
1976*	36	13
1980	31	19
1984	35	15

* Excludes 1 independent state governor

Diagram A: Voting in presidential elections, 1932-1984

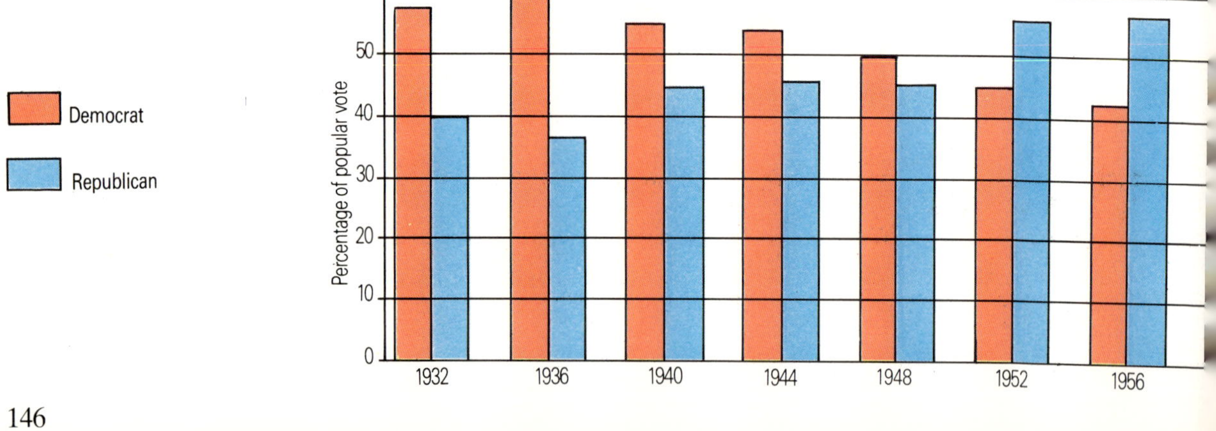

those who are registered, approximately one-quarter fail to do so. Votes cast in the 1984 presidential election numbered 92.6 million, about 53 percent of possible (including nonregistered) voters. The percentage figure was almost identical in the 1932 election. In spite of efforts to persuade more eligible people (especially blacks in the South) to register, little progress had been made toward making elections more fully democratic.

Of the 16 presidential elections between 1924 and 1984, 8 were won by candidates of each party. This equilibrium surprises middle-aged Democrats in particular, who tend to think of the Republicans as essentially a minority party (between 1932 and 1968 there was only one successful Republican presidential candidate, Eisenhower).

Diagram A shows that Democratic candidates in general took a higher share of the popular vote between 1932 and 1984, which is confirmed by the results of Congressional elections and by the Democratic predominance among state governors (Table A). President Reagan's victory over Carter by a large majority in 1980, the first defeat of an elected incumbent president since 1932, appears all the more remarkable.

An interesting feature revealed in Diagram A is the high proportion of presidential elections that have been won by either a very narrow or a very substantial majority.

The two-party system has remained deeply entrenched since the early years of the twentieth century and shows no signs of changing. Nevertheless, on two occasions in particular a third candidate has made a considerable impact. In 1968 Governor Wallace of Alabama attracted nearly 10 million votes; in 1980 John Anderson secured nearly 6 million. In the 1984 election, however, a number of fringe candidates managed only 0.7 percent of the popular vote between them.

Sources: U.S. Bureau of the Census;
U.S. Information Service

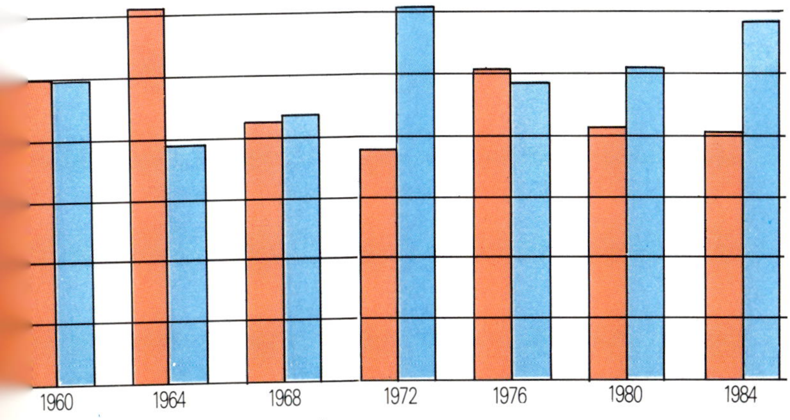

INTERNATIONAL TRADE

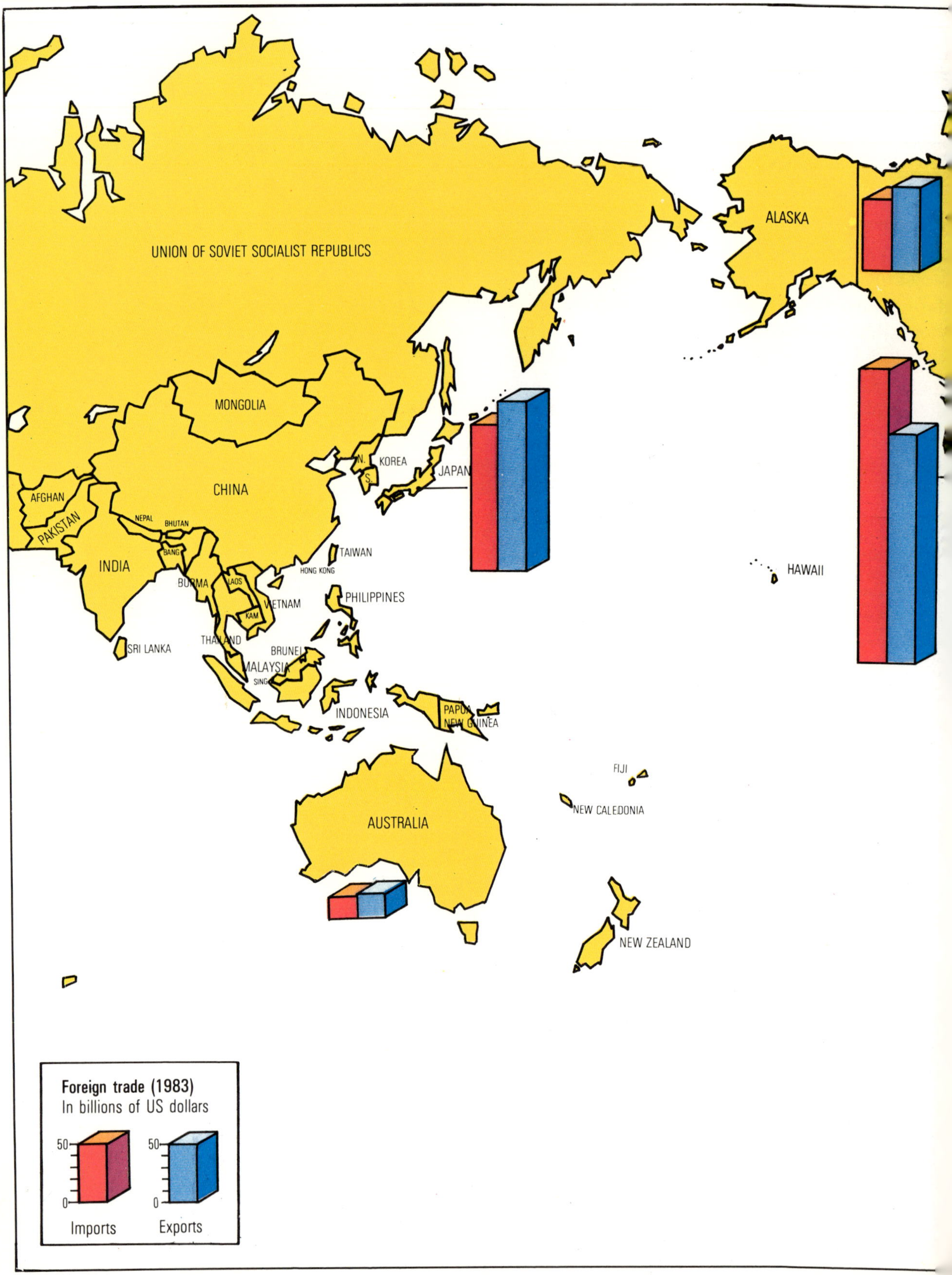

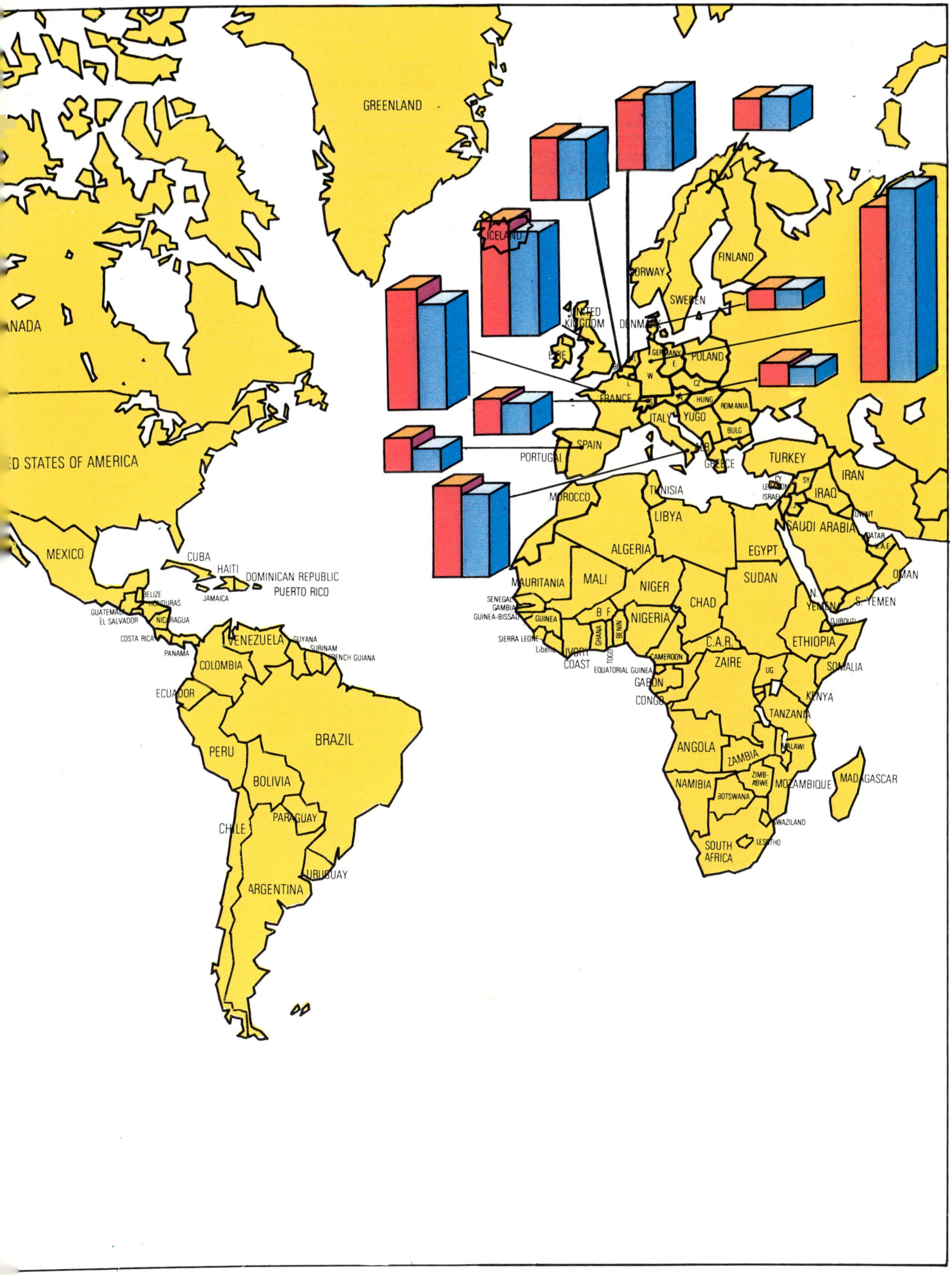
GREENLAND
ICELAND
FINLAND
NORWAY
SWEDEN
UNITED KINGDOM
DENMARK
EIRE
GERMANY
POLAND
FRANCE
CZ
HUNG
ROMANIA
ITALY
YUGO
BULG
SPAIN
PORTUGAL
GREECE
TURKEY
IRAN
IRAQ
SY
ISRAEL
LEBANON
CY
MOROCCO
TUNISIA
LIBYA
ALGERIA
EGYPT
SAUDI ARABIA
KUWAIT
QATAR
U.A.E.
OMAN
MAURITANIA
MALI
NIGER
CHAD
SUDAN
SENEGAL
GAMBIA
GUINEA-BISSAU
GUINEA
SIERRA LEONE
Liberia
IVORY COAST
GHANA
TOGO
BENIN
NIGERIA
CAMEROON
EQUATORIAL GUINEA
GABON
CONGO
C.A.R.
ZAIRE
UG
KENYA
ETHIOPIA
SOMALIA
DJIBOUTI
N. YEMEN
S. YEMEN
TANZANIA
ANGOLA
ZAMBIA
MALAWI
ZIMBABWE
MOZAMBIQUE
MADAGASCAR
NAMIBIA
BOTSWANA
SWAZILAND
LESOTHO
SOUTH AFRICA
MEXICO
CUBA
HAITI
DOMINICAN REPUBLIC
PUERTO RICO
JAMAICA
BELIZE
HONDURAS
GUATEMALA
EL SALVADOR
NICARAGUA
COSTA RICA
PANAMA
VENEZUELA
GUYANA
SURINAM
FRENCH GUIANA
COLOMBIA
ECUADOR
PERU
BRAZIL
BOLIVIA
PARAGUAY
CHILE
URUGUAY
ARGENTINA

INTERNATIONAL TRADE

This map shows the imports and exports of the major trading countries in 1983, in billions of dollars. The difference between the heights of the two blocks in each country gives the trade balance for that year — a deficit if the left-hand block is the higher, and a surplus if the right-hand block is the higher.

Trade with the United States accounted for nearly 12 percent of total world trade, and resulted in a U.S. net trade deficit of $57.5 billion. In the following year, this deficit increased still further, to over $120 billion. In 1983, on the other hand, Japan showed an overall trade surplus of $20.6 billion, and West Germany achieved a $16.8 billion surplus.

The rise in total world exports since 1950 has been tremendous. But the increase has varied between countries or groups of countries and the proportion of the total accounted for by each has changed considerably. The proportion due to the trade of the United States fell from 1950 from 17 to 12 percent, that due to Western Europe rose from 25 percent to 41 percent. Japan, which in 1950 accounted for under 2 percent of world trade, was approaching 9 percent in 1983. The oil-producing countries accounted for about 7 percent in 1950, and this was still the case in 1973. But in 1975 the rise in oil prices brought about a rapid increase in the proportion to over 13 percent, a figure that remained unchanged in 1983.

Diagram A shows the imports and exports of the United States by region. Diagram B elaborates on this, giving the international picture showing the trade in 1983 between the United States,

Diagram A: United States imports and exports, 1984, by region

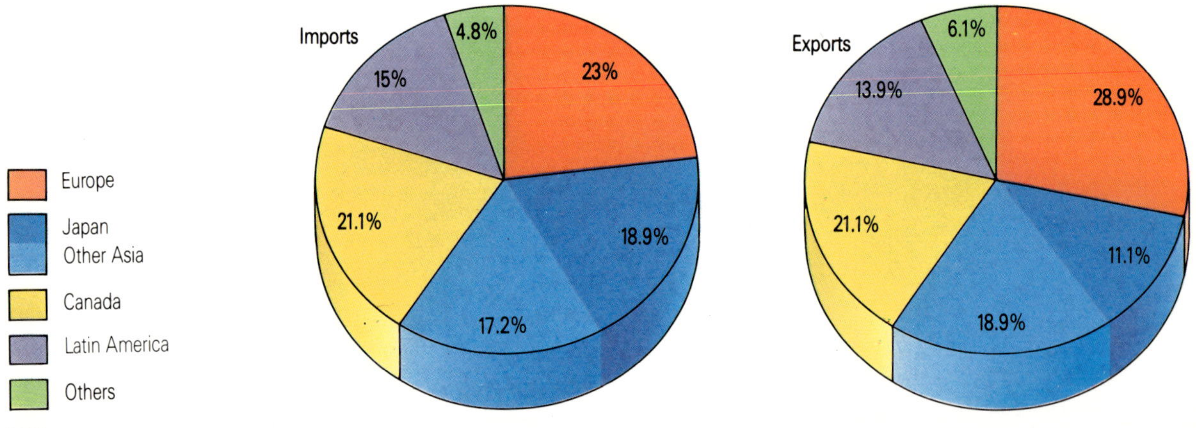

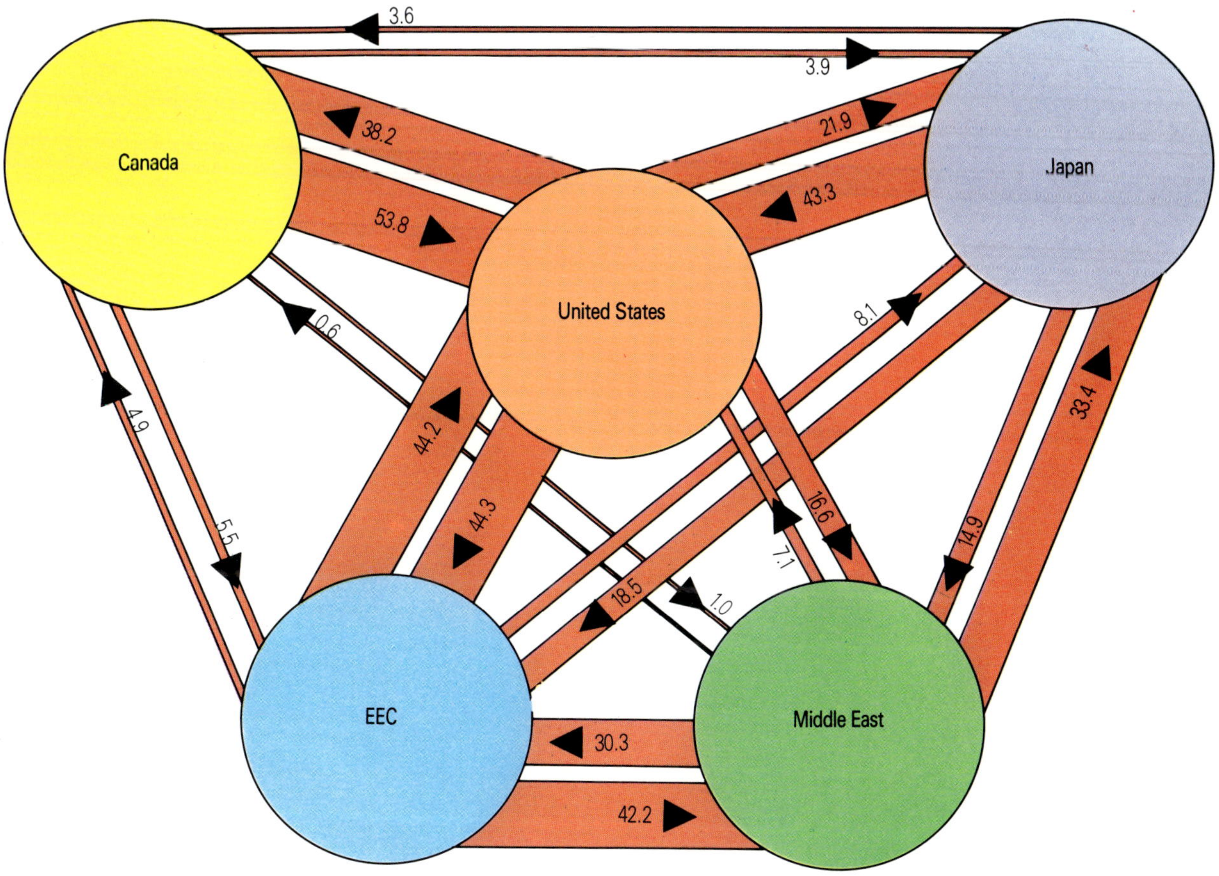

Canada, the countries of the European Economic Community (EEC), Japan, and the Middle East. U.S. imports from Canada form the largest single component of this picture, at $53.8 billion, followed by exports from the United States to the EEC countries ($44.3 billion).

The troublesome imbalance between Japan and the United States is clear to see — a deficit for the United States of $20.4 billion. And in 1984 this gap widened still further, to $36.8 billion. Japan showed trade surpluses of nearly this size in 1983 both with the EEC countries and with the Middle East.

Sources: Organization for Economic Co-operation and Development; U.S. Bureau of the Census

Diagram B: International trade by selected countries in 1983, in billions of dollars

FOREIGN INVESTMENT

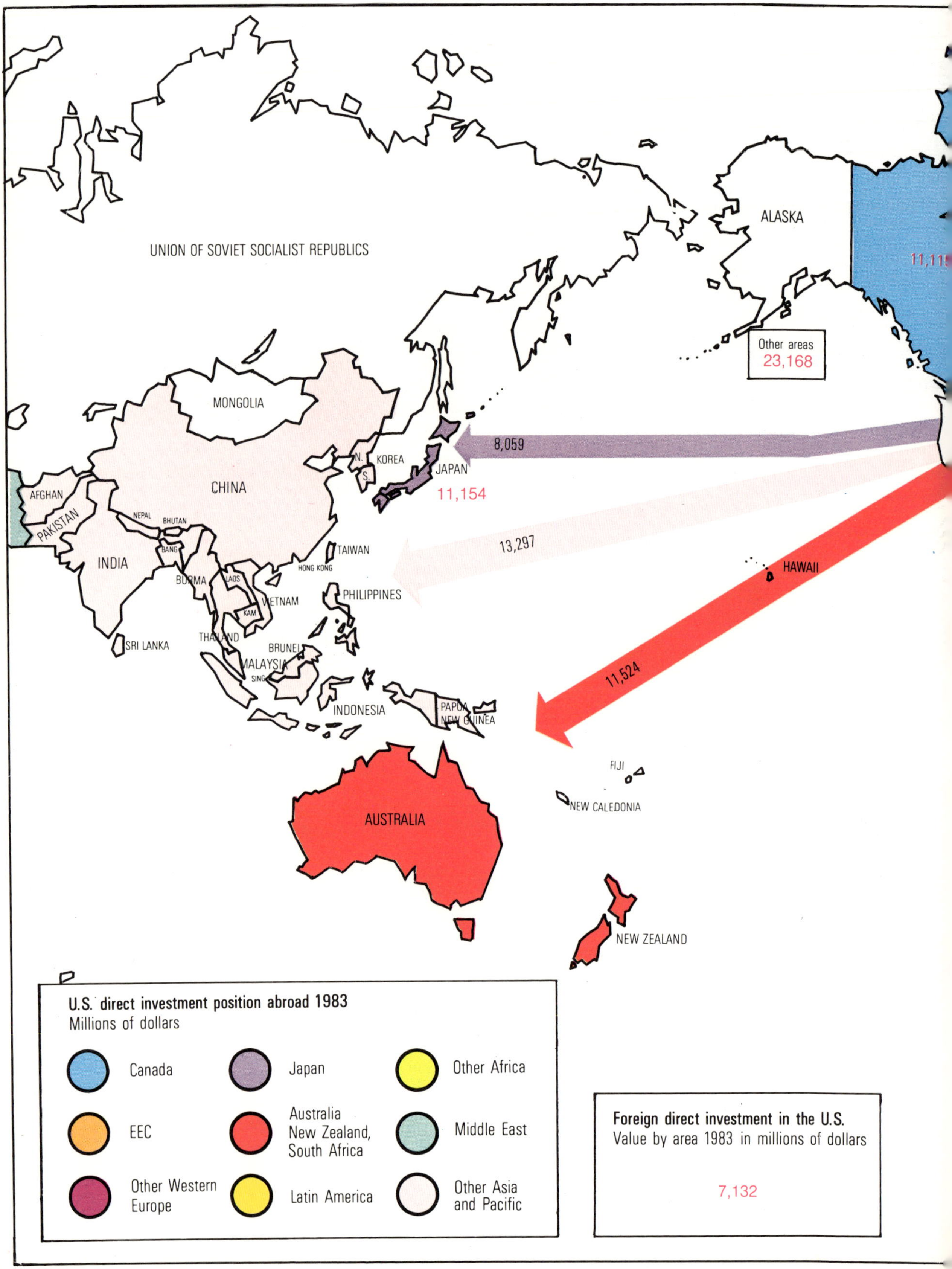

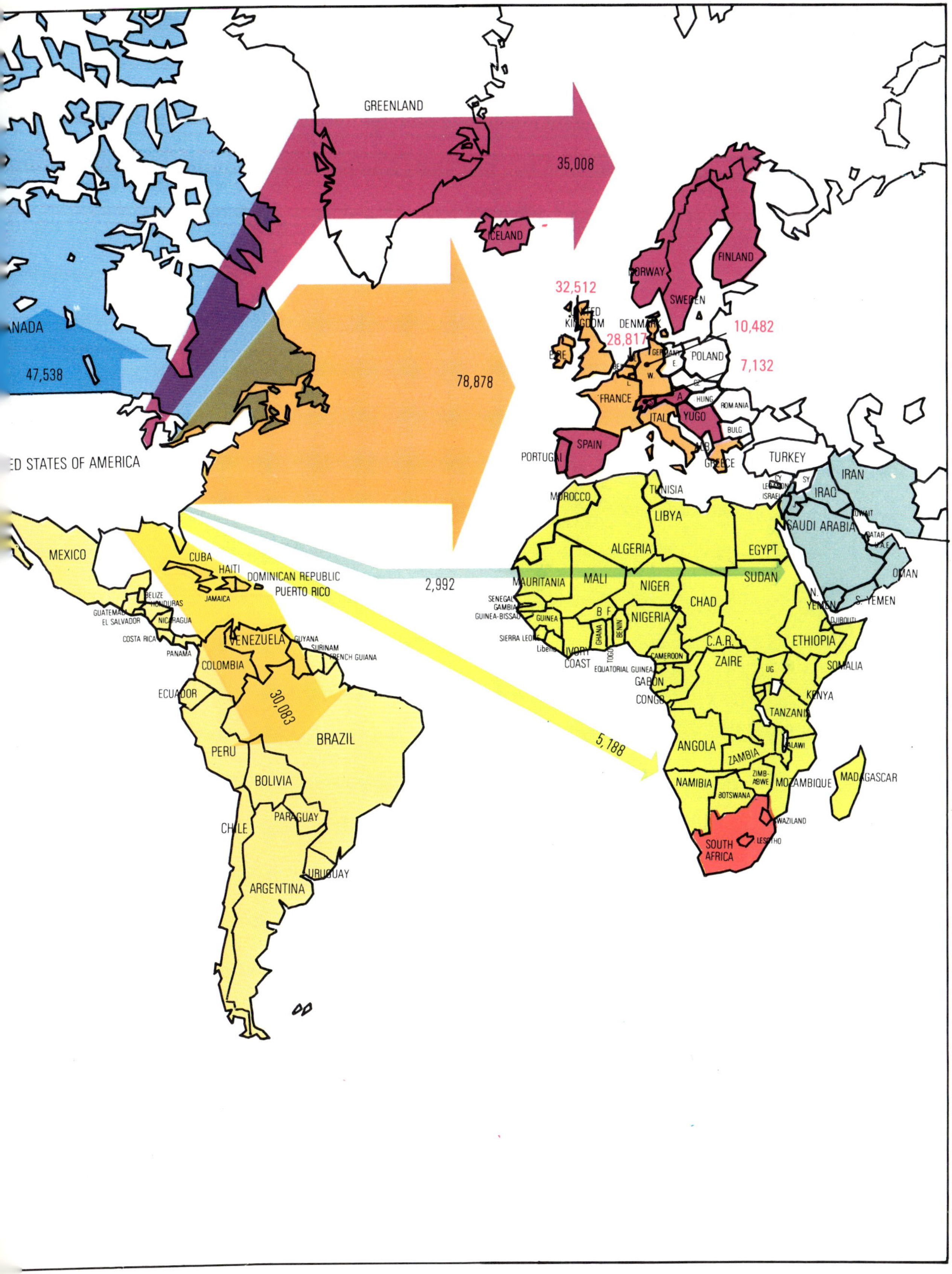
GREENLAND
35,008
ICELAND
NORWAY
SWEDEN
FINLAND
32,512
UNITED KINGDOM
DENMARK
10,482
28,817
EIRE
GERMANY
POLAND
7,132
47,538
78,878
FRANCE
HUNG
ROMANIA
YUGO
ITALY
BULG
SPAIN
PORTUGAL
GREECE
TURKEY
ED STATES OF AMERICA
IRAN
IRAQ
MOROCCO
TUNISIA
LIBYA
SAUDI ARABIA
ALGERIA
EGYPT
MEXICO
CUBA
HAITI
DOMINICAN REPUBLIC
PUERTO RICO
JAMAICA
2,992
MAURITANIA
MALI
NIGER
SUDAN
OMAN
S. YEMEN
CHAD
NIGERIA
ETHIOPIA
BELIZE
HONDURAS
GUATEMALA
EL SALVADOR
NICARAGUA
COSTA RICA
PANAMA
VENEZUELA
GUYANA
SURINAM
FRENCH GUIANA
COLOMBIA
ECUADOR
30,083
SENEGAL
GAMBIA
GUINEA-BISSAU
GUINEA
SIERRA LEONE
IVORY COAST
GHANA
TOGO
BENIN
CAMEROON
EQUATORIAL GUINEA
GABON
CONGO
C.A.R.
ZAIRE
SOMALIA
KENYA
TANZANIA
BRAZIL
PERU
5,188
ANGOLA
ZAMBIA
MALAWI
BOLIVIA
NAMIBIA
BOTSWANA
MOZAMBIQUE
MADAGASCAR
PARAGUAY
CHILE
SWAZILAND
SOUTH AFRICA
LESOTHO
URUGUAY
ARGENTINA

FOREIGN INVESTMENT

This map is concerned with foreign investment, both investments of U.S. companies in other countries, and direct investments of foreign companies in the United States. The amounts represented refer to the situation in 1983.

Direct investment abroad is defined as the "ownership or control, direct or indirect, by one U.S. person or business enterprise of 10 percent or more of the voting securities of an incorporated foreign business enterprise".

Foreign direct investment in the United States means "the ownership or control, directly or indirectly, by one foreign individual, branch, partnership, association, trust, corporation, or government of 10 percent or more of the voting securities of a U.S. business enterprise, or an equivalent interest in an unincorporated one.'' Only enterprises with assets of over $1 million, or owning 200 acres of land in the United States, are included. Book values of direct investments are given for the end of each year.

In 1983, the value of investments of U.S. companies overseas amounted to a total of $226 billion. Over one-fifth of this was in Canada, and almost exactly one-half in Western Europe. Of the European countries, the United Kingdom accounted for the largest single part, with nearly $31 billion U.S. investment. U.S. direct investment in Latin America totalled $30 million, $9 billion of this in Brazil.

On the other side of the coin, foreign investment in the United States in 1983 reached a total of $136 billion. The United Kingdom, with $32.5 billion, was the country with the largest single investment. It was closely followed by the Netherlands, whose nationals had $29 billion invested in the United States. A large proportion of this was in the petroleum industry. However, the 1983 situation represented a fall for the United Kingdom since 1970, as for Canada, while the Netherlands showed a sharp rise over the same period.

Diagram A is a pie chart, showing the distribution of foreign direct investment in the United States, among Canada, Europe, Japan, and the rest of the world. The predominance of European investors is clear, accounting for 68 percent of the total. In 1970, Japanese investment in the United States made up less than 2 percent of the total foreign direct investment, but by 1983, it equalled Canadian investment in importance.

The position of the United States as a world investor has changed dramatically over the past century as it became a world power. Before 1900, U.S. overseas investment was negligible. By 1908, it had risen to $2.5 billion. In 1929, the total of U.S. foreign investments was $7.5 billion, and of this total, $3.5 billion — 45

Diagram A: Distribution of foreign direct investment in the United States, 1983

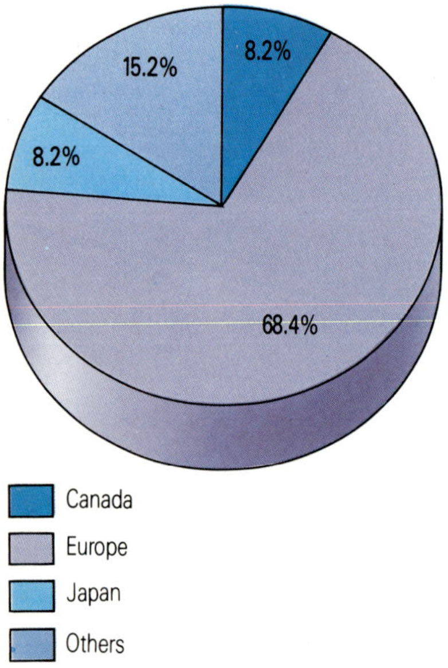

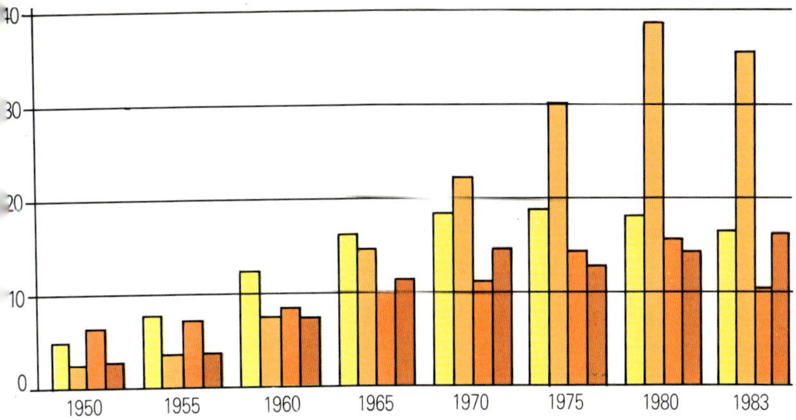

Diagram B: U.S. direct investment overseas, 1950-1983

percent — was in Latin America. In 1950, the Latin American proportion still stood at 40 percent. But investment in Europe, which in 1929 had represented only 15 percent of the total, rose rapidly in the 1950s and 1960s, overtaking the Latin American figure in 1962, and soon far outstripping it. In 1970, the income from U.S. investment abroad amounted to over $8 billion; in 1983 it was $21 billion.

Diagram B graphs part of this history. It shows the value of U.S. direct foreign investment, expressed in constant (1967) dollars, over the period 1950-1983, for Canada, Western Europe, Latin America, and other countries. The tremendous increase in the amount of U.S. investment in Europe, and the decline in U.S. investment in South American countries, stands out clearly.

Diagram C shows the distribution of investments abroad directly owned by U.S. companies. Again, the importance of Europe taken as a whole is obvious. A significant proportion of the "other" category refers to U.S. investment in the Middle East.

Diagram D gives the proportions of the total U.S. investment abroad in manufacturing, oil, finance, and other enterprises. Manufacturing makes up 40 percent of the total, followed by oil with 26 percent.

Source: U.S. Bureau of Economic Analysis

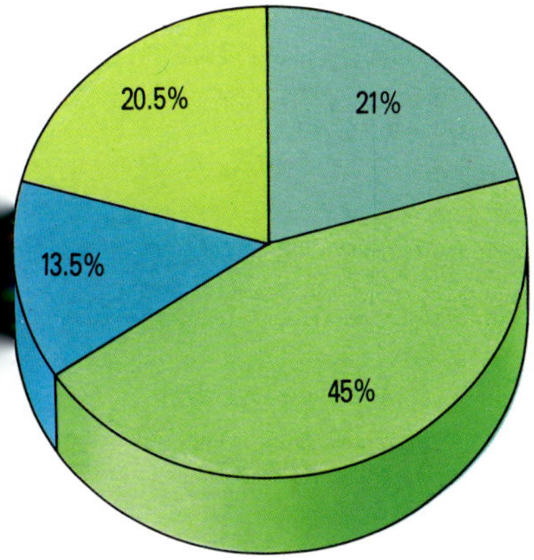

Diagram C

Diagram C: Distribution of U.S. direct investment overseas in 1983, by region

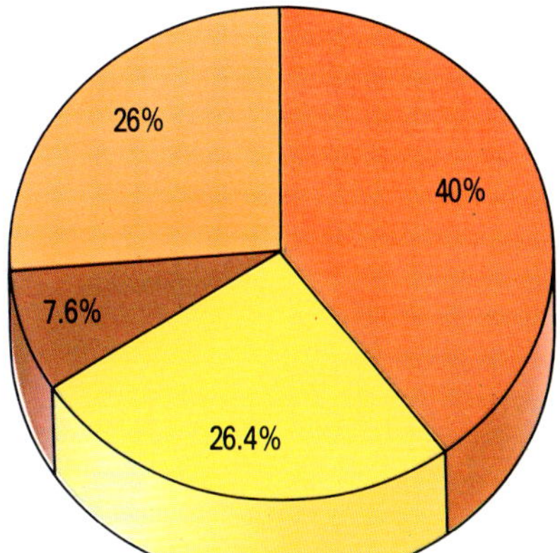

Diagram D

Diagram D: Distribution of U.S. direct investment overseas in 1983, by industry

FOREIGN AID

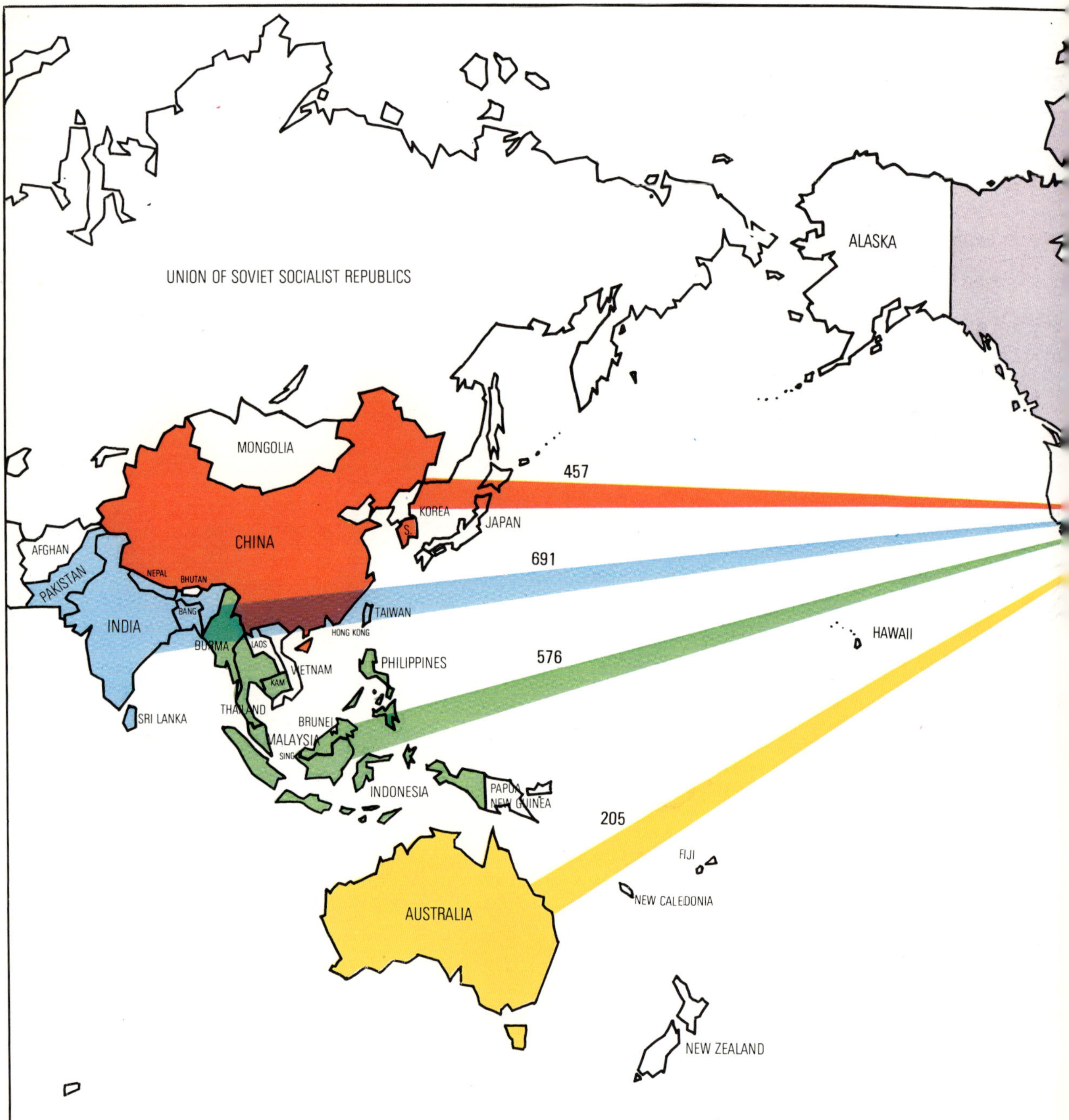

Direction of US foreign aid

Millions of dollars excluding international and regional organizations

- Western Europe
- Eastern Europe
- Near and Middle East
- Indian sub-continent
- South East Asia
- Far East
- Australia and Pacific Islands
- Canada
- Central America and the Caribbean
- South America
- Israel
- Africa

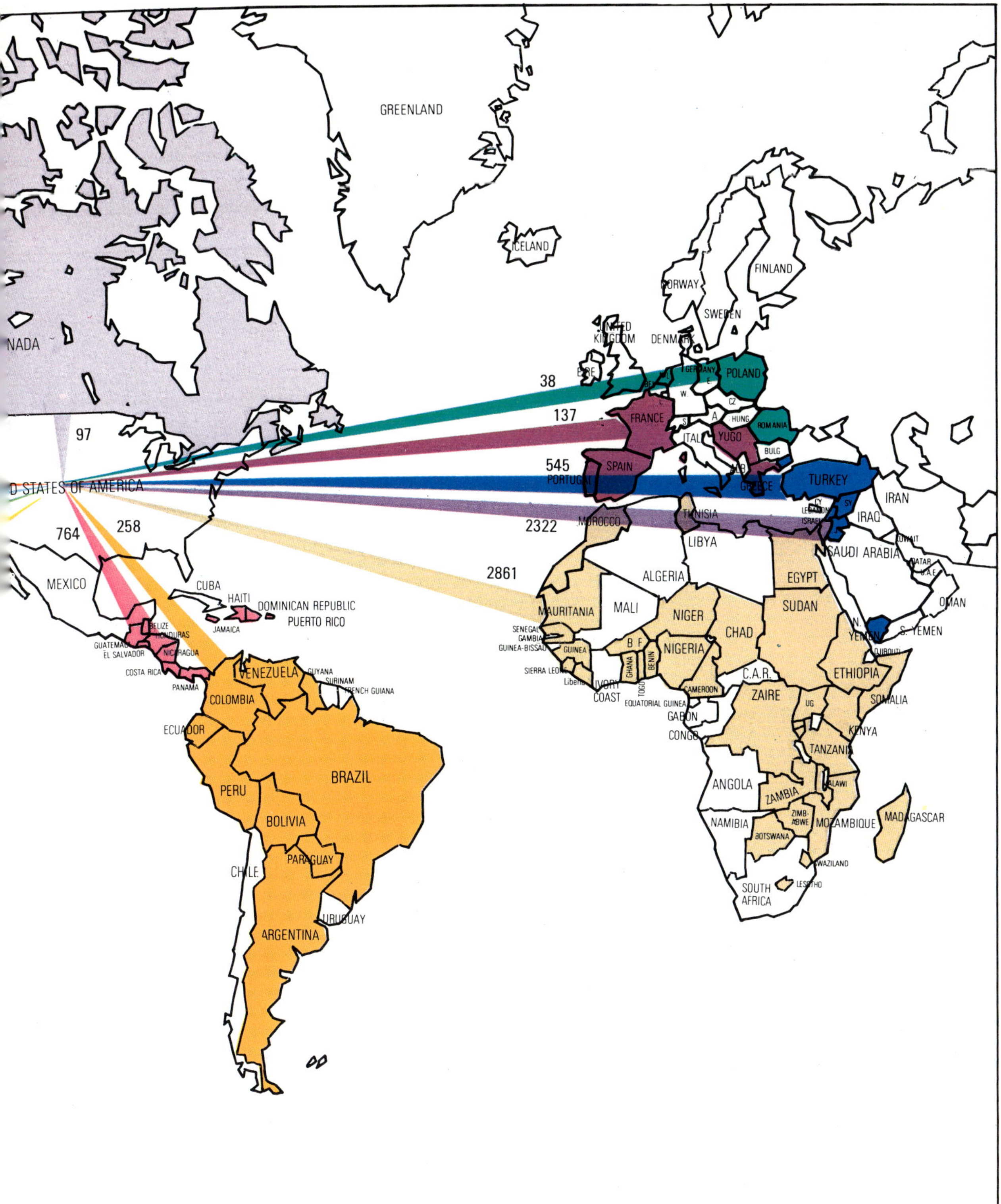
GREENLAND
ICELAND
NORWAY
SWEDEN
FINLAND
UNITED KINGDOM
DENMARK
EIRE
NADA
38
137
97
545
D STATES OF AMERICA
POLAND
GERMANY
FRANCE
ROMANIA
HUNG
CZ
YUGO
BULG
ITALY
SPAIN
PORTUGAL
GREECE
TURKEY
IRAN
IRAQ
ISRAEL
TUNISIA
MOROCCO
2322
LIBYA
SAUDI ARABIA
KUWAIT
QATAR
U.A.E.
OMAN
764
258
2861
ALGERIA
EGYPT
MEXICO
CUBA
HAITI
DOMINICAN REPUBLIC
PUERTO RICO
JAMAICA
BELIZE
HONDURAS
GUATEMALA
EL SALVADOR
NICARAGUA
COSTA RICA
PANAMA
MAURITANIA
MALI
NIGER
CHAD
SUDAN
N. YEMEN
S. YEMEN
SENEGAL
GAMBIA
GUINEA-BISSAU
GUINEA
SIERRA LEONE
Liberia
IVORY COAST
GHANA
TOGO
BENIN
NIGERIA
CAMEROON
EQUATORIAL GUINEA
GABON
CONGO
C.A.R.
ETHIOPIA
DJIBOUTI
SOMALIA
ZAIRE
UG
KENYA
TANZANIA
VENEZUELA
GUYANA
SURINAM
FRENCH GUIANA
COLOMBIA
ECUADOR
BRAZIL
PERU
BOLIVIA
PARAGUAY
CHILE
URUGUAY
ARGENTINA
ANGOLA
ZAMBIA
MALAWI
ZIMBABWE
NAMIBIA
BOTSWANA
MOZAMBIQUE
MADAGASCAR
SWAZILAND
LESOTHO
SOUTH AFRICA

FOREIGN AID

This map illustrates the distribution of U.S. government aid to foreign countries in 1983, in the form of grants and credits. Well over half of the total went to the countries of the Near East. Israel received the largest single amount, $2.3 billion, and Egypt received $1.8 billion. Of the $457 million aid going to the Far East, $448 million went to South Korea. Of the $576 million aid going to South East Asia, $251 million went to Indonesia and $215 million to the Philippines. These figures cover both military and economic aid programs.

Foreign assistance is divided into three groups. Grants are transfers for which no payment is expected. These include military supplies and services. Credits are loans with specific obligations for repayment. Finally, there is the transfer of U.S. farm products in exchange for foreign currencies.

Military aid to friendly countries is given under the Mutual Defense Assistance Program, set up in 1949. Between World War II and 1983, the United States gave a total of $100.5 billion in such aid, $74.6 billion of this as grants. In 1983, military aid totalled $5.6 billion, $4.2 billion of this going to the Near East and South Asia.

Total economic aid in 1983 was $8.6 billion, just over one-third of this being given to Near Eastern and South Asian countries. $1.1 billion went to the African continent, $2 million of this to Ethiopia.

Diagram A: U.S. foreign aid compared with other leading countries, 1983

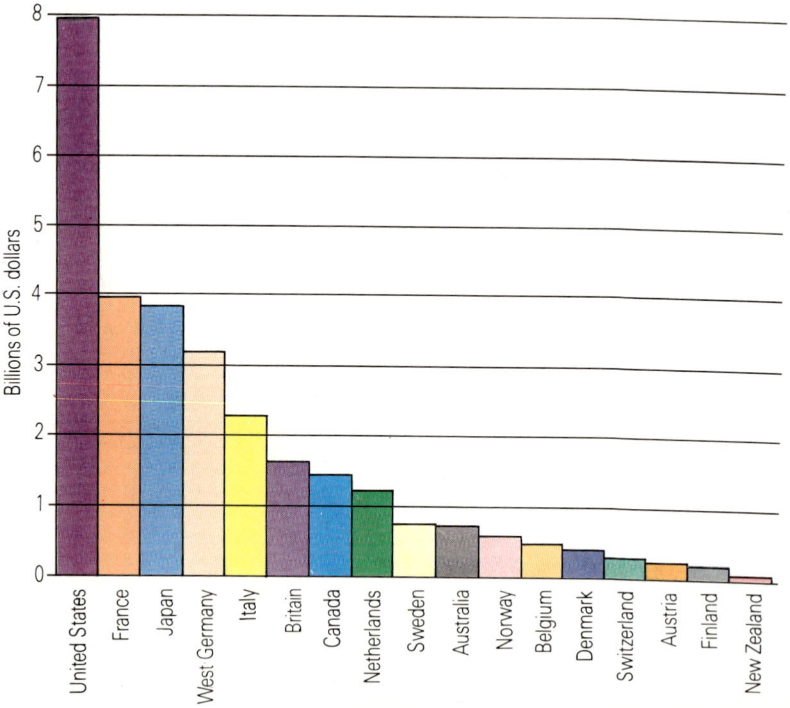

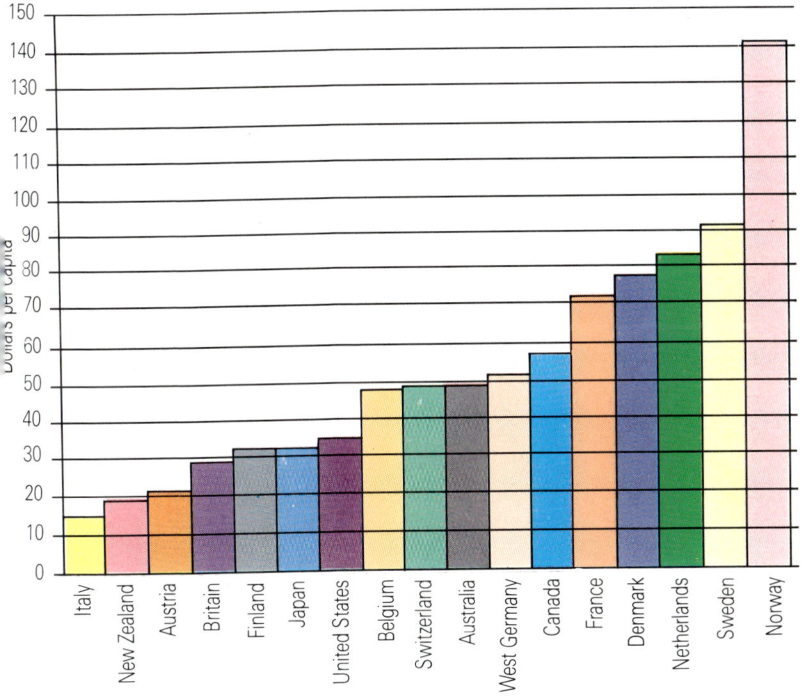

Diagram B: Per capita public aid to developing countries, 1983 (excluding military aid)

The distribution of U.S. government aid to foreign countries has changed considerably since the years immediately following World War II. From 1945 to 1954, aid to Western Europe accounted for the vast majority of the total U.S. foreign aid. After 1954, the Near East, South Asia, and the Far East represent the largest categories, the Far East playing a less important part since the mid-1970s.

Diagrams A and B show international aid to developing countries in 1983, excluding military aid. Diagram A gives the total amounts of such aid from different countries. The U.S. figure of $8 billion is by far the highest. Only France ($3.9 billion), Japan ($3.8 billion) and West Germany ($3.2 billion) come anywhere near it. Diagram B, however, expresses the same figures as amounts per capita: the United States appears farther down on this list.

Sources: U.S. Agency for International Development;
U.S. Bureau of Economic Analysis